REINTERPRETING
REVELATION
and
TRADITION

*Jews and Christians
in Conversation*

THE BERNARDIN CENTER SERIES
GENERAL EDITOR: ROBERT J. SCHREITER, C.PP.S.

The Bernardin Center Series presents works of scholarly and general interest that grow out of activities at the Joseph Cardinal Bernardin Center for Theology and Ministry at Catholic Theological Union.

Areas of activity and interest of the Bernardin Center include the ongoing interpretation and implementation of the Second Vatican Council, church leadership, the consistent ethic of life, Catholic health care, the Catholic Common Ground Initiative, interreligious dialogue, and religion in American public life.

REINTERPRETING
REVELATION
and
TRADITION

Jews and Christians
in Conversation

Edited with an introduction by
JOHN T. PAWLIKOWSKI, O.S.M.
and
HAYIM GOREN PERELMUTER

SHEED & WARD
Franklin, Wisconsin

2000

SHEED & WARD

7373 South Lovers Lane Road
Franklin, Wisconsin 53132
1-800-266-5564

Printed in the United States of America

Cover and interior design by Robin Booth
Cover drawing "Brother Joseph" by Robin Booth
    Copyright ©1997 Catholic Theological Union

Library of Congress Cataloging-in-Publication Data

    Reinterpreting revelation and tradition : Jews and Christians
in conversation / edited and with an introduction by
John T. Pawlikowski and Hayim Goren Perelmuter.
        p. cm. — (The Bernardin Center series)
    Includes bibliographical references and index.
    ISBN 1-58051-042-6 (hardcover : alk. paper)
    1. Judaism—Relations—Christianity. 2. Christianity and other religions—
Judaism. I. Pawlikowski, John. II. Perelmuter, Hayim Goren. III. Series.
    BM535.R415 2000
    261.2'6—dc21   00-024753

TABLE OF CONTENTS

INTRODUCTION
John T. Pawlikowski and Hayim Goren Perelmuter
vii

CONVERSATION ONE
One Covenant or Two: Can We Sing a New Song?
MICHAEL SIGNER
3

*The Search for a New Paradigm for the
Christian-Jewish Relationship: A Response to Michael Signer*
JOHN T. PAWLIKOWSKI
25

CONVERSATION TWO
Differences with the Church in the Rabbinic Parables
CLEMENS THOMA
51

A Response to Clemens Thoma
HAYIM GOREN PERELMUTER
63

CONVERSATION THREE
Gazing Beneath the Veil: Apocalyptic Envisioning the End
ELLIOT R. WOLFSON
77

*Apocalyptic Impulse in Judaism and Christianity:
A Response to Elliot R. Wolfson*
LESLIE J. HOPPE, O.F.M.
105

CONVERSATION FOUR
*One Covenant or Two: Paul and Early Christianity on
Universalism and Cultural Pluralism*
ALAN F. SEGAL
113

The Apostolic Decree in Acts: A Response to Alan F. Segal
CELIA DEUTSCH
141

CONVERSATION FIVE
Hatred for and Attraction to Jews in Classical Antiquity
LOUIS H. FELDMAN
167

A Response to Louis H. Feldman
KEVIN MADIGAN
191

CONVERSATION SIX
*Halakic Correspondence in Antiquity: Qumran, Paul,
and the Babylonian Talmud*
PETER J. TOMSON
201

A Response to Peter J. Tomson
BARBARA E. BOWE
231

CONTRIBUTORS
239

INDEX
241

INTRODUCTION

JOHN T. PAWLIKOWSKI
and
HAYIM GOREN PERELMUTER

When the Catholic Theological Union was founded after Vatican II in 1968, committed to shaping theological education in the spirit of the Council, Jewish Studies was included in its program. It began modestly with a single course taught by a rabbi as an adjunct, and some preliminary and tentative ventures into interfaith dialogue by a young ethicist who joined the faculty as a newly-minted Ph.D. when his religious order became part of the corporation.

That is how the editors of this volume began their collaboration. From the tiny seeds of tentative beginnings, a full program of Jewish Studies and interfaith discourse has developed. The Catholic-Jewish dialogue and Jewish Studies have grown and flourished at C.T.U.

What we have experienced in those three decades is a seismic shift in Christian-Jewish relations that is particularly apparent in the direction the dialogue has taken. Those relations have moved from deep hostility, mutual contempt, the unspeakable tragedy that culminated in World War II, with the Shoah and the questions it raised, to a capacity to communicate, to reason together. The dialogue has achieved a depth of mutual understanding that makes possible the ability to confront the most painful issues with an openness and understanding. Its underpinnings are deep and confident friendship.

The present volume, the distillation of a scholarly exploration of the relation to each other and of the mutual validity of the Christian and Jewish covenants, is evidence of where things have arrived. In early May of 1998, four eminent scholars—experts in Jewish theology, first-century Christian-Jewish relations, the area of mysticism and apocalypticism, and midrash as a reflection on the Christian-Jewish encounter—met to exchange views.

Responding to them was a group of four other scholars, Catholic and Jewish like the first four. The conversation went from presentation to response and then to discussion which continued, beyond the sessions, at lunch and dinner. The impact was deep and lasting, and readers will capture its spirit as they enter the conversation. Each was looking for something precious in the "other" that was needed to validate his or her self: not to convert but to strengthen and clarify self-acceptance and self-awareness.

A wealth of insights have resulted from the process. Michael Signer saw the relationship of the two covenants as being most effective when grounded in a mutual hermeneutical effort applied to their central texts. This turning of their respective hermeneutical traditions towards each other could have consequences of the greatest possibilities for healing. Although John Pawlikowski considers such mutual reflection on common texts valuable, he is of the opinion that the question of mutual origins needs to be confronted, the pain in the process notwithstanding.

Clemens Thoma, in effect, acts on Signer's suggestion. He examines Jewish texts and parallels in Jewish midrashim, to extrapolate from them, through a brilliant hermeneutical process, the rabbinic response to the claims of emerging Christianity. It is a subtle and insightful hermeneutic that indeed illumines the conversation. As he so perceptively puts it, these rabbinic parables have two aims: to teach Torah to the people on the popular level, and to confront the claims of the new movement. Hayim Perelmuter reflects on the anthological structure that brings Jewish texts together and on the choral role of midrashic commentary in plumbing their meaning. Tradition carefully exegeted becomes an important building block for the interacting and communicating covenants.

Elliot Wolfson examines the evidence for a link in the Christian and Jewish apocalyptic and mystical enterprise. The links between the underpinnings of Daniel and Revelation suggest a common thread. He makes the point that both in Jewish and Christian apocalypses, the spiritual elite are described in terms of eschatological transmutation. There appears to be the same motivation for both: "The world is out of joint, one must look beyond it for a solution." Leslie Hoppe is of the opinion that, unlike Wolfson's suggestion that the apocalyptic impulse in Judaism leads to mysticism, this is not the case for Christianity. Christians, he opines, who are involved in apocalyptic exercise, do so as "an act of desperation against a system that was perceived as oppressive, in order to assert that the soon-to-come end will bring the destruction of evil powers and create a new world."

On the question of the two covenants, Segal sees significance in the Rabbinic view that makes room for non-Jews in the world-to-come. That is to say, there is one covenant but gentiles can be included without conversion. He then proceeds to examine questions from the Christian perspective, specifically the perspective of Paul and Luke/Acts. Celia Deutsch examines more closely Segal's use of the sources in Luke/Acts with respect to the Apostolic Decree dealing with converts. From her perspective this Decree displays to the outside world "a relationship of continuity between the Way and the parent."

We have added two additional papers and responses to the conversation. One was given earlier in the same year by Louis Feldman as a Shapiro Lecture at the Bernardin Center. The other, by Peter Tomson, was given several years earlier in a conference at Catholic Theological Union examining the letters of Paul in relation to the Rabbinic response genre. Both, in the view of the editors, added significantly to the dialogue.

In his analysis of Christian-Jewish relations through a critique of gentile perceptions of Jews in the Roman Empire of the first century, Louis Feldman sees a germ of possibilities for the contemporary scene. Indeed, he finds a remarkable appreciation of the qualities of the Jewish people from outside sources. One gets a sense of his conviction that the Roman-Jewish relationship was at bottom secure and mutually self-confident, a strong hint of what we are beginning to experience in our time. Kevin Madigan analyzes Feldman's presentation with a deep sense of appreciation of his work, while dwelling upon the challenges to his claims for a widespread Jewish missionary activity and the role of "God-fearers" as converts. The delicate balance of certainty and doubt hovers in the background.

The conventional picture of Paul vis-à-vis Judaism is that he broke sharply with it and created something radically new. Peter Tomson examines Paul's letters to see how they might relate to the genre of rabbinic response.

To see how he takes a close look at this possibility, finding deep roots of halakhic method and approach in what appears to be Paul's antinomian role, is intriguing. In this connection, he examines the Qumran MMT document and observes that it testifies to the early existence of halakhic terminology in various Jewish sects. He skillfully compares this with Paul's "halakhic letter" to the gentiles in 1 Corinthians. For Barbara Bowe some qualification is required before we can draw such conclusions. When Paul replies to a question, is he not also indulging in polemic? How can we be sure that halakhic topics are presented in response when, in fact, Paul "may not be answering questions, but questioning answers"?

The conversation in these papers moves in many directions and covers a wide area, but the connective glue is the concern for the inner relationship between Judaism and Christianity in the attempt to overcome the aftermath of the painful schism of the early years of the siblings in their covenantal struggle. Beyond supersessionism, beyond rejection, the possibilities of One Covenant interpreted two different ways, or Two Covenants separate but deeply related, animate our purpose and inform our conversation.

And in the end, perhaps the resolution of the ancient Hillel-Shammai debate will resonate for us all: "These and these are the words of the Living God!"

CONVERSATION ONE

MICHAEL A. SIGNER

JOHN T. PAWLIKOWSKI

CONVERSATION ONE

One Covenant or Two: Can We Sing a New Song?

MICHAEL A. SIGNER

The Nature of Theological Reflection in our Time

Nostra Aetate, the name of the Second Vatican Council's Declaration on Non-Christian Religions, provides a leitmotif for an understanding of the nature of theological reflection over the past thirty years. "In our time" reminds us that when we speak critically about matters human and divine we may address the eternal, but we are located in temporality. The words "our time" no longer have the optimistic ring of progress. We have become more tentative about making universal claims. We seek communities for our reflection.

Thanks to the spirit of the Council, Catholics were urged to seek out those in the ecumene of the Christian Churches and members of the Jewish community. "In our time" theological reflection in mixed confessional groups has become more or less routine. We teach in one another's institutions, gather for scholarly meetings, and travel to international conferences. Theological reflection draws from a variety of disciplines such as philosophy, literature, and history. Perusing the journals and periodicals, we can observe that there is no longer a regnant discourse or genre for writing theology.

Does this mixing of disciplines and genres and confessions indicate a retreat from the proud position that theology in the Church held as *regina artium*? From the perspective of the Jewish community there are some of my colleagues who adamantly claim that "Jews don't *do* theology." An extension of the claim by the skeptics might be that this "mixture" is simply further evidence of either community abandoning its responsibility to the past in order to rush headlong into an uncertain future.

There might be a more affirmative foundation for the mingling of communities and discourses. We do theology in the presence of others because

our era has witnessed the political and social results of absolutist or exclu-
sivist claims. Fifty years after the Shoah we are more humble and tentative in
our predication about the relationship between God and humanity—a relationship that we shall claim is the basis for "covenant." We mix—indeed we
juxtapose our thoughts and traditions—because we recognize that when we
seek God, our glimpse comes only in fragments, in traces of a shattered
humanity. Our great challenge as Jews and Christians after the Shoah is how
to engage in any theological reflection in our time when shadow seems to
overwhelm the light.

   My own perspective on theological efforts by Jews or Christians since
the Shoah is that they are most successful when they are grounded in a
hermeneutical effort. We engage the texts of our separate traditions, teach
them to one another, and appropriate them for our own communities so that
the texts become part of daily life. As we work toward that goal, we can then
develop our common efforts to understand one other without becoming one
another. In my own efforts to realize this program I have found David Tracy's
book, *The Analogical Imagination*, to be a most important guide as I have
entered theological conversations.[1] Tracy's description of the theological tasks
emboldens those who have been trained in other disciplines, particularly history and philology, to take their place among those who seek to explain the
relationship between the divine and human in an era when the conversation
has become so fragmented.

   When viewed from the perspective of Tracy's *Analogical Imagination*,
theology is a hermeneutical reflection upon the sacred texts of one's tradition.
It moves from reading those texts to their contextualization, and ultimately to an
appropriation which respects both their origin and our own contemporaneity.
The boldness of our efforts during the past thirty years as Christians and Jews
is that we do our theology both separately and together. We simultaneously
engage in conversation with our own tradition and with the traditions of the
community of others.

   Theological reflection calls us to a hermeneutics of juxtaposition of our
traditions, and encourages us to observe their dialectical tensions, rather than
a hermeneutics of identity or sameness. In this manner we can appreciate the

full implication of Walter Benjamin's assertion: "It isn't that the past casts its light on the present or the present casts its light on the past; rather, an image is that in which the Then and the Now come into a constellation like a flash of lightning."[2] It has been my experience that the arc of light between ideas that seem to be asymmetrical or incommensurate often produces new insights. To put this idea into a biblical metaphor: God is glorified by the multitude of differences in the world, not the continuing discovery of homogeneity or the need to impose it on everyone.

In the examination of the question of "one covenant or two," I will not review much of the literature which has engaged many of the fine theologians who have posed this question such as Norbert Lohfink, John Pawlikowski, F. W. Marquardt, Bertold Klappert, or others.[3] I will instead assume that many Christian theologians—among them Joseph Cardinal Ratzinger and John Paul II—are convinced that the covenant with the Jewish people "has never been revoked."[4] My paper will move in another direction. It will provide, I hope, a meditation or speculation on how the position of each community, Jews and Christians, in space and time illuminates the problems of how people can relate to God and to other communities.

The Problem of this Paper: One Covenant or Two

A theology which is conversational implies a series of relationships:
- a relationship to the text;
- a relationship to the world of life;
- a relationship to the community that is created out of the text and life-world.

It is in the intersection of the relationship between text, world, and community that the rabbinic tradition enters the discussion of the concept of "covenant." The text which contains the sacred narratives and practices of biblical Israel enjoins its readers to realize its stories and precepts in their own world. The activity of reading/transmitting and the activity of interpreting/living constitute the complex network of the dynamic world of the Jewish people. This social group is therefore in conversation between God and humanity and one another. As they live through space and time they engage with others who do not share their worlds of conversation—but who are engaged in analogous conversations.

The focal point of all of these conversations for the Jewish people is the idea of *berit* or covenant. This word or concept maps the boundaries for relationships: between individual Jews and their God, between the community of Jews and its God, between Jews and non-Jews, and between non-Jews and the God of Israel. Within the Jewish tradition, the term "covenant" may be used to describe any of these relationships. All covenants are one in their origin— with the God of Israel. However, as we shall observe, as various boundary relationships are established between the originator of the covenant and the human partners, a complex hierarchy of covenants appears. What is one in origin becomes multiple in its realization.

From the perspective of the Jewish tradition, the covenant indicates a relationship of mutual obligation. However, these mutual obligations do not obscure the clear hierarchy between God and humanity. The Jewish people approach God through their Scripture and oral Torah in a dialogical relationship. Rabbinic expansions on biblical passages often elaborate on divine words and human responses—filling in the gaps, as it were. In the covenantal relationship God is kind, caring, and concerned for Israel's welfare. However, the God of Israel is also concerned about justice and loyalty. This leads to the possibility and realization that Israel may sin and even be exiled as a consequence of falling from its obligations. The "punishment" does not indicate a breaking of the relationship, but the opportunity to return to God which is held out as an ever-present possibility.

In Jewish liturgical texts and lectionary, the foundation of the communal covenant derives from the narrative of Egyptian redemption, theophany at Sinai, desert wandering, and the entry into the land. Within the perspectives of the Scripture and the Rabbis it is the ability to dwell within the land of Israel that becomes the paradigm for loyalty to the covenant. Both written and Oral Torah provide evidence that the loss of sovereignty in the land and subsequent diaspora did not stretch the loving kindness of God beyond the breaking point with Israel. This continuing relationship may be discerned within the scriptural treatment of the presence of God in Egypt with Jeremiah and in Babylonia with Ezekiel. Return from the Babylonian exile is described as a new Exodus and a period of the renewal of the prior intensity of Israel's relationship with God. The universal power of God among the nations is discerned in the second and third Isaiah as well as in 2 Chronicles as the God of Israel is revealed in relationship with non-Jewish rulers who bring Israel back to the land.

In the evidence from Scripture of the oscillation between the exclusive nature of Israel's relationship with God and the description of the God as creator of the universe and ruler of all nations, we can observe the origin of the problem for the Jewish people who are torn between God's singular care for them and the divine relationship to non-Israelite peoples. In the texts of Scripture, non-Israelite peoples appear as idolaters and oppressors; they also often appear as favored by God and fulfill the obligations that God imposes upon them. Thus, even the greatest betrayal by Israel, which is idolatry, does not separate the non-Israelite nations from God or divine favor. Idolatry does not separate peoples from their creator.

The polyphony of the canon about non-Israelite peoples, their relationship to God and to Israel, is set in ambiguity: they are beloved of God, yet distanced from God. Might we discern here a homology between Israel's own relationship with God? This Scriptural aporia became the inheritance of the rabbinic tradition from the tannaitic period through modernity.[5] The question of covenant for the Jewish people becomes for me an exploration of multiple perspectives. It might be described as a mapping of possibilities which are contingent upon where Israel or another community, like Christianity, stands with respect to the God of Scripture. We might describe these perspectives through the dynamic movement of "turning" or moments of Teshuvah—a moment in which we can return and renew the relationship with God. At each turn the perspective of covenant will change and open different horizons or possibilities.

The remainder of this paper will focus on three "turnings" or moments of Teshuvah: the first turn occurs when Israel as the Jewish people faces its creator; the second turn, when the Jewish people turns toward other peoples;

the third turn arises when the Jewish people discerns their message reflected
in another people which also cherishes their Scripture.

Covenant and Turning: The First Two Turns

The first turn occurs when Israel, the Jewish people, faces its creator.
There is an intimacy and exclusiveness to this relationship which views no
other people on the horizon. Put simply: only Israel, the Jewish people, has
Israel's relationship with God. Many statements in Scripture focus exclusively
upon Israel and its relationship with God. Fidelity or lack of fidelity creates
the dramatic tension which drives much of the narrative in the historical and
prophetic books. Israel is loved by God not because it is the greatest or most
powerful of nations, but because it is the smallest among them. Yet, this
exclusive favor brings with it the most stringent demand: absolute loyalty to
the God of Israel. Therefore, idolatry becomes Israel's greatest sin because it
is the most obvious action of infidelity. In the book of Exodus we can observe
this covenantal tension between loyalty and betrayal in the following narrative: the exclusive covenant of Israel and God at Mt. Sinai (Ex 19–24), which
is immediately transgressed by the very same people with the creation of the
golden calf (Ex 32), with the subsequent intervention by Moses and the reconciliation with God (Ex 33–34). All of the tension, dissolution, and reconciliation is then resolved by the establishment of the tabernacle (Ex 35–39), which
then becomes the permanent locus where the people can reconcile with God.

In the third section of the Jewish canonical order, Ketuvim, the term
"covenant" appears with less frequency. The sovereignty of God over all
creation and peoples is manifest in the books of Ezra and Chronicles where
Cyrus of Persia expresses his fidelity to Israel's divinity. The community of
returned exiles turns to a life of fidelity to Torah as interpreted by an authoritative body of elders as we read in Nehemiah 8–9.

It is in the history of Israel restored under Cyrus that we come to the
second "turning": the turn of Israel from its exclusive relationship to God as
it negotiates its relationship with other peoples. During this "turn" we shall
observe the development of covenental theologies in post-biblical Judaism. It
is during this "turning" outward that we shall observe those who lay claim to

the name Israel reinterpret the nature of how the exclusive relationship to God is to be maintained.

The narrative framework for understanding the relationship of fidelity to the God of Israel among the nations emerges during the interaction between the community in Judea and its neighbors in Syria and Egypt during the Hellenistic period. The book of Daniel reveals appropriate behavior among non-Jewish nations and the miraculous demonstration of God's power before their rulers. One and 2 Maccabees provide testimony to the tensions over what constituted idolatry, or the betrayal of Israel's God in the face of claims to divinity by the Seleucid rulers. Two Maccabees introduces the concept of death rather than compromise with idolatry as the paradigmatic form of loyalty to the covenant.

The literatures of interpreting the Hebrew Bible during this period provide juridical frameworks for the boundaries of covenant and community. Turning outward toward the other required the development of behaviors and attitudes where those loyal to the covenant could demonstrate their separation from others. We can observe these frameworks in the manuals of discipline in the Qumran community, the Gospels and Epistles of the New Testament, and in the traditions of the Oral Torah in rabbinic Judaism.

Turning toward the Other and fidelity to the covenant can be observed in the literature of the early Christian communities. When early Christians turned to the God of Israel, the demands of loyalty to and separation from biblical Israel weighed upon them. The Gospels provide one answer: Jesus Christ is the fulfillment, and transformation of the variety of divine commandments to Israel opened the door to their self-assessment as the new or true Israel. The tension between the claims of Israel and God's relationship with all other nations is made more explicit in the writings of St. Paul in Galatians 3 or Romans 9–11.

However, the need to focus on the relationship with Israel as the Jewish people or the community of believers in Jesus Christ reaches a significant resolution in the Epistle to the Hebrews. In this book the rites of Israel and the Scripture of Israel are absorbed into the person of Christ who becomes the key to understanding the message of the Hebrew Bible. What has happened before in diverse ways has been accomplished once and for all time by Jesus of Nazareth. In Jesus, the many become one.

Two streams of interpretation emerge from Hebrews and develop in the Christian tradition of interpretation of the Hebrew Bible. The first stream which may be found in the Epistle of Barnabas and Melito of Sardis constitutes what I would call the *via negativa*: those who lay claim to the Hebrew Bible as Israel according to the rabbis go in the wrong path. Those who insist on fulfilling the precepts of the Hebrew Bible betray the covenant, and their lives are without value. A second stream discerns a profound value in the place of those who interpret the Hebrew Bible as the Jewish people. For these theologians, represented in the early Church by Augustine and Gregory the Great, the Jewish people are part of the economy of divine salvation. They "carry" the "books" of the Church and are witnesses to the "victory" of Christian faith.[6]

The rabbis, like the communities of early Christians, also wrestled with competing claims for how the covenants in Hebrew Scripture might be formulated. As the rabbis transmitted the oral traditions they focused on juridical boundary issues. They elevated biblical denunciations of idolatry and attempted to define the boundaries of what constituted *'avodah zara.'* The pagan worship practices of the ancient world provided the rabbis with a most convenient, indeed plain meaning through the interpretation of the biblical prohibitions against idolatry. Those who would be part of Israel's continuing covenant were to separate themselves from all participation in pagan cultic activity. However, they also suspected that the pagans who engaged in commercial transactions with Jews might put their profit into cultic activity. Therefore, proscriptions against "idolatry" extend beyond cultic activity into the spheres of commerce and property law. We can then observe a homology between the biblical laws against idolatry and those developed by the rabbis. Idolatry was the boundary between Israel and others: cult, property, and commerce all required some form of regulation to maintain the sanctity of the Jewish community.

Within the web of rabbinic prohibitions about idolatry we can detect an ambivalence or apologetic motif. One statement argues, "R. Hisda said to

Avimi: There is a tradition that the tractate Avodah Zarah of our father Abraham consisted of four hundred chapters. We have learned only five and yet we do not know what we are saying (Avodah Zara 14b)." Several motifs of rabbinic thought are evident in this passage. First is the existence of oral Torah during the period of the patriarchs. Before Sinai, the patriarchs eagerly studied the oral law. Second, the tractate concerning the laws of idolatry in Abraham's time was much more extensive, four hundred chapters. Presumably the reason for these extensive delineations of laws was that in Abraham's time idolatry was a very serious problem. To belong to Abraham's people in that period required an intimate knowledge of the practices of idolaters. By contrast, the five chapters available in the rabbis' time indicated that either knowledge might have been lost or, most likely, that they required less detailed knowledge. This contrast brings us to the third observation about this passage: If the rabbis claimed, "we don't know what we are saying," they admit that the problem of idolatry might be entirely less dangerous. Further indication of the lack of salience of idolatry in their time is evident in the rabbinic statement, "God created two evil inclinations in the world: one toward idolatry and the other toward incest. The former has already been uprooted while the later still holds sway" (Canticles Rabba 7:8). Rabbinic statements of such an apodictic nature should always be understood with a measure of caution. However, the idea that "idolatry has already been uprooted" may provide us with a hint that when the Rabbis observed idolatry in their own era, it was of a different order of magnitude than idolatry during the biblical period.[7]

One might argue that the rabbis developed their ideas of idolatry in order to set limits on the contacts between Jews and non-Jews. They did not deny that non-Jews had a relationship with the God of Israel. We can observe this relationship between God and non-Jews in the rabbinic extensions of biblical peoples to identify them as Edom, Moab, and Ishmael. By the Middle Ages the use of Edom for Christianity and Ishmael for Islam had become commonplace.

Some of the earliest rabbinic texts such as Mekhilta on Exodus emphasize that the Jewish people/Israel's relationship with God is unique. They were the center of the drama of the theophany at Sinai. However, each nation also was given an opportunity to become part of the same covenant. Their behavior is contrasted to the behavior of Israel. Each of them asks the content of the covenant, and God responds with a particular commandment: Ishmaelites-"robbery"; Moabites-"incest"; Edomites-"murder." When they discover the specific behavioral prohibition, they refuse to enter the covenant. Each people must refuse because, ironically, they obey the fate assigned to them by the rabbis. Only Israel accepts the covenant without any pre-conditions, pledging that "All that the Lord has said, we will obey."[8]

In the course of these deliberations about entering the covenant, the compilers of the Mekhilta and their successors presumed that the written Torah and all of its potential explanations (Oral Torah) were transmitted to Moses at Mt. Sinai. This two-fold covenant then becomes the exclusive possession of the Jewish people. The obedience to Torah as appropriated by the Oral Torah remains the exclusive provenance and privilege of the Jewish people. Those who do not accept its validity are not required to observe the Scripture as understood by Jews.

However, the exclusive possession of the dual Torah covenant has never precluded the possibility that God has covenants in the sense of relationship and dialogue with other groups. These relationships were gathered in rabbinic literature under the rubric of the Noachide commandments. These commandments, often seven in number, provide the standard of conduct for all the nations of the world. Through this covenant non-Jews are given the status of semi-converts—*ger toshav*. In soteriological terms, the righteous man of the gentile nations has a share in the world to come even without being a Jew (Maimonides). On a social level, the non-Jew was entitled to full charitable support from the Jewish community. David Novak has provided an extensive treatment of these Noachide commandments.[9] However, even these brief summary statements about the Noachide commandments indicate that the rabbis expanded their juridical framework to bring all nations into the covenant with God.

For our argument in this paper, the Noachide commandments provide the rabbinic resolution of the aporia presented in turning to others. When the rabbis view the divine horizon through Scriptures, they see themselves alone in the light of the covenant. All other nations share in the light, but not with the intensity of Israel. In this way, the tension between the Scriptural rejection of idolatrous practices of the nations, and yet the obedience of their sovereigns to God, is relieved by the fact that non-Israelite nations have a homologous relationship to God. They, like Israel, are under the yoke of commandments. However, the demands upon them are not as extensive as those upon Israel.

We can discern in this second turning, the turning toward others, the following asymmetry: the Jewish people reflects only upon its relationship with God as the most beloved. Other nations have the potential and are indeed engaged in relationships with God. They become, through the Noachide commandments, *ger toshav*, partial converts. To be God's most beloved meant the marginalization of others but not their abandonment. As we have just indicated: They were beloved of God, but not as beloved as Israel. In this manner the primary source of the oral law—Mishnah and Talmud—presenting halakha in a timeless manner rarely mentions other religious claims. As Jews turned toward Christians, their oppressors and protectors, they developed a series of approaches that modified rigid separation in the life-world, while reserving the most stringent separations in the realm of worship and symbolism. From the writings of Katz and Novak, Jewish theologians can observe the conscious effort that Jews had to make with respect to Christians, while Christians immediately had to contend—often with erasure—with the reality of the Jewish people when they made their claim to be the true Israel.

The Third Turning: Turning Together To Be a Blessing

We now have come to the point where I would suggest a third "turning." This turn stands in contrast to the first turn toward God in covenantal relationship as biblical Israel. It expands upon the second turn which is the realization by the inheritors of biblical Israel of their relationship toward others with its hierarchy of covenants or erasure of other covenants. The third turning is accomplished by Jews and Christians as they turn their respective hermeneutical traditions toward each other, and then toward other groups which do not share their common Scriptural source. This third turning by Christians and Jews together has been articulated by John Paul II, who expressed his hope that Jews and Christians become first a blessing toward one another and then together, a blessing to all the nations in fulfillment of the promise to Abraham.

How might we realize this aspiration in our current condition? It surely seems to be a self-explicit demand of our Scriptural heritage. However, within both of our two communities and in the broader fellowship of world religions there remains the fear that a common demand for unity implies a homogeneity of practice. The past practice of Christian mission would seem to underscore these fears. Rev. Peter Phan has described the situation in sixteenth-century China where the indigenous population considered Jews, Christians, and Muslims to be one religion. Within a few generations the catechetical instruction insisted on the supersession of the Jewish covenant by Christians. The prejudices of western Christendom toward Judaism came to the East where they were previously unknown.[10] For Christians to turn to Jews in blessing will require the continuing effort of a new generation of teachers to present Judaism with respect and love.

As a non-missionary religion, Jews would argue that the election of Israel does not imply the erasure or replacement of God's covenant with other nations. However, in the post-Shoah world, the delicate issue of Jewish power has appeared. The birth of the State of Israel has provided a new opportunity for the Jewish people. They might consider rephrasing Irving Greenberg's famous dictum that after the Shoah, no theological statements should be formulated that cannot be pronounced in the presence of burning children. Fifty years after the birth of the State of Israel, Jews must come to terms with the reality of their own power over religious minorities. This new reality raises issues which Western European and American Jews might have considered consigned to the rubble of history. The reinsertion into a commonly used Israeli prayer book, *Rinat Yisrael*, of the phrase in the prayer *'Aleinu leshabeach,'* which concludes every service, which denounces Christianity is a case in point. This prayer had been excised from most prayer books of all streams of modern Jewry, and its reintroduction is disturbing. Naturally, one may argue that there is no necessary link between a derisive phrase and violence. However, the reappearance of this phrase is problematic in building toward a renewed encounter between our two communities. In our era, Jewish and Christian communities have many members for whom the rethinking of the continuity of the covenant for Jews by Christians and the relationship of the Jewish God toward non-Jews as idolaters is not at all desirable. People who hold these opinions denounce more generous interpretations of the covenant as compromise or relativism.[11]

Is there an understanding of our covenant with God in a way that permits both communities to turn toward one another in love and respect that might avoid the accusations of relativism or compromise? I believe that there is, and that our fragmented world requires our common effort. Let me delineate three paths:

The first path is well grounded in our past experience. We might summarize this path in the following manner: *There is only one covenant. Even though God is capable of establishing an infinite number of covenants, all other covenants are truly secondary and only shadows of the first.* The history of the Jewish-Christian relationship has used this argument until the modern period. Both communities have successfully created rigid boundaries between them. The only form of conversation possible was disputation which often, though not inevitably, led to violence—and always, at some point, to the erasure of the Jewish population through expulsion. It is precisely against this exclusive formulation that Michael Wyschogrod argues in his book, *The Body of Faith*:

> There is value in talking to one another in and by itself, apart from any results' achieved.....To be with fellow (human beings) is to become aware of (their) mode of being in the world, of the reality of (their) being . . . .Let us realize that the alternative to speaking is violence. There really is no such thing as ignoring a fellow human being....Not to speak with my neighbors is a mode of relating to (them), and even if the mode does not immediately express itself in violence, it points toward it because the alternative to speech is communication by deed, violent deed.[12]

The logic of Wyschogrod's statement belies its simplicity. We move toward violence when we do not encounter another human being in conversation. However, when we engage in disputation, there can be no conversation because our Truth drowns out any possibility of hearing the other person. The first path leads us into the endless repetition of the past. It may very well protect our communities from outside influence, but it renders them vulnerable to violence.

The second path urges dialogue and conversation between Christians and Jews. Its goal is not the erasure of the Other, but to describe the historical situation of the early Church and the "parting of the ways" between Judaism and Christianity. This path had its origins in the nineteenth century with the works of Abraham Geiger and reached its greatest intensity just before the Shoah.[13] Its principal question was, "Did Jesus belong to Jerusalem or Athens? Was the essence of Christian teaching grounded in Judaism, or did Jesus move beyond the parochialism of the Hebrew Bible toward a universal philosophical truth?" The answer to this question produced contestatory scholarship by Jews and Christians. Adolph Harnack and his followers argued that it was the estrangement of Jesus from Judaism that made Christianity the bearer of the unique truth of Israel's God. From the Jewish community we have the writings of Leo Baeck, Martin Buber, Joseph Klausner, and others who argued that Jesus was indeed true to the Jewish prophetic tradition, while Paul, influenced by Hellenistic mystery cults, led early Christians away from their Jewish roots.[14] For our question of covenant, the writings of Franz Rosenzweig have special importance. For Rosenzweig, Judaism and Christianity have reciprocal roles. Judaism is the center of the star. It provides the "heat." Christianity presents the rays of the star reaching outward through space and time. Both communities have their task:

> Before God, then, Jew and Christian both labor at the
> same task. He cannot dispense with either. He has set
> enmity between the two for all time, and withal has most
> intimately bound each to each. To us (Jews) he gave eter-
> nal life by kindling the fire of the Star of his truth in our

hearts. Them (the Christians) he set on the eternal way by causing them to pursue the rays of that Star of his truth for all time unto the eternal end. We (Jews) thus espy in our hearts the true image of the truth, yet on the other hand we turn our backs on temporal life and the life of the times turns away from us. They (the Christians), for their part, run after the current of time, but the truth remains at their back; though led by it, since they follow its raise, they do not see it with their eyes. The truth, the whole truth, belongs neither to them nor to us. For we too, though we bear it within us, must for that very reason first immerse our glance into our own interior if we would see it, and there, while we see the Star, we do not see the rays. And the whole truth would demand not only seeing its light but also what was illuminated by it. They (the Christians), however, are in any event already destined for all time to see what is illuminated and not the light. And thus we both have but a part of the whole truth. . . . A direct view of the whole truth is granted only to him who sees it in God. That, however, is a view beyond this life . . . Thus both of us, they as much as we . . . are creatures precisely for the reason that we do not see the whole truth.[15]

I have quoted at length from Rosenzwieg because he presents such a rich and complex image of the Jewish-Christian relationship. From his perspective both Jews and Christians have received the same revelation from God. However, they understand the revelation and realize it in diverse ways. In the *Star of Redemption* the highest form of the revelation comes to the Jews, while Christians have a secondary comprehension. What strikes me about Rosenzweig's image of the Jewish-Christian relationship is that the reciprocity is grounded in what he calls *Feindschaft*, which means "enmity," "hatred," or "hostility." It seems odd that the divine plan would provide for a reciprocal relationship between Jews and Christians which is driven by hatred between them. Therefore, I would like to suggest another path which would retain the notion of reciprocity and transcend the necessity of "eternal hatred" (*in aller Zeit Feindschaft*).

The third path is grounded in the reality of a reciprocal relationship between Jews and Christians. However, it would lead them away from an obsession with the problem of the origins of Christianity and toward a study of their traditions of interpreting the Hebrew Bible, not just the historicizing interpretations born in the modern university but their full histories of interpretation. This path would lead both of our communities back to their common root. For Jews and Christians to return to their interpretive traditions of the Hebrew Bible would fulfill the idea that Abraham Joshua Heschel claimed: that great reformulations of Judaism and Christianity begin with a study of the Hebrew Bible.[16] To follow the diverging paths of interpretation throughout our history together, and doing this in the living presence of one another, will provide both an atmosphere of dialogue and its content.

The theme of one covenant or two may be illuminated by a study of Psalm 62:12, "God has spoken once, we have heard it twice." This verse speaks to a significant motif both in the Jewish and Christian traditions. How do we resolve the gap between the claim to divine revelation in the language of Scripture and the arduous human task of explicating what is heard and read—and then bringing the interpretation to realization in our daily lives?

The auditory element in Psalm 62 is salient. We humans rely not only on what we see or read, but what we hear. When the text is read we must bring the word to life within our community. We invite the "to and fro" of conversation. However, the conversation is not without boundaries. We want to have a conversation in which both Christians and Jews would bring forward what our traditions have gathered, and make this the subject for further conversation.

When we emphasize the Scriptural text and its interpretation we follow both the world of speech and the echoes of that speech in the writings of our exegetical traditions. We can admit the gap between ourselves and our ancestors. We can freely acknowledge the fragmentation in our understanding of language that has been so debased by the Shoah.

The third path has already been taken by some brave pioneers. Rabbi David Hartman has gathered Jewish and Christian theologians at the Shalom Hartman Institute in Jerusalem for serious study. The Institute for Christian-Jewish Studies in Baltimore holds annual institutes where rabbis and Christian clergy study text on which they will preach sermons. Paul van Buren's *Theology of the Jewish-Christian Reality* demonstrates the results of his years of study with Jews.[17] Jeremy Cohen's book, *Be Fertile and Increase*, demonstrates how much we can learn about the development of attitudes toward sexuality and the body in both traditions.[18]

We now can return to Psalm 62:12 and its implications. I would argue that it suggests only one covenant from the perspective of God. This one covenant stands both revealed and concealed in the language of Hebrew Scripture. There are, however, two distinct yet recognizably analogous realizations of the covenant: one in Oral Torah for Jews, and one in the incarnate word for Christians. Both of these realizations present a challenge to either community's urge to dominate their conversation with each other.

I do not advocate flattening the diversity of the two realizations of the divine words, but to emphasize the divergent traditions which produce continued learning and conversation. It is in the third path that Jews and Christians can realize fully the complex nature of divine revelation. *Yalqut Shim'oni*, a thirteenth century compendium of Jewish interpretations, explains our verse as follows:

> "God has spoken once, we have heard it twice." One Scriptural verse may provide two meanings but two verses have only one meaning. Rabbi Ishmael taught, "Like a hammer striking on a rock" (Jer. 23:29). Just as the hammer (striking) divides into many sparks, so a scriptural verse may have several meanings. (Furthermore) the ways of the Holy One are not like those of human beings. A human being may not say two things at once, but the One Who Spoke and the World Came into Being spoke ten commandments in one word . . . . A human being cannot

hear two other human beings when they are shouting as
one, but God is able to hear all the peoples of the earth cry
out before the divine presence.[19]

The contrast between human and divine speech is also the subject of the
Glossa Ordinaria's excerpt from St. Augustine on Psalm 62:12:

"Once" God has spoken eternally. This means that he has
set forth all things which I have heard two. It would seem
to be a contrary statement that one could speak once and
hear twice . . . . But among humans God has created in the
divine self one word through which all things have been
made and in which all things are created at the same time.[20]

Both of these exegetical statements speak of the divine word and its disposition in our lives across the traditions. In analogous manner, Christians and
Jews may understand that the reality of the differences are grounded in a
language which eludes any singularly dominant and exclusive interpretation.

In turning toward one another to become a blessing to each other we
have a long journey of study ahead. It will require perduring tenacity, good
humor, and patience. It will never shape itself as a homogenous reading or
collapse into singularity. The third path may lead us to sing a new song which
will be both dialogue and argument, polyphony and monod. As we listen to
each other's differing yet similar interpretations of our common text, we will
be able to invite more voices into the song.

ENDNOTES

Scripture references are the author's own translation.

1. David Tracy, *The Analogical Imagination: Christian Theology and the Culture of Pluralism* (New York: Crossroads, 1981), and *Plurality and Ambiguity: Hermeneutics, Religion and Hope* (San Francisco: Harper and Row, 1987).

2. Walter Benjamin, "Theory of Knowledge" (N 2a, 3) quoted in Susan Handelman, *Fragments of Redemption; Jewish Thought and Theory in Benjamin, Scholem and Levinas* (Bloomington: Indiana University Press, 1991) p. 7.

3. Norbert Lohfink, *The Covenant Never Revoked* (New York: Paulist Press, 1991); John Pawlikowski, *Christ in the Light of the Jewish-Christian Dialogue* (New York: Paulist Press, 1982); Friedrich-Wilhelm Marquardt, *Das christliche Bekenntnis zu Jesu dem Juden: eine Christologie*, 2 vols. (Munich: Ch. Kaiser, 1990) ; Bertold Klappert, *Worauf wir hoffen? Das Kommen Gottes und der Weg Jesu* (Gütersloh: Gerd Mohn, 1997).

4. Joseph Ratzinger, *Gospel, Catechesis, Catechism: Sidelights on the Catechism of the Catholic Church* (San Francisco: Ignatius Press, 1997); John Paul II, *Spiritual Pilgrimage: Texts on Jews and Judaism 1979-1995* (New York: Crossroads, 1995).

5. Jakob Katz, *Exclusiveness and Tolerance: Jewish-Gentile Relations in Medieval and Modern Times* (New York: Schocken Press, 1962) presents the most sophisticated analysis of the ambiguities of this relationship.

6. Joseph Hayyim Yerushalmi in "Response to Rosemary Ruether" in *Auschwitz: Beginning of a New Era* (New York: Ktav, 1974) pointed out that this idea of the Jews as "witness people" has often provided a bulwark of protection for the Jewish people against the more negative stream. Steven R. Haynes, *Reluctant Witnesses: Jews and the Christian Imagination* (Louisville, KY: Westminster John Knox Press, 1995)

demonstrates the darker elements in this "protective" doctrine in contemporary Christian thought.

7. Moshe Halbertal, *Idolatry* (Cambridge, MA: Harvard University Press, 1992).

8. *Mekilta de-Rabbi Ishmael*, translated by Jacob Lauterbach. Philadelphia: (Jewish Publication Society, 1967), vol. 2, pp. 234–237.

9. David Novak, *The Image of the Non-Jew and Judaism: An Historical and Constructive Study of the Noachide Laws* (New York: The Mellen Press, 1988).

10. Peter Phan, *Mission and Catechesis: Alexandre de Rhodes and Inculturation in Seventeenth-Century Vietnam* (Maryknoll, NY: Orbis Books, 1998).

11. See the comments by Clemens Thoma, *A Christian Theology of Judaism*, translated by Helga Croner (New York: Paulist Press, 1980), pp. 85–92, and also *Theologische Beziehungen zwischen Christentum und Judentum* (Darmstadt: Wissenschaftliche Buchgesellschaft, 1989), pp. 45–62, 157–163.

12. Michael Wyschogrod, *The Body of Faith: Judaism as Corporeal Election* (New York: The Seabury Press, 1983), p. 242.

13. Susannah Heschel, *Abraham Geiger and the Jewish Jesus* (Chicago: University of Chicago Press, 1998).

14. Hans Joachim Schoeps, *Jüdisch-christliches Religionsgespräch im neunzehnten Jahrhundert*, mit einem Nachwort von Edna Brocke (Munich and Frankfurt am Main: Jüdischer Verlag Athenäum, 1961), pp. 115–184 and the concluding remarks by Dr. Brocke, pp. 200–208.

15. This translation from Franz Rosenzweig's *Star of Redemption* Part III, Book 3, is quoted in *Jewish Perspectives on Christianity: Leo Baeck, Martin Buber, Franz Rosenzweig, Will Herberg, Abraham J. Heschel* (New York: Crossroad, 1990), pp. 224–225. The translation of the *Star of Redemption* is by William Hallo (New York: Holt, Rineheart, Winston, 1971) pp. 415–416.

16. Abraham Joshua Heschel, "No Religion is an Island" and "The God of Israel and Christian Renewal" in *Moral Grandeur and Spiritual*

Audacity, edited by Susannah Heschel (New York: Farrar, Straus and Giroux, 1996), pp. 235–250 and 268–285.

17. Paul van Buren, *A Theology of the Jewish-Christian Reality*, 3 volumes (New York: Seabury Press, 1980).

18. Jeremy Cohen, *Be Fertile and Increase. Fill the Earth and Master It: The Ancient and Medieval Career of a Biblical Text* (Ithaca: Cornell University Press, 1989).

19. *Yalqut Shim'oni* to Psalm 62 (Berlin: Horeb, 1936) paragraph 783.

20. *Biblia Latina cum Glossa Ordinaria*, Facsimile Reprint of the Editio Princeps Adolph Rusch of Strassburg 1480/81 (Turnhout: Brepols, 1992).

CONVERSATION ONE

The Search for a New Paradigm for the Christian-Jewish Relationship: A Response to Michael Signer

JOHN T. PAWLIKOWSKI

Chapter Four of the Second Vatican Council's Declaration *Nostra Aetate*, which addressed the relationship of the Church and the Jewish People, represents one of the most decided shifts in Catholic thinking emerging from the Council. Since at least the second century of the common era the prevalent position in Christian thought was that Jews had been replaced in the covenantal relationship with God by the newly emergent Christian community, the "true Israel," because of Jewish failure to acknowledge Jesus as the expected Messiah and Jewish responsibility for his eventual death on the Cross. In contrast, *Nostra Aetate* affirmed the continuity of the Jewish People in the covenantal relationship, underscored the constructive influence of the Jewish tradition on Jesus and the early Church, and said that there never was a basis in fact for the historic deicide accusation against the Jews that over the centuries was the source of their persecution and at times even death. In making their argument for a total reversal in Catholic thinking on Jews and Judaism, the bishops of the Council bypassed almost all the teachings about Jews and Judaism in Christian thought prior to Vatican II and returned to chapters 9–11 of Paul's Letter to the Romans where the Apostle reaffirms the continued inclusion of the Jews in the covenant after the coming of Christ even though this remains for him a "mystery" that defies complete theological explanation. In one sense, the bishops in *Nostra Aetate* were picking up where St. Paul left off in the first century.[1]

I welcome the opportunity to respond to Professor Signer's rich text because it parallels in many ways the road I believe we must walk together if both our communities are to reevaluate the Jewish-Christian relationship in light of the profound change in thought generated by *Nostra Aetate* and a host of similar Protestant documents.[2] While I think the process of reformulation will prove much easier for Jews on a theological level, given that the Jewish community never gave meaning to its own existence in terms of the obliteration of Christianity, Jews certainly will find such reevaluation painful in light of their historic experience of Christian antisemitism.[3] For Christians the effort will also prove painful in a somewhat different way since it must involve a fundamental reassessment of their identity as a religious community. If they are no longer the "true Israel," as they once proclaimed, what constitutes their basic identity as a religious community? On the theological and catechetical level the Christian churches have begun some rethinking of their classical position. But at the level of worship—perhaps the most critical area because it is where Christian proclamation touches the ordinary believer on an ongoing basis—little has been done so far to incorporate the fundamental theological about-face introduced by *Nostra Aetate*. The liturgical texts, especially for the crucial seasons of Advent, Lent, and Easter, still proclaim subtly (and sometimes not so subtly) fundamental aspects of the pre-Vatican II theology of the Church as the fulfillment of the old Israel.

Professor Signer lays out three approaches from the Jewish side towards the rethinking of Judaism's relationship with Christianity. While he seems sympathetic to aspects of the first two approaches, he believes that in the end they wind up in theological polarization that serves neither community very well. The third approach, which he appears to favor, would downplay the discussion of origins in favor of a mutual reflection on common texts. I do believe that such mutual reflection is indeed valuable, whether it takes place relative to the Hebrew Scriptures or to the impact of Jewish texts and practice on early Christian writings and perhaps vice versa to a lesser extent.[4] It certainly may help build a sense of religious bonding. But in my judgment it is insufficient. We do need to confront more directly the question of origins. This is especially the case for the Christian community since theological anti-Judaism has been so central to our historic self-expression. I do feel nonetheless that following the third path of joint reflection on common texts is vital not only for the inherently new understandings it will provide both for Jews and Christians but also for the improved climate it can create for a discussion of the question of origins.

The challenge now facing Christianity in light of *Nostra Aetate* and parallel Protestant documents is how we can both honor classical theological claims about "newness" in Christ while remaining faithful at the same time to Vatican II's insistence that this "newness" does not involve the termination of the original covenant with the Jewish people as the Churches have often argued. Additionally, we shall have to decide whether the "old covenant-new covenant" terminology, so widespread in Christianity, helps or hinders our ability to face up to the post-conciliar theological challenge.

As individual Catholic and Protestant (and recently a few Orthodox) theologians, as well as official Church documents, have begun to grapple with restating the theology of the Christian-Jewish relationship in a more positive way, no clear consensus has emerged as yet. The pre-conciliar approach advocated by several scholars in the vanguard of improved Christian-Jewish understanding, such as Charles Journet,[5] initially became attractive to a wider group within the Church. Rooted in Paul's "mystery" approach to Jewish-Christian relations, this viewpoint was appropriated by the likes of Jean Daniélou,[6] Hans Urs von Balthasar,[7] Augustin Cardinal Bea,[8] and several others. While each of these scholars had a distinctive twist on the Pauline perspective, they all remained uncompromising on the question of the centrality of Christ and the fulfillment that his coming brought to salvation history. Although they all found ways to leave some theological space for Judaism after the Christ event, they made no sustained effort to reconcile the apparent tension resulting from these two assertions. Rather, they simply fell back on the Pauline contention that their compatibility remains a "mystery" in the divinely instituted plan of human salvation.

A decade or so after the Council Catholic theologians began to move away from this "mystery" paradigm and to search for bolder ways to restate the church-synagogue bond theologically. In general, two models have surfaced, though a few have advocated a third option. The two major models have generally been designated the "single" and "double" covenant theories. Each has several variants.

The Single Covenant Model

The single covenant model holds that Jews and Christians basically belong to one ongoing covenantal tradition that began at Sinai. In this perspective the Christ event represented the decisive moment when the Gentiles were able to enter fully into the special relationship with God which Jews already enjoyed and in which they continued. Some holding this viewpoint maintain that the decisive features of the Christ event have universal application, including to Jews. Others are more inclined to argue that the Christian appropriation and reinterpretation of the original covenantal tradition, in and through Jesus, applies primarily to non-Jews.

A single covenantal perspective has clearly dominated the many statements and speeches of Pope John Paul II on the theology of the Church's relationship to the Jewish people. He has now spoken more on this topic than any other pontiff in history. While a certain lack of clarity remains in the corpus of John Paul's writings on several issues related to the theology of Christian-Jewish relations, there is little doubt that the Pope firmly believes in the continued bonding between church and synagogue after the Christ event. This bonding exists as a core element of Christian self-identity for John Paul II who regards the Jewish-Christian relationship as "sui generis." It is quite different in his mind, particularly on the theological level, from the relationship that the Church has with any other world religion.[9]

Several prominent Christian scholars have supported the single covenantal model. One is the American theologian Monika Hellwig. While she has not pursued this question in earnest in recent years, her earlier writings portrayed Judaism and Christianity as both pointing toward the same fundamental eschatological reality which still lies ahead. The two faith communities share a common messianic mission in terms of this reality, though each may work somewhat differently in carrying it out. For Hellwig there is "a most important sense in which Jesus is not yet Messiah. The eschatological tension has not been resolved . . . . Logically the Messianic Event should be seen as lengthy, complex, unfinished and mysterious."[10]

In Hellwig's paradigm, the one covenant forged at Sinai continues in force. This affirmation of continuing divine faithfulness to the covenant with the Jewish people forces Hellwig into rethinking the fundamental significance of Jesus as the Christ. Her response is to see in the Christ event not primarily the completion of messianic prophecies, but the possibility of all Gentiles encountering the God of Abraham, Sarah, and Isaac. Jesus the Jew opened the gates for Gentiles to enter the covenantal election first granted the Jewish people and to experience the intimacy with God that this election brought them. Hence Christians must look to God's continuing revelation in contemporary Jewish experience to grasp fully God's self-communication today. While some ambiguity remains in Hellwig's thought on this point, she also seems to imply that the revelation given humankind in and through the Christ event serves as one barometer for Jewish faith expression as well. Her theology of Jewish-Christian linkage thus ultimately involves some rethinking of respective self-definitions by both communities.

Hellwig is willing to grant that in the end it does not matter all that much whether we speak of one or two covenants in terms of the Jewish-Christian relationship. The crucial question is whether people in the Church describe Christianity as fulfilling everything valuable in Judaism so that the latter no longer retains any salvific role or whether, instead, Christians understand themselves as simultaneous participants with Jews in an ongoing covenantal relationship with God. She still prefers to stay with the vocabulary and imagery of a single covenant because it has a solid biblical basis and has the possibility of unfolding in newly constructive ways.[11]

An internationally known voice in theological discussion for the past several decades (now deceased) was the Episcopal scholar Paul van Buren. His is without question the most comprehensive effort at constructing a new theological model for the Jewish-Christian relationship. *The Burden of Freedom* was his first, rather preliminary statement in which he mainly emphasized the deficiencies in previous models.[12] This work was followed by his major trilogy on the topic which includes *Discerning The Way*,[13] *A Christian Theology of the People of Israel*,[14] and *A Theology of the Jewish Christian Reality, Part III: Christ in Context*.[15]

Van Buren argued that Christianity has more or less eradicated all Jewish elements from its faith expression in favor of a pagan-Christian tradition. The

Holocaust represents the pinnacle of this Christian tradition. The Church must now rejoin Judaism, no easy task in light of the "cover-up" which van Buren believed took place during the first century of Christian existence. When the Christian leadership realized that the promised signs of the messianic era were nowhere to be seen, the response was not to modify the Church's initial theological claims about the Christ event but rather to push the actual realization of these claims to the metahistorical, "higher" realm. This metahistorical realm of messianic fulfillment was penetrable through faith. It was not subject to historical verification of any kind. With the completion of this transfer, the path was cleared for the proclamation of the Easter mystery as an unqualified triumph on the part of Christ, a triumph in which the Jewish people had no continuing role.

In his more recent writings van Buren has increasingly insisted on the need to recognize that Israel consists of two connected but distinct branches. Both are essential to a full definition of the term. Christianity represents the community of Gentile believers drawn by the God of the Jewish people to worship him and to make his love known among the peoples of the world. For van Buren it is not a question of the Church now suddenly abandoning its historic proclamation of Jesus Christ as the Son of God. But Jesus was not the Christ in one crucial sense. He was not the long-awaited Jewish Messiah. And so post-Easter Judaism remains a religion of legitimate messianic hope rather than of spiritual blindness or outdated messianic expectation.

The shared messianic vision of Judaism and Christianity leads van Buren to advocate the notion of the "co-formation" of the two faith communities. By this he meant that both of the branches of Israel must grow and develop alongside each other rather than in isolation. Let me add at this point that Rabbi Signer's proposed joint study of sacred texts would certainly fit in well here, but in my judgment only if both Christianity and Judaism clearly acknowledged the necessity of such co-formation as a result of a theological about-face regarding the nature of their interrelationship. Obviously the about-face for Christianity will prove far more challenging as I have already underlined. In the van Buren perspective, each religious community would continue to retain a measure of distinctiveness while at the same time experiencing

a developing mutuality characterized by understanding and love. This growing together in love would increase each partner's freedom to be its distinctive self while maintaining an awareness of the necessity of mutual
cooperation.

In his later years van Buren began to give some in-depth attention to the
significance of Christ within his theology of Israel. His interpretation of the
"new" revelation in Jesus focused on the manifestation of the divine will that
Gentiles too are welcome to walk in God's way. Through Jesus the Gentiles
were summoned for the first time as full participants in the ongoing covenantal plan of salvation. But the Gentiles' appropriation of this plan, van Buren
admitted, took them well beyond the circles of God's eternal covenant with
the Jewish people. In no way, however, did it annul the original covenant. Nor
can Christians bypass the original covenantal people in their quest for bonding with the God of Abraham, Sarah, and Isaac who was revealed to them
through the ministry and person of the Jew Jesus.

Jesus did not expect a future in the ordinary sense of the word. From
that perspective his message is ahistorical, much like the rabbis of his time.
He anxiously awaited the coming of God's reign which would replace the
present era. He did reveal a deep, personal intimacy with God, but his relationship with God maintained a clear line of demarcation between himself
and the Father, a view that a scripture scholar such as the late Raymond
Brown would contest. For Brown the relationship is far more ambiguous and
the separation not as clearcut as van Buren maintains.[16] As van Buren saw it,
Jesus' sense of intimacy with the divine was very Jewish. Van Buren put it
this way:

> We can only speculate about what went on in Jesus' own
> soul, but we can know how the early witness presents him.
> It presents him as we could expect Jews to present a Jew
> wholly devoted to God. It presents him as one whose will
> was to do God's will. His cause was nothing but the cause
> of God. In this sense and in no other, he had no will of his
> own and no cause of his own to defend. In other words, he

was strong-willed and stubborn in the cause of God. In
short, he was a Jew.[17]

For van Buren any Christological proclamation today, particularly in
view of the Holocaust, must make it abundantly clear that the divine authori-
zation Jesus enjoyed to speak and act in the name of the Father did not exempt
him from the realities of the human condition, and that the powers of death
and darkness continued to hold sway after the Easter event. In short, a major
modification of many Christological claims is demanded by a new understanding of Jesus' relationship to the Jewish community of his day, by the
Jewish people's return to the historical existence in the modern State of Israel,
and by the Holocaust.[18] If we are to take one traditional Christological doctrine with utmost seriousness, it is the incarnation. The Council of Chalcedon
insisted that the Word "became" flesh, not merely that the Word had "put on"
flesh. Jesus' participation in the human condition was total and real in every
sense of the term.

Where van Buren ultimately wound up on the Christological question
in his published writings was the proclamation of Jesus as "Israel's gift to the
Gentile church." Jesus' primary mission was to reconcile the Gentiles with
God. This remains a hard saying for most Christians still victimized by the
Church's erroneous first-century belief that Jesus was expelled rather than
given by Israel.

Van Buren acknowledged that Jews might have some difficulty with his
claim because Judaism never recognized Jesus as its gift to the Church. But
this latter situation is largely the result of the sufferings endured for centuries
by the Jewish people in the name of Jesus. But as the Church begins to move
away from the "expulsion" theology of Israel, Jews, van Buren believed,
would begin to rethink their traditional posture towards Jesus as well. For if
Israel remains bound to God, and if it is God who gives the Church the gift of
the Jew Jesus, then Israel remains clearly implicated in this gift.

In giving their special allegiance in faith to Jesus, van Buren argued,
Christians follow, in the words of Paul to the Romans (see 15:8), a person
who "became a servant to the Jewish people." Herein lies the basis of Israel's

claim upon Christianity, a claim sealed through Jesus Christ. The Church can never escape this profound debt to Israel and profoundly corrupts itself anytime it tries:

> To acknowledge the claim of God's love, with which the Church is confronted in the witness to Christ, is therefore always to acknowledge the legitimate claim of Israel. No Jew need repeat that claim today, since it is repeated to the church again and again, whenever it rehearses the things concerning Jesus of Nazareth, by his reality as a Jew. It comes as his call to follow him in his service to his people.[19]

In some presentations to the Christian Study Group of Scholars which is dedicated to the ongoing exploration of Christian understandings of Jews and Judaism, van Buren, a longtime member along with myself, attempted to respond to criticism, including mine, that he failed to explain adequately the uniquely Christian appropriation of the covenant with Israel in and through Christ.[20] He put forth the notion that the revelation in Christ involved making God "transparent" to humanity in a away that surpassed the revelation present in the initial covenantal disclosure. Van Buren did not appear to pursue this track very much further prior to his death. If he had, it would have positioned him closer to those sometimes categorized as "double covenant" proponents, for he would have been arguing that the Christ event involved not only the opportunity for Gentiles to enter the covenanted community but also the exposure to an enhanced understanding of the divine link to humanity. Instead he began to pursue a somewhat more traditional path, trying to understand the Christ event in terms of the "binding of Isaac" narrative. This shift, which he admitted was moving him away from the viewpoint in his major trilogy, was occasioned by his reading of Jon Levenson's volume *The Death and Resurrection of the Beloved Son*.[21]

Another important representative of the single covenant position has been Norbert Lohfink. Much as van Buren, Lohfink's view of the single covenantal tradition embracing Jews and Christians is more complex than first imagined. Unlike van Buren he does not expand the term "Israel." Rather, he speaks of a twofold way to salvation within a single covenantal framework.[22] In concert with van Buren he holds to the view that Christians and Jews appropriate this single covenant in different ways. The Christian way is strongly rooted in the New Testament's understanding that the eschatological fullness of the "new covenant" promised in the book of Jeremiah has already begun. But this sense of the dawn of eschatological covenantal renewal is not absent from post-biblical Jewry. So one cannot posit a hard and fast distinction between Jews and Christians in this regard.

Lohfink interprets the "parallel" ways of Israel and the Church in a dynamic sense. They are not destined to remain separated permanently; otherwise God's salvific design for the creation would be thwarted. Hence his rejection of a double covenant approach which he regards as a form of permanent separation between Jews and Christians that would undermine their jointly necessary witness against the forces of power and sin in the world. He concludes that:

> One must speak of a "twofold way to salvation" in such a way that one does not deny to the other that it is God's instrument. But to condemn the two ways, facts that they are, to permanent parallelism for all time on the ground that there are simply countless ways to salvation would be to despair of the possibility of the actual salvation of this world, of that salvation of which the Bible speaks. This ends up, hard as it sounds, in unbelief before God's biblical world.[23]

Double Covenant Perspectives

The double covenant perspective is frequently misrepresented. It is often understood in a way that renders the two covenants totally dichotomous. Lohfink appears to fall into such a misrepresentation. In fact, the double covenant model generally begins at the same point as its single covenant counterpart, namely, with a strong affirmation of the continuing bonds between Jews and Christians. But then it prefers to underline the distinctiveness of the two traditions and communities, particularly in terms of their experiences after the gradual separation in the first century C.E. Christians associated with this perspective insist on maintaining the view that through the ministry, teachings, and person of Jesus a vision of God emerged that was distinctively new in terms of its central features. Even though there may well have been important groundwork laid for this emergence in Second Temple or Middle Judaism, what came to be understood regarding the divine-human relationship as a result of Jesus has to be regarded as unprecedented.

A historical note must be introduced at this point. Increasingly Christian and Jewish scholars are stressing the fluidity of the first century of the Common Era. A major transformation was occurring within Judaism. New groups were arising, one of which was the community of Christian Jews. This fact makes it impossible to speak of a single covenant in a linear way. Christianity and Judaism, as they emerged at the dawn of the second century, were post-biblical phenomena. While they remained in most cases deeply rooted in the biblical tradition, including the covenantal tradition, their intense separation which we now know from scholars such as Robert Wilken, Anthony Saldarini, and Robin Scroggs lasted for most of the first century (and even longer in some regions) and left them quite distinctive faith communities. While the Church clearly began as a community of Christian Jews, as scholars such as James Charlesworth and Cardinal Carlo Martini have insisted,[24] this was no longer the case, except in a few areas, by the second century. This reality has been recognized both by Christians and Jews throughout the centuries. It accounts for one of my principal problems with the single covenant perspective, a problem that neither Hellwig nor van Buren nor Lohfink have addressed in any significant way.[25]

One of this century's early pioneers in the effort of rethinking Christianity's theological stance toward the Jewish people was the Anglican James Parkes. Over the years Parkes developed his outline of the double covenant theory on the basis of what he regarded as the two different but complementary revelations given humankind through Sinai and Calvary respectively.[26]

One area in which Parkes' model has been frequently faulted is the scriptural. It does not seem clearly enough rooted in scriptural data. This certainly was not the case with another early proponent of the double covenant theory, the University of Chicago biblical scholar J. Coert Rylaarsdam. His approach was developed almost entirely out of the scriptural tradition. He argued that any adequate theological viewpoint regarding the Jewish-Christian relationship must begin with an acknowledgement of the presence of two distinctive covenants within the Hebrew Scriptures.

The first of these covenants, the one with Israel, focused on God's union with the covenanted community in history. At its core stood a fact of mutual faithfulness and responsibility between God and the Jewish people. This covenant was future-oriented. Divine intervention in history on behalf of the chosen people was an ongoing, openended process. Since its basic élan did not mesh well with the initial proclamation of finality in the Christ event within the apostolic Church, it tended to be downplayed in the New Testament.

The second covenant revolved around the figure of David. It bore a far more eschatological cast. In this covenantal strain religious meaning was rooted in the holiness tradition associated with Mount Zion and the divine presence revealed through the Davidic dynasty. It looked to and celebrated a supra-temporal order of meaning. God was depicted as king of creation and of the nation. The earlier biblical stress on Torah and history is largely abandoned. The tension between these two covenantal traditions in late biblical Judaism led, Rylaarsdam believes, to the growth of several sectarian religious groups. One of these was the eschatologically oriented Christian Church which arose out of the preaching of Jesus. This new faith community quickly found itself beset with some of the same tensions as Judaism. But in early Christianity the Davidic covenantal tradition rapidly gained ascendancy.

Rylaarsdam thus posits the existence of twin biblical covenants. But they are not two chronologically successive covenants in the way Christians have traditionally explained them. Rather these two covenantal traditions permeate both the Hebrew Scriptures and the New Testament. Recognition of these simultaneous rather than consecutive covenants forces upon the Church a radical reshaping of its understanding of the Christ event and the related model of the Jewish-Christian relationship. For if both Judaism and Christianity continue to revolve around the same two covenants that are intimately linked, albeit in paradoxical fashion, then the Church-synagogue relationship, whatever its specific tensions at any given moment, must be understood as one of mutual interdependence.[27]

Though there are valuable insights to be gained from the perspectives of both Parkes and Rylaarsdam, subsequent scholars have judged their models inadequate as the basis for building a new theological relationship between Jews and Christians. Somewhat more promising have been the viewpoints presented by a contributor to this volume, Clemens Thoma, and by the German Catholic theologian Franz Mussner. I include both of them within the "double covenant" category (not something they expressly do themselves) because of their insistence on a distinctive revelation in and through Jesus that clearly goes beyond that of the original covenant with Israel.

Clemens Thoma's approach to the Christian-Jewish relationship is deeply rooted in the Scriptures. He strongly emphasizes the profound connections between Jesus' teachings and the Jewish tradition both prior to and contemporaneous with him. The Hebrew Scriptures also occupy a central role in any expression of Christian faith for Thoma. He emphatically rejects any effort to describe the basic theological tensions between the Church and Israel as rooted in the acceptance/rejection of Jesus. There was no consistent, univocal notion of the messiah in Jewish thought at the time of Jesus. Many diverse understandings surfaced in a period of great creative renewal within Judaism. Some Jews had even reached the conclusion that the notion of messiah should be permanently discarded. Hence there exists no one Jewish expectation to which Jesus can be compared and no grounds for alleging Jewish rejection of Jesus' fulfillment of this expectation:

> It is not correct to say that the decisive or even the sole dif-
> ference between Judaism and Christianity consists in the

> Christian affirmation of Jesus as the messiah and its denial
> by Jews. There are certain asymmetries and considerations
> on both sides that render unacceptable such absolute state-
> ments of the messianic question. For a better evaluation we
> must consider and compare the relative importance and
> place accorded the question in Judaism and Christianity....
> In the last resort, neither in Judaism nor in Christianity is it
> a question of the messiah but of the Kingdom of God, of
> "God who is all in all" (1 Cor 15:28).[28]

For Thoma the uniqueness of Jesus is ultimately located in the unqualified fashion in which he tied the kingdom of God to his own activities and
person. In so doing he was following a trend already present in apocalyptic
interpretations of Judaism. But his sense of intimacy with the Father went
beyond what any branch of Judaism was prepared to acknowledge. Thoma
puts it this way:

> In his relationship to the God and Father, Jesus gathered
> together Old testament Jewish traditions of piety in an
> original way and endowed them with a new beauty. Yet, it
> would be a radical mistake to represent Jesus, on principle
> and in any way at all, as being in opposition to the God of
> Torah. However, he did experience this God in a uniquely
> close and intimate way.[29]

Franz Mussner's perspective bears many similarities to Thoma's. He
shares the same conviction about Jesus' deep, positive links to the Jewish tradition. He likewise rejects any interpretation of the Christ event over against
Judaism in terms of Jesus' fulfillment of biblical messianic prophecies.
Rather the uniqueness of the Christ event arises from the complete identity of
the work of Jesus, as well as his words and actions, with the work of God. As
a result of the revelatory vision in Christ, the New Testament is able to speak

about God with an anthropomorphic boldness not found to the same degree in the Hebrew Scriptures.[30]

In answer to the question what the disciples finally experienced through their close association with Jesus, Mussner speaks of "a unity of action extending to the point of congruence of Jesus with God, an unprecedented existential imitation of God by Jesus."[31] But this imitation, Mussner insists, is quite in keeping with Jewish thinking, a contention that many Jewish scholars would no doubt challenge. The uniqueness of Jesus is to be found in the depth of his imitation of God. So the most distinctive feature of Christianity for Mussner, when contrasted with Judaism, is the notion of incarnation rather than the fulfillment of the messianic prophecies. But even this Christian particularity is an outgrowth of a sensibility profoundly Jewish at its core.

Having laid out the basic principles of his approach to a theological expression of the Jewish-Christian relationship, Mussner amplifies his model with a discussion of what he calls "prophet Christology" and "Son Christology." The "prophet Christology" is chronologically the older. It views Jesus as belonging to the line of prophets who manifested the "pathos" of God and joined their words and actions to the divine plan for human salvation. Christianity never completely abandoned this "prophet Christology," not even in the gospel of John where the "Son Christology" most clearly predominates. The two Christologies do not stand in fundamental opposition. But the "Son Christology" adds a dimension of superiority to Jesus as prophet that makes the differentiation between Christian and Jewish belief more pronounced.

But even this "Son Christology" in Mussner's analysis has some roots in the Jewish tradition. The claims in the past for an essentially non-Jewish basis for this "high" Christology are unfounded in Mussner's view. In fact, he argues, this "Son Christology" owes much of its language and imagery to the Wisdom literature. Mussner has no illusions that calling attention to the connection between "Son Christology" and the Jewish tradition will remove all opposition to it on the part of Jews. But such an understanding might provide an opening for discussing the issue within the framework of the Christian-Jewish dialogue.

From the above survey of recent scholarship on the theology of the Christian-Jewish relationship, it is apparent that the line of demarcation between the single and double covenant perspectives is far from rigid. Both perspectives acknowledge some measure of continued bonding because of the common footage in the Jewish biblical and Second Temple traditions. Both likewise point to a degree of distinctiveness in Christianity's covenantal participation, even if this participation comes through the original covenant with Israel. Many scholars, myself included, remain dissatisfied with the present options of "single" and "double" covenantal language, and we are not quite ready to move to the multicovenantal approach advocated by Rosemary Ruether and in a somewhat different way by Paul Knitter. Nor am I for one completely convinced by Norbert Lohfink's effort to bridge the gap by speaking of two paths to salvation within a single covenantal framework. Proposals for a "siblings" paradigm by Hayim Perelmuter[32] or a "fraternal twins" model being developed by Mary Boys may eventually prove far more fruitful.

At this point, if I am forced to choose between the single and double covenantal models I have a decided preference for the latter. The double covenantal model, despite its evident drawbacks, more faithfully represents the reality of the Christian-Jewish relationship both historically and theologically. Too many of single covenant proponents are excessively locked into a biblical framework.

The double covenant perspective helps to underline the distinctiveness of the revelation experienced in and through Christ. Jesus certainly represented the point of entry for the Gentiles into the covenantal tradition of Israel. But the Christ event involved something more than that. A new understanding emerged over time of the profound linkage between humanity and divinity. Whether we express it in the "transparency of God" language of a Paul van Buren, in the more biblically based terminology of a Clemens Thoma, in the "Son Christology" of a Franz Mussner, or in the "Christology of the Divine-Human Nexus" which I have proposed in my own writings,[33] the Christ event involves more than "Judaism for the gentiles." That is why I have objected, for example, to the title of what is otherwise a very fine book, Clark M. Williamson's *A Guest in the House of Israel: Post-Holocaust Church*

Theology.[34] While the single covenant paradigm may somewhat better protect the sense of linkage between Jews and Christians, it fails to safeguard the unique contribution of the revelation in Christ. Christianity has something distinctive to offer to the covenantal partnership with Jews. Language such as the title of Williamson's book obscures that reality.

Several points need to be made about Christianity's distinctive revelation. First of all, it did not come instantly, but over a period of time. Hence the weakness of theological models of the Jewish-Christian relationship which basically confine themselves to the biblical tradition. As Raymond Brown correctly argued, the awareness of the enhanced divine-human nexus does not really appear until the latter part of the first century C.E. where it very likely had liturgical origins.[35] Prior to that, as Robin Scroggs has insisted, the Jerusalem/Palestinian community had little consciousness of a separate identity from Judaism.[36] So when we wish to speak today about the theology of the Christian-Jewish relationship, we cannot become excessively biblical in our approach. We must consider the historical developments that took place, both positively and negatively. A return to a "pure" Jewish Christianity is neither theologically desirable nor practically possible. This means, for one, that we must pursue the emergence of Christianity's distinctive revelation through the drawnout process of Christian-Jewish separation into the second century and its gradual formulation in philosophical categories by the Church Fathers and the early Church Councils. Contemporary discussions about covenantal theology cannot totally discard this development. It is part of the authentic identity of Christianity. Neither, on the other hand, can we restrict discussions of covenantal theology from the Jewish side to the biblical period. The Jewish community that emerged out of the renewal movements of the first century C.E. was not simply a reincarnation of biblical Judaism. That is the ultimate import of the research of Neusner, Shmueli, and Perelmuter.

But the process of developing a double covenantal theology will involve the purging of certain prevalent trends in articulating the distinctive Christian revelation. All forms of displacement theology must be jettisoned. Certainly that is demanded by chapter four of *Nostra Aetate*. So must an excessive sense of "victory" or "triumphalism" as Johannes Metz and the late

A. Roy Eckardt emphasized. Finally, we shall have to pursue the issue of the distinctiveness of Judaism. Here the early reflections of James Parkes and J. Coert Rylaarsdam have some continuing value, even though we must take the question beyond their formulations. The sense of community, peoplehood, the dignity of creation, the importance of history—these are core theological values that have been seriously underplayed, or even obfuscated, in much of Christian covenantal theology.

While stressing the distinctiveness of the revelation of divine intimacy in and through Christ we must emphasize, as Mussner has and I do in my writings, that there do exist connections between this Christian sense of a new divine intimacy and developments in Second Temple Judaism. I have emphasized in particular the connections with perspectives found within Pharisaism as explained by the Jewish historian Ellis Rivkin.[37] It is not true to say, however, that Jesus' sense of divine intimacy was no different from the understanding shared by many of his Jewish contemporaries. But proof of this does not depend on a claim that Jesus had a special sense of God as "Abba," as Schillebeeckx incorrectly argued, but on a panoply of sayings and actions on the part of Jesus.

My final reason for preferring the double covenant paradigm over the single covenant model at present is that it better safeguards the distinctive experiences of the two communities since separation. Following the *1985 Notes on the Correct Way to Present Jews and Judaism in Christian Preaching and Catechesis* which underscore the importance of the post-biblical Jewish experience for Christian reflection, we must recognize the history of antisemitism, the Holocaust, and other events which have impacted the communities in different ways. As a result, the vast majority of Christians and Jews now see the two faiths as quite separate, something we cannot totally ignore in our theological reflections.

Let me add three additional comments. First of all, discussions of covenantal theology will have to be filtered through the experience of the Holocaust. Johannes Metz is absolutely correct on this point. In doing this, we must begin with the question of God and then move to Christology. No covenantal theology can bypass the Holocaust. I have begun to address both

the God and Christology questions in recent publications.[38] Second, in the
end, Monika Hellwig may be correct in saying we should not overemphasize
the issue of single vs. double covenant. Perhaps we should be content with the
formulations of a Perelmuter, Boys, or Williamson (who introduces the notion
of Jews and Christians as "partners in waiting"). Finally, whether one selects
the single or the double covenant paradigm as a framework for theological
reflection on the Jewish-Christian relationship, it is clear that the language of
"old covenant/new covenant" is seriously flawed. First Covenant is probably
the most acceptable terminology for the theological discussion. If it is used,
then New Covenant may remain viable, though we must be aware of how a
scholar such as Lohfink interprets its origins in the book of Jeremiah.

In closing let me repeat my appreciation for Rabbi Signer's approach to
the covenantal question. Scholars such as Zev Garber and James Moore have
given us some excellent examples of how to pursue such a path.[39] But let me
also reemphasize my conviction that pursuing the theological discussion
about the covenantal relationship between Jews and Christians cannot be put
on hold. I would voice my admiration for the efforts Rabbi Signer has under-
taken to interest his Jewish colleagues in such a discussion. How we view the
theological relationship will significantly influence how we interpret the texts
Rabbi Signer has encouraged us to study together. While this may be more the
case for Christians than for Jews, Jews also are affected in the final analysis
by the theological perspective on Christianity. The encounter theologies of a
Levinas or a Buber will certainly aid our effort greatly. But they cannot sub-
stitute for the far more difficult task of reconstructing our theological relationship. While we pursue this, we certainly can develop a handedness that
transcends our current theological impasse and will enable us to become partners in human responsibility for the world. Solidarity between Jews and
Christians need not, in fact should not, await doctrinal restatement.

ENDNOTES

1.   On the unique argumentation of *Nostra Aetate*, cf. Eugene J. Fisher,
      "The Evolution of a Tradition: From *Nostra Aetate* to the Notes,'" in
      International Catholic-Jewish Liaison Committee *Fifteen Years of
      Catholic-Jewish Dialogue 1970-1985: Selected Papers*. Rome: Libreria
      Editrice Lateranense, 1988, 239–254.

2.   Cf. Allan Brockway, Paul van Buren, Rolf Rendtorff, and Simon
      Schoon (eds.), *The Theology of the Churches and the Jewish People:
      Statements by the World Council of Churches and Its Member
      Churches*. Geneva: WCC Publications, 1988.

3.   Cf. Eugene B. Borowitz, "Jesus the Jew in Light of the Jewish-
      Christian Dialogue" and "The Challenge of Jesus the Jew for the
      Church," in *Proceedings of the Center for Jewish Christian Learning* 2
      (Spring 1987), 16–18, 24–26.

4.   Cf. Hayim Goren Perelmuter and Wilhelm Wuellner (eds.),
      *Proceedings of a Conference on the Question of the Letters of Paul
      Viewed from the Perspective of the Jewish Responsa Mode*. Chicago:
      Catholic Theological Union, 1991.

5.   Charles Journet, "The Mysterious Destinies of Israel," in *The Bridge*,
      vol. II, ed. John Oesterreicher. New York: Pantheon, 1956; 35–90.

6.   Jean Daniélou, *Dialogue with Israel*. Baltimore: Helicon, 1966; *The
      Theology of Jewish Christianity*. Chicago: Henry Regnery, 1964. Also
      cf. Jean Daniélou and André Chouraqui, *The Jews: Views and Counter-
      views*. New York: Newman, 1967.

7.   Hans Urs von Balthasar, *Church and World*. New York: Herder and
      Herder, 1967.

8.   Augustin Cardinal Bea, *The Church and the Jewish People*. London:
      Geoffrey Chapman, 1966.

9.   Cf. John Paul II, *On Jews and Judaism*: 19791986, eds. Eugene J.
      Fisher and Leon Klenicki. Washington: United States Catholic
      Conference, 1987; *Spiritual Pilgrimage: Texts on Jews and Judaism:*

1979-1995, eds. Eugene J. Fisher and Leon Klenicki. New York: Crossroad, 1995.

10. Monika Hellwig, "Christian Theology and the Covenant of Israel," in *Journal of Ecumenical Studies* 7 (Winter 1970), 49.

11. Monika Hellwig, "From the Jesus of Story to the Christ of Dogma," in *Anti-Semitism and the Foundations of Christianity*, ed. Alan T. Davies. New York/Ramsey, NJ/Toronto: Paulist, 1979, 118–136.

12. Paul van Buren, *The Burden of Freedom*. New York: Seabury, 1976.

13. Paul van Buren, *Discerning the Way*: New York: Seabury, 1980.

14. Paul van Buren, *A Christian Theology of the People of Israel*. New York: Seabury, 1983.

15. Paul van Buren, *A Theology of the Jewish-Christian Reality, Part III: Christ in Context.* San Francisco: Harper & Row, 1988. Also cf. "The Context of Jesus Christ: Israel," in *Religion & Intellectual Life* III:4 (Summer 1986), 31–50.

16. Raymond E. Brown, "Does the New Testament Call Jesus God?" in *Theological Studies*, 26:4 (December 1965), 546.

17. Paul van Buren, "The Context of Jesus Christ: Israel," 47.

18. I have always maintained that van Buren's understanding of the Holocaust's impact on theology was inadequate. Cf. my essay, "Christology after the Holocaust," in *Encounter* 59:3 (Summer 1998), 345–368.

19. Paul van Buren, "The Context of Jesus Christ: Israel," 50.

20. Van Buren, relying on a Barthian perspective, presented an inadequate picture of my position. Cf. Paul van Buren, *A Theology of the Jewish-Christian Reality*, Part III, 221. His position on the "transparency of God" in Christ and my understanding of the Christ event do not in fact seem all that far apart. And my overall presentation of Christology hardly merits the humanistic label that van Buren applied to it. Cf. my volume *Christ in the Light of the Christian-Jewish Dialogue*. New York/Ramsey, NJ: Paulist, 1982.

21. Cf. Jon Levenson, *The Death and Resurrection of the Beloved Son: The Transformation of Child Sacrifice in Judaism and Christianity.* New Haven: Yale University Press, 1993.

22. Nobert Lohfink, *The Covenant Never Revoked: Biblical Reflections on Christian-Jewish Dialogue.* New York/Mahwah: Paulist, 1991. Nobert Lofink, *Das Jüdische im Christentum: Die verlorene Dimension.* Freiburg/Basel/Wien: Herder, 1987.

23. Nobert Lohfink, *The Covenant Never Revoked*, 93.

24. Cf. James H. Charlesworth, ed., *Jesus' Jewishness: Exploring the Place of Jesus in Early Judaism.* New York and Philadelphia: Crossroad and the American Interfaith Institute, 1991, and Cardinal Carlo Maria Martini, "Christianity and Judaism: A Historical and Theological Overview," in James H. Charlesworth, et al., *Jews and Christians: Exploring the Past, Present, and Future.* New York: Crossroad, 1990.

25. Cf. Wayne A. Meeks and Robert L. Wilken, *Jews and Christians in Antioch in the First Four Centuries.* Missoula, MT: Scholars Press,1978; Robert L.Wilken, *John Chrysostom and the Jews: Rhetoric and Reality in the Late 4th Century.* Berkeley: University of California Press, 1983; Anthony J. Saldarini, "Jews and Christians in the First Two Centuries: The Changing Paradigm," in *Shofar* 10 (1992), and Robin Scroggs, "The Judaizing of the New Testament," in *The Chicago Theological Seminary Register,* 75:1 (Winter 1986). On developments within Judaism, cf. Jacob Neusner, *Death and Birth of Judaism: The Impact of Christianity, Secularism, and the Holocaust on Jewish Faith.* New York: Basic Books, 1987; Efrain Shmueli, *Seven Jewish Cultures: A Reinterpretation of Jewish History and Thought.* Cambridge & New York: Cambridge University Press, 1990, and Hayim Goren Perelmuter, *Siblings: Rabbinic Judaism and Early Christianity at their Beginnings.* New York: Paulist, 1989.

26. Cf. James Parkes, *Judaism and Christianity.* Chicago: University of Chicago Press, 1948, and *The Foundations of Judaism and Christianity.* London: Vallentine Mitchell, 1960. Also cf. John T. Pawlikowski, "The

Church and Judaism: The Thought of James Parkes," in *Journal of Ecumenical Studies* 6 (Fall 1969), 673–697.

27. Cf. J. Coert Rylaarsdam, "Jewish-Christian Relationship: The Two Covenants and the Dilemmas of Christology," in *Journal of Ecumenical Studies* 9 (Spring 1972), 239–260.

28. Clemens Thoma, *A Christian Theology of Judaism*. New York/Ramsey, NJ: Paulist, 1980, 134–135.

29. Clemens Thoma; *A Christian Theology of Judaism,* 115.

30. Franz Mussner, *Tractate on the Jews: The Significance of Judaism for Christian Faith.* Philadelphia: Fortress, 1984. Also "From Jesus the 'Prophet' to Jesus 'The Son,'" in Abdoldjavad Falaturi, Jacob J. Etuchowski; and Walter Strolz (eds.), *Three Ways to the One God: The Faith Experience in Judaism, Christianity and Islam.* New York: Crossroad, 1987, 76–85.

31. Franz Mussner, *Tractate on the Jews*, 226.

32. Cf. Hayim Goren Perelmuter, *Siblings.* Mary Boys' views will appear in a forthcoming volume from Paulist Press.

33. Cf. John T. Pawlikowski, *Christ in the Light of the Christian-Jewish Dialogue.* New York/Ramsey, NJ: Paulist, 1982, and *Jesus and the Theology of Israel.* Wilmington: Michael Glazier, 1989.

34. Clark M. Williamson, *A Guest in the House of Israel: Post-Holocaust Church Theology.* Louisville: Westminster/John Knox, 1993.

35. Raymond E. Brown, "Does the New Testament Call Jesus God?" 546.

36. Robin Scroggs, "The Judaizing of the New Testament," 8.

37. Ellis Rivkin, *A Hidden Revolution: The Pharisees' Search for the Kingdom Within.* Nashville, Abingdon, 1978.

38. Cf. John T. Pawlikowski, "Christian Theological Concerns After the Holocaust," in Eugene J. Fisher, et al., *Visions of the Other: Jewish and Christian Theologians Assess the Dialogue.* New York/Mahwah: Paulist, 1994, 28–51; "The SHOAH: Continuing Theological Challenge for Christianity," in Steven L. Jacobs, et al., *Contemporary Christian Religious Responses to the Shoah.* Lanham/New York/London: University Press of America, 1993, 139–165. "Christology in Light of the

Jewish-Christian Dialogue," in *Proceedings of the Forty-ninth Annual Convention*, Catholic Theological Society of America, 49:1994, 120–134.

39. James F. Moore, "Wrestling with Two Texts: Genesis 32:22–33 and Matthew 26:36–46—a Morning Roundtable," and Zev Garber, "Disorder in Order: The Interlocution of Shoah in the Passover Haggadah and Seder," in Henry F. Knight and Marcia Sachs Littell (eds.), *The Uses and Abuses of Knowledge: Proceeds of the 23rd Annual Scholars' Conference on the Holocaust and the German Church Struggle*, Studies in the Shoah XVII. Lanham/NewYork/London: University Press of America, 1997, 255–272; 273–292.

CONVERSATION TWO

CLEMENS THOMA

HAYIM GOREN PERELMUTER

CONVERSATION TWO

Differences with the Church in the Rabbinic Parables
CLEMENS THOMA

The title of this exposition could also run as follows: Arguments against Christianity in Rabbinic parables. Or: Rabbinic reactions against the attractive preaching of the Early Church expounding the New Testament parables. Or: Polemics of the Rabbis against the Christian preachers by formulating parables similar to those of their Christian competitors.

Introduction

More than two thousand rabbinic parables were written between the first and the tenth century of the common era. They provide valuable elements for reconstructing the history of Jewish literature and theology from the end of the ancient world into the early Middle Ages. Many of those parables result partly from differences with early Christianity. Because of this they can inform us about Jewish-Christian literary and theological history.

The religious history of early Jewish-Christian differences has not yet been explored thoroughly. Historical as well as theological reasons have caused this gap. Several early Christian interpretations of rabbinic literature contained dangerous anti-Jewish comments and theological approaches which led to medieval Talmud burnings. Today's scholars, therefore, prefer to set aside polemic statements of the rabbis against gentiles and the Church, and also do their best to avoid commenting on anti-Jewish attacks against rabbis in the Talmud. Thus there has been a certain muteness surrounding these matters. Nevertheless, for the sake of religious dialogue, it should be possible, without any rhetoric or dogmatism, to excavate differences which go back to the rabbis and to the Fathers of the Church. Rabbinic parables suit this purpose admirably. They did not only result from self-sufficient Jewish reflections, nay, many parables were brilliant reactions and answers to Christian conceptions about Judaism, Christian hostility against Judaism, or Christian attempts at familiarity with Judaism.

I base my opinion, first of all, upon the three hundred and seventy-seven rabbinic parables which have been worked on, commented on, and edited since 1981 by the Lucerne Institute for Jewish-Christian Studies under the direction of a Christian and a Jew.[1] In the meantime, thirty more have been made ready for publication, so that we now have at our disposal a total number of about four hundred parables, especially out of the *Midrash Pesilta deRay Kahana (PesK)* and of the rabbinic comment of Genesis *(BerR)* and Exodus *(ShemR)*. Some parts of *ShemR* were written later, during the tenth century, whereas the larger *BerR* and the *Midrash PesK* go back to classical rabbinic time (from the third to the sixth century).

The Lucerne research project is not our only basis. The first person who led us in investigating rabbinic parables was the Jewish scholar David Flusser, who spent a year and a half in Lucerne as our guide and collaborator.[2] The Jewish parable researchers David Stern[3] and Jonah Fraenkel[4] were two more interlocutors.

After a brief introduction into the nature of rabbinic parables, I shall quote and comment on five of them. They all give evidence of dispute with the competing Church, and I would like to draw conclusions for today's dialogue.

The Nature of Rabbinic Parables

A simple rabbinic parable, the *parable of the captive bird (BerR 19:11)*, can lead us to a definition of the rabbinic parables:

> It is like a bird which had been caught by a hunter. The man met someone and asked him: What shall I do with this bird? Shall it live or shall it die? The other man told him: If you want it to live, then it will, and if you want it to die, then it will![5]

The parable of the captive bird may show us the nature and connections of a rabbinic parable. It is told just after quoting Ezekiel 37:3: "Son of man, can these bones live? And I answered: O Lord God, thou knowest." This parable, just like every rabbinic parable, is a short worldly transformation of a biblical revelation.

The point of this parable *(the mashal: the worldly story)* is its decisive element of decision. The hunter asks the unknown man a nonsensical question: it only depends upon the hunter's will whether he crushes the bird fluttering in his fist, or whether he sets it free. He would have killed it a long time ago if he really had wished to do so. The stranger, therefore, gives the one correct answer: the bird's fate depends solely upon the hunter's will and power.

You cannot tell this clever short story without considering its intention. This parable aims at something which is meant in the biblical revelation *(nimshal: the meaning, the intention of the preaching)*, namely belief in the resurrection of the dead as lying entirely in God's power. One has to believe that human beings will live quite freely after death by dint of God's strength and will. A worldly story has to make this belief clear. The parable of the captive bird arose from the wish to support belief in the resurrection of the dead. It was told in the fourth century. We cannot find out whether it was addressed to skeptical Jews or to gentiles who denied resurrection. It surely did not focus on Christianity, in which that belief was in full bloom during the fourth century.

Is Israel or the Church God's Chosen People?

Many rabbinic parables deal with election by God. I shall discuss here the *parable of the wheat and the chaff (BerR 83:5)*[6] which is told after quoting the following Torah verse: "One of the chiefs was Magdiel, the father of Esau/Edom" (Genesis 36:43, OB). This verse is commented together with the Song of Solomon 7:3 "Your belly is a heap of wheat."

Both verses, if combined, hint at the two interconnected topics of the parable: only the wheat pile, that is Israel, is chosen, and Edom, its enemy, who senselessly competes with Israel, shall be humiliated.

This can be compared with the quarrel of the straw, the chaff, and the stubble. Each of them said: The field was sown because of *me*. The wheat told them: Just wait until harvest comes, and we shall know with which intention the field was sown. Harvest came. Everything was brought into the barn. The possessor came to sort his crop. The chaff went with the wind. The possessor threw the stubble to the floor and the straw into the fire.Then he took the wheat and made a wheat pile. People came and kissed it. So the peoples of the earth. Each one says: *We* are Israel, and the earth was created because of us. Israel told them: Just wait until the day of the Holy One, blessed be He, comes.Then we shall know because of whom the earth was created.

The point is that the wheat in the field does not interfere in the meaningless dispute whether the possessor has sown to get straw, chaff, or stubble. The growing wheat, knowing that the man only wanted wheat, keeps silent and hopeful until its confidence is confirmed when harvest comes. The possessor will then sort his crop, reject all competitors of wheat, and manifest before them that silent hope was right.

The parable of the wheat and the chaff implies a twostage harvest. In the first phase, the wheat is ready for harvesting; sheaves will soon be brought into the barn. The second phase starts afterwards, when they are being threshed, and it becomes clear that the sower only wished to get wheat: he sorts it out as the only field crop, and he takes pleasure in it. The parable thus deals with two topics: first, Israel's unique election in our worldly time, the end of which is just showing, and secondly eschatological confirmation by God of Israel's belief in this election.

We can probably explain the rise of this parable as follows. On some Sunday in the fourth century, a Jew heard a Christian clergyman preaching about the parable of the weed in the midst of the wheat (Matthew 13:24–30 and 36–43). He thus told the Jewish *darshan* about it. The clergyman might have used the Gospel story to treat the belief in Christian unique election: *"Extra ecclesiam nulla salus"* (Outside the Church there is no salvation). Maybe he interpreted another passage instead, such as John the Baptist's words in Matthew 3:11 f. and Luke 3:16–17: "He (the Messiah) will baptize you with the Holy Spirit and with fire. His winnowing fork is in his hand, and he will clear his threshing floor and gather his wheat into the granary, but the chaff he will burn with unquenchable fire."

Anyway, the *darshan* thus decided to write a corrective sermon about the topic: *"Extra Israel nulla salus"* (Outside Israel there is no salvation) in order to counter a possible feeling of insecurity among his congregation. Of course, we cannot know whether he used the Gospel or not. But he did realize the importance of the subject, since his own tradition confronted him with similar concepts and stories. Wheat as a symbol of election, and its growth until it was ripe, were popular Jewish topics; in this respect, the Song of Solomon 7:3 animated rabbinic literary tradition. According to *TanB ki tissa* 2 (II 104 f), for instance, Israel is a heap of wheat grains without which the world would cease to exist; God counts them all and will bring each grain into the land of its destiny.

Our *darshan* surely finished off his parable with preaching. His (Christian) competitors used to claim election loud and clear. Our preacher instead stressed that faithful Jews, though aware of their unique election, did not broadcast it as Christians did. Election could not be proved; only final judgment would be able to announce the divine election. Furthermore, the *darshan* tried to be a better rhetorician than Christian parable exegetes. He embellished his description of Israel, as justified by the final judgment, with the bride's thighs and breasts, and the bridegroom's bliss according to the Song of Solomon (7:2 and 7:8). Israel will be an attractive wheat pile. The passersby who kiss the pile are celestial angels. They are described much more kindly than the servants in the Gospel who gather the weed from the midst of the wheat and burn it. The *darshan* described the angels as lovers of the justified Israelites.

Christians and Jews have changed their views about many a pretension to exclusive election. Christians, for instance in *Nostra Aetate* (no. 4, beginning), now try to stress a common election of all the faithful since Abraham. Jews point out that Abraham's Covenant (Gen 12:15) may include Christianity as a complementary movement to Israel according to Isaiah 49:6 ("I will give you as a light to the nations, that my salvation may reach to the end of the earth," OB) and 55:5 ("Behold you shall call nations that you know not, and nations that knew you not shall run to you, because of the Lord, your God, and of the Holy One of Israel, for he has glorified you," OB). The old quarrel about election was often fought ruthlessly. Today, instead, both religions have to emphasize their common ground under God's mercy, and to encourage each other to be faithful. When God created human beings and religions and sent them into earth, He did not expect them to admire themselves in an autistic way nor to despise the rest of humanity. The point is that they have to recognize one another.

Does Israel or the Church Have Better Ministries?

From the fourth century on, Jewish and Christian authorities indirectly competed about the question which of both religions had better management or better office bearers. I shall quote and comment on two parables to explain this competition: the building on the rock *(Yalk Balak 766)*[7] and the favorite son *(BerR 98:8)*.[8]

The parable of the building on the rock: "It is like a king who wanted to erect a building. He dug down deeper and deeper and wanted to lay foundations. In many places, he struck swamps. He did not care about it, but dug at a certain place, and struck upon a rock (poppa). He said: I shall build here. He laid foundations and built. So the Holy One, blessed be He: He wanted to create the earth. He sat and thought during the time of Enosh and the time of the Flood. He said: How can I create the world? Those blasphemers will rise and anger Me. Then He looked at Abraham, who was bound to rise later. The Holy One, blessed be He, said: 'Now I have found a rock (poppa) on which I can build.' And He created the world. He thus called Abraham a rock, for the Bible says: 'Look to the rock from which you were hewn' (Isaiah 51:1). The Holy One, blessed be He, also called rocks the children of Israel, for the Bible says: 'Remember thy congregation, which thou hast gotten of old' (Psalm 74:2). God's thought of the children of Israel preceded every other thing."

This parable was elaborated at the beginning of Carolingian time on the basis of an earlier parable to be found in *ShemR* 15:7. Most surprising in that rewriting is the Grecian word "tampa" (rock) in Hebrew letters, though the Jewish Bible and the earlier parable use *"tsar."* The author probably referred with a polemic intention to Matthew 16:18: "You are Peter, and on this rock *(petra)* I will build my church. And the powers of death shall not prevail against it." Some rabbis proposed Abraham, as the "rock," against the Roman Pope's pretension of being the successor of another "rock." For ages Abraham has been the rock on which the world is built. Israel, as an orderly building on that rock, is founded on Abraham who ties that house of living stones into the Covenant with God. According to an other parable, Abraham "was created in the middle of generations, in order to bear the earlier and the later ones on his shoulders."[9] Therefore, Jews need no Pope; their rock is Abraham! The Jewish people is borne by Abraham as a rock, and therefore can go on its way without any authoritarian leader. Jewish people is a community that is following the Torah, not a human authority.

The parable of the favorite son (BerR 98:8): "It is like a king who had twelve sons. He loved one of them more than every other one. In addition to the common inheritance of his twelve sons, he gave his favorite an extra share."

This parable interprets Genesis 49:8f. "Judah, your brothers shall praise you; your hand shall be on the neck of your enemies; your father's sons shall bow down before you. Judah is a lion's whelp!" The original text of this prophecy begins with an onomatopoeia: *"Yehudah 'atta, Yodukha . . ."* A literal translation would be: "Judah, you! They will recognize you as Judah."

Reading this parable, one has the suspicion that its authors knew quotations from the Gospel, or at least preachings about them. The rabbinic parable of the favorite son looks like a Jewish antithesis to John 21:15–17: "Jesus said to Simon Peter: Simon, son of John, do you love me more than these? He said to him: Yes, Lord, you know that I love you! He said to him: Feed my lambs! A second time he said to him: Simon, son of John, do you love me? He said to him: Yes, Lord, you know that I love you! He said to him: Tend my sheep . . ." Jesus thus asks Peter the same question for the third time, and Peter protests his love again and again in an effusive, humble way.

The authors of our parable mean that Jews have a *primacy in love* too, nay, a better one than the Christians' primacy. Judah ties them together to one loving, orderly congregation.

If we consider the two parables of the building on the rock and of the favorite son, we have the growing desire to carry on a dialogue with Jews about religious ministries. Such a dialogue would bring about good results to a forgetful Christianity.

God Suffers with Israel

Many rabbinic parables interpret God's sufferings because of Israel and for Israel's sake. They refer especially to Exodus 3:7, Psalm 91:15, and Isaiah 63:9. The Torah verse is important because of its last part: "I have seen the affliction of my people who are in Egypt, and I have heard their cry because of their taskmasters; I *know their sufferings*." According to Psalm 91:15, God says about His faithful ones who trust in Him in the hour of need: "When he calls to me, I will answer him; I will be with him in trouble." Isaiah's report on God is even more farreaching: "In all their affliction He was afflicted, and the angel of His presence saved them; in His love and in His pity He redeemed them; He lifted them up and carried them all the days of old."

The *twin parables of common sufferings (ShemR 2:5)* give quite concise examples of God's commiserating affliction.

> 1. It is like two twins: if one has a headache, the other has it as well.
> 2. It is like somebody who took a stick and struck two people with it. Both of them were flogged, and both of them had pain.[10]

The *nimshal* quotes the three biblical verses mentioned to show that God suffers with people like a fellow creature, and that He is also in need when they are in need.

Christians and Jews would greatly contribute to the spiritual enrichment of our time if they followed together the marks of the suffering and commiserating God in their respective traditions. It is a distorted picture of the Jewish God to represent Him as a pure, inaccessible, unapproachable spirit. In the Torah, and even more in rabbinic literature, He bends towards people, is vulnerable, and escorts and cures them in their ordeals.

It is a Jewish *and* a Christian item to imagine God suffering with us. The idea of Trinity instead is explicitly rejected by Jews in and out of rabbinic parables. The contrastive parable of the family king says *(ShemR 29:5)*: "God is the beginning and has no end, no father, and no son."

The End of Days

In rabbinic literature, we can find several conceptions of the way how only Israel will be saved, whereas idolatrous, anti-Semitic peoples of the earth will be damned or exterminated. Similar conceptions are to be found on the Christian side. Jews and heretics are pictured as evil, doomed figures; true Christians instead will be glorified.

Nevertheless, a famous sentence of the third century common era has come down to us: "Among gentiles, there are righteous people who will share in the world to come" (tSan 13:2). In the thirteenth benediction of the *Amidah*, a central prayer of Jewish congregational services, those claimants to eternal salvation are mentioned together with Israel as "the righteous, the pious, and the upright strangers."

The long parable of the wood in the public bath (*ShemR 15:17* [here only in summary]) has quite a strong theological expressiveness (11). It imagines the end of days in a way which strikingly reminds us of Romans 11:25–36, so that this parable could be called a Jewish answer to St. Paul.

> A public bath in a certain province had a good wooden
> floor which every bather used to trample. However, neither
> the bathers' sandals nor their dirt were able to damage the
> wood. The king once sent to the province a stone image of

himself and ordered an icon of it to be made of the best wood. It turned out that in the whole province there was no better wood than the one which used to be trampled on in the public bath. Artists carved their king's icon out of that wood. It was then exhibited in the province palace, and the provincials came in rows and bowed to the king's icon. An artist shook his head and said to the venerators of the icon: "You used to trample scornfully on this very wood till yesterday, and now you bow to it." They answered: "We do not bow for the sake of the wood, but because of the king's bust which is pictured in it."

This parable was probably elaborated in Carolingian time, somewhere in what is now southern France. The Jewish author was acquainted with the Christian iconoclastic controversy; he refers to it when calling Israel the true, holy icon behind which God hides to test and to save gentiles. At the end of days, nations will gather before God and worship Him (within the meaning of Zechariah 14:9); they will recognize him through Israel, i.e. through looking at Israel.

Saint Paul firmly believed that Israel would be saved on the Last Day, even though it formerly refused to recognize Christ: "A hardening has come upon a part of Israel, until the full number of Gentiles come in, and so all Israel will be saved" (Romans 11: 25 ff.). In the parable of the wood in the public bath, Israel and the gentiles interchange the attitudes in which St. Paul pictured them; the hardening has come upon the nations, but at the end they will reject anti-Semitism and turn to Israel and via Israel to God. This parable is evidence of a serious dialogue between Jews and Christians at the beginning of the Middle Ages. The point for Jews was Christian anti-Semitism and Israel's recognition as God's own people who are joined by gentiles. The history of humankind deals with "all Israel" and with the peoples of the earth who associate with Israel. According to Christian dogma, Christ established a radical connection with Israel through His propitiation.

The rabbinic parables I have just related and commented upon could spur us to give a fresh impetus to modern dialogue between Jews and Christians, and to avoid every form of supersession.

With respect to supersessionism, the point (*nimshal*) of the parable reads as follows: "The kings speak so: We used to trample Israel in a forbidden way, now we bow to it instead. And the Holy One, blessed be He, told them: Yes, for the sake of My name which is written on the children of Israel! For the prophet says: '. . . because of the Lord, who is faithful, the Holy One of Israel, who has chosen you' (Isaiah 49: 7). And Moses says: 'And all the peoples of the earth shall see that you are called by the name of the Lord'" (Deuteronomy 28:10).[11] In other words, rabbinic Judaism is urging Christianity to say "no" to supersessionism

The examples mentioned here show that the rabbinic parables are not solely artificial productions for the embellishment of the preaching. They are short tales that represent two aims of rabbinic thinking. First, they are appropriate expressions for the instruction on Torah for the listeners. On the second level, they are literary rabbinic instruments to avoid spiritual and dogmatic influences from the outside of Judaism and to stress the unique rabbinic doctrine.

ENDNOTES

Scripture references are from the *New Oxford Bible*. New York: Oxford University Press, 1991.

1. Clemens Thoma and Simon Lauer, *Die Gleichnisse der Rabbinen*, vol. 1–2, JudChr 10.13, Bern: Peter Lang, 1986–1991; Clemens Thoma and Hanspeter Ernst, *Die Gleichnisse der Rabbinen*, vol. 3, Judaica et Christiana 16, Bern 1996.

2. David Flusser, *Die rabbinischen Gleichnisse und der Gleichniserzähler Jesus*. 1st part: *Das Wesen der Gleichnisse*, Judaica et Christiana 4, Bern: Peter Lang, 1981.

3. David Stern, *Parables in Midrash. Narrative and Exegesis in Rabbinic Literature*, Cambridge, MA: Harvard University Press, 1991.

4. Jonah Fraenkel, *Darke ha'aggadah wehammidrash*, 2 vol. Jerusalem: 1991-1996 Yad l'Talmud. See also: Clemens Thoma and Michael Wyschogrod, *Parable and Story in Judaism and Christianity*, New York: Paulist Press, 1989.

5. Thoma/Lauer, *Gleichnisse* 2, 180f., 336.

6. Thoma/Ernst, *Gleichnisse* 3, 86–91.

7. Thoma/Ernst, *Gleichnisse* 3, 199–203.

8. Thoma/Ernst, *Gleichnisse* 3, 141–143.

9. Parable of the supporting beam: *BerR* 14:6; Thoma/Lauer 2, 163f.

10. Thoma/Ernst, *Gleichnisse* 3, 154–156.

11. Thoma/Ernst, *Gleichnisse* 3, 236–240.

CONVERSATION TWO

A Response to Clemens Thoma
HAYIM GOREN PERELMUTER

Clemens Thoma last visited Catholic Theological Union fifteen years ago, and I was called upon to respond to his paper. Subsequent circumstances brought me to Lucerne where I could see at first hand his extraordinary work as Director of the Institute for Jewish-Christian Studies. I cherish our friendship and salute him for his achievements. We warmly welcome him back to this Conference and are delighted beyond words that he can be here.

What Clemens Thoma and Simon Lauer have done[1] in their monumental task of reading into the heart of the rabbinic parable as they explored it in a vast range of midrashic texts, brings the Christian-Jewish dialogue to an apogee of constructive communication and adorns the world of scholarship with the grace of their quest.

It is dialogue at its best as Christian and Jew read each other's texts critically, perceptively, but with an irenic spirit. Without rancor, without anger, without bitterness, yet not without bite; with compassion, with understanding, and with a capacity to see each other's point of view and recognize each other's common goal, yet not without a skeptical eye. The routes through history may differ, but that common goal beckons to suggest that we began in common roots, journeyed along diverse paths, and in the end the "mountain of the Lord" might well be a spacious and welcome terminus where the covenants that diverged find equal justification in the end. The words of the eternal Hillel-Shammai debate: "these and these are the words of the living God"[2] would ring out as reconciliation reigns.

Thoma makes his points tellingly by his choices of parables from the rabbinic oeuvre. He shows how significant theological principles are embedded in parable, and similarly how the realities of the Christian-Jewish encounter are encapsulated therein. Finally, he shows that the midrashic view of God suffering for Israel touches a nerve of identification with Christian experience.

It is clear that the midrashic parable mode of encompassing the people's historic experience is a unique phenomenon, and one must wonder why. Why this form of communication and not another? Recent work of competent scholars in the field points to the anthological tendency in Judaism, a tendency to preserve by anthologizing its historic experience. I refer to the extraordinary recent two-issue study in Prooftexts on the anthological imagination.[3] It deals with the fact that all the major texts that shape Judaism are in fact anthologies. From this perspective, it considers each of them: Bible, Talmud, Midrash, and Prayer Book. Anthologists and editors seem to become as important as the author, and crucial to that importance is their role in preserving and transmitting traditions and decoding them.

Gershom Scholem has said that in Judaism commentary or exegesis is the fundamental approach to the expression of the lasting insights of faith.[4] The flash of direct revelation was but a brief moment in the history of our religious experience. After that, commentary became the pathway to insight and experience. Thoma operates within this tradition. It is a tradition of commentary and anthology, and the capacity to read it correctly can open the door to an understanding of what Judaism and the Jewish-Christian dialogue is all about.

It can be argued that this is a risky business. Interpretation of parables as a route to revealing historic truths? Theorizing on the basis of the unspoken or the implied? The archaeology of obiter dicta? What kind of evidence is that? Can you safely build a whole theory on a shard? I think so, if you have enough well-placed shards and you know how to put them together. Thoma is that kind of a "parabolic archeologist"!

Yes, I think we can and we must use this approach, and certainly in the field of Judaism and of Christian-Jewish relations. The fragments of tradition that are preserved in our literature need to be taken seriously. In many ways they are all we have. The mouth-to-ear tradition goes back a long way and only much later was captured in writing. Thanks to that anthological genius we have it in our literature and begging to be decoded.

Let me offer a few examples to show what I mean and then conclude with a reflection on why midrash as such is a crucial vehicle for Jewish communication. I have selected a number of literary traditions of the Javneh generation, from the years 70–90, when the core leadership of Rabbinic Judaism left Jerusalem and went west to a prisoner of war camp on the Mediterranean to shape a mutated Judaism, while the earliest Jewish-Christians went east through Emmaus to organize Christianity. They all involve the Christian-Jewish dialogue.

I

We begin with a tradition about Johanan ben Zakkai which appears twice in the Talmud.[5] These versions differ slightly from each other and the differences are instructive. They both tell us about Hillel's disciples and list them in three categories: the very best, very good, and average. In both versions Johanan is at the bottom of the list. Perhaps this is a kind of understatement, a superlative in reverse. The suggestion is that if Johanan was at the bottom of the class—what a class!

Of all the scholars mentioned, only in the case of Johanan is mention made of the curriculum of study. In the Aboth d'Rabbi Nathan version we are told:

> He mastered Scripture, Mishnah, Gemara, Halakhot,
> Agadot, Toseftot, the minutiae of Torah, the minutiae of
> the Scribes, and the hermeneutical rules of the Sages . . .

In Suka and Baba Batra, both possibly earlier sources, we read the following variant:

> They say of Rabbi Johanan been Zakkai, that he did not
> leave unstudied Scripture, Mishnah, Gemara, Halakhah,
> Agada, details of the Scribes, inferences a minori ad
> majus, analogies, calendrical compositions, *gematrias, the*
> *speech of ministering angels, the speech of spirits, and the*

> *speech of palm trees, fullers, fables and fox fables, great*
> *matters and small matters. Great matters mean ma 'aseh*
> *merkaba and small matters mean the discussions of Abaye*
> *and Rava . . .* (emphasis mine)

Does the first version reflect an accidental omission, or is it post-Javnean, reflecting the trauma of the destruction of the Temple and the beginnings of the Christian schism? Does it perhaps reflect the unease about extreme apocalypticism and messianic extremism that brought on the zealot revolutions, Bar Cochba and the schismatic messianism of the Jesus movement? Does it reflect the chain of events whose consequence was the elimination of the Apocrypha from the Scriptural canon? And does the latter text reflect the pre-Javnean very early Christian period when the messianic movements, political and spiritual, coexisted and were accepted? Indeed, the omission may well reflect the tension between extreme and moderate messianism, which was a constant issue in the development of Rabbinic Judaism, as Gershom Scholem has suggested.

II

In the Aboth d'Rabbi Nathan version, cited above, and where reference to study of merkaba mysticism has been significantly omitted, there is a very interesting coda.[6] Immediately following the account of Hillel's disciples that focuses on Jochanan ben Zakkai, we are told of the death of his sons, and how each disciple tried to console him. Each of them pointed to some figure in the Bible who suffered as he did, but who got over it. In his grief, Jochanan brusquely turned them aside. But El'azar teen Arakh, surpassed his colleagues with this parable:

> To what is the matter like? To a man with whom a king
> had deposited an article of value. Daily the man wept and
> exclaimed: "Woe is me! When will I be free from the
> responsibility of this trust?" You too, my master, had a son
> versed in the Torah . . . He has departed sinless from this

world. Surely you should derive comfort from returning our trust intact! Rabban Jochanan said to him: "El'azar, you have comforted me as men can comfort!"[7]

And the account continues:

> When they left his presence Rabbi El'azar said to his colleagues: 'I go to Dimsith, a delectable place with excellent and refreshing waters." The others said: "We will go to Javneh." Because he went to Dimsith, his fame in the Torah waned, whereas those who went to Javneh . . . the renown of Torah increased.[8]

Dimsith is Emmaus. Early Christianity moved east through Emmaus up to Antioch. Rabbinic Judaism moved west to Javneh. Is this passage a faint footprint of this fact?

III

During this 70–90 Javneh period there is another significant Talmudic reference to an early encounter of Rabbinic Judaism with early Christianity.[9] It concerns Eliezer been Hyrcanus, Jochanan's best student, who became his successor as Nasi of the Sanhedrin. This passage records that he was once arrested by the Roman authorities on the suspicion that he was a Christian. He was interrogated and acquitted. He expressed embarrassment at this episode and wondered how it could have come about. One of his disciples, Akiba, jogged his memory:

> "Master," said he, perhaps some of the teaching of the *Minim* (in this case, Christians) had been transmitted to you and you approved it, and because of that you were arrested?" He exclaimed: "Akiba, you have reminded me!"

And he went on to say that one day, while in Sepphoris, he encountered James the Less, a disciple of Jesus, who quoted something his Master had said, and Johanan liked what he heard. This was the episode the Romans had witnessed that caused his arrest. Even though the conclusion of the text warns Johanan's followers to keep away from Christians, it is clear that there was still some civil communication. We can read this in connection with Paul's crisis with the Jerusalem Church in Acts, to see traces of the gradual moving apart.

IV

From the brush with Christianity in Sepphoris to the violent argument over the Oven of Aknai may be a short distance but it runs deep. The conventional wisdom about this well-known passage in the Tractate b. Baba Mezia[10] is that it represented a revolt of Eliezer's colleagues in the Sanhedrin against an authoritarian and dictatorial presiding officer, his impeachment and the introduction of democratic rule in that august body.

> The tone is set at the beginning of the passage: It has been taught: On that day Rabbi Eliezer brought forth every imaginable argument, but they did not accept them. . .[11]

Eliezer, the successor of Johahan ben Zakkai, was opposed at every turn. Finally he turned to the desperate expedient of invoking miracles (successfully) to support his position. In every case the stratagem failed, and the colleagues continued to vote nay. He then played his trump card with an appeal for direct divine inspiration via a *bat kol*, a voice from heaven. It confirmed Eliezer's positions. At this point, Joshua ben Hananiam, an eloquent spokesperson for the Jewish cause in the Empire and a leader of the opposition, intervened, crying out:

> "It is not in heaven!" What did he mean by this? Rabbi Jeremiah said that since the Torah had already been given on Sinai we pay no attention to a heavenly voice. . .[12]

The miracles of Eliezer, a tree jumping, a river flowing backwards, walls tottering, all had a touch of the absurd. This is underscored by a post-script to this story where someone present at this extraordinary event is reported to have met Elijah the prophet after the event. He asked him what God's reaction had been, and received the reply: "God smiled and said: 'My children have bested me!'" [13] All of which underscores the parable method of recording a significant, watershed event. And exactly what was it? From the perspective of the Javnean period and Joshua's role as a polemicist with "*minim*," it is not unreasonable to conclude that this was directed at the new messianic cult that was moving away from Judaism.

V

Let us reverse the direction of the process, look at a New Testament passage, and see how this may work.

Among the last words of Jesus as recorded in the Gospel of Mark are words from the first verse of Psalm 22, quoted in the Christian tradition as: "*Eloi Eloi lama sabachtani!*" [14] We know that a widely practiced midrashic technique going back to the early Tannaitic period was to quote a Bible text partially, expecting the audience to be able to fill in the rest, and making the exegetical point in the unquoted portion.

Knowing that Psalm 22 begins with despair and ends with hope, we could hazard a premise that Jesus, a midrash and parable expert par excellence, was doing just that and that this presumed cry of despair was really a clarion summons to hope. Psalm 22 indeed!

The five episodes here cited, four from Talmudic traditions of the Javnean period and one New Testament tradition from approximately the same time, have this in common: A careful reading of texts to isolate traditions as bearers of the kernels of historic fact and process is what Clemens Thoma attempts to demonstrate, and to which this responder adds a hearty amen!

And now a final thought. The shift from direct revelation and prophetic communication, to the technique of achieving this through midrash, has set its stamp on how Rabbinic Judaism operates. Midrash is the revolutionary, transforming process. That means commentary, explanation, exegesis, allegory,

parable. How does this become the language of divine truth and divine revelation? Where did direct communication go, and why this special kind of
mediation?

It may well be that the parable and, for that matter, the midrashic
approach (exegesis as the only way to confront the reality behind the text
which is, ultimately, God) is the other side of the coin of the Jewish intoxica-
tion with the idea of the one, ineffable God.

"No man can see My Face and live," Moses was told at such a sublime
moment. God cannot be seen, expressed, described in words. Thus, this "inef-
fability," this "en-sof-ness" can only be captured and expressed by parable.
Symbolic insight is the only way that we can capture the ultimate reality, and
at best for a fleeting instant. This holds for midrash in Halakha, in Agada, in
Kabbalah. Indeed, the letters that comprise the entire Torah contain in fact the
real name of God, Nachmanides tells us in the introduction of his commentary to Genesis.[15] This process is at the very infrastructure of living Judaism.
And so, to deepen our understanding and make the dialogue work, we grasp
the strand of interpretation fossilized in parable, and Torah comes alive, trail-
ing in its glory insights of the Divine. I think Thoma has helped us see a
glimpse of this.

At the conclusion of *Major Trends in Jewish Mysticism*, Gershom
Scholem relates a Hasidic story which is relevant to this conversation:

> When the Baal Shem had a difficult task before him, he
> would go to a certain place in the woods, light a fire and
> meditate in prayer and what he had set out to perform was
> done. When a generation later the "Maggid" of Meseritz
> was faced with the same task, he would go to the same
> place in the woods and say: "We can no longer light the
> fire, but we can still speak the prayers"—and what he
> wanted done became reality. Again a generation later Rabbi
> Moshe Leib of Sasov had to perform the task. And he too
> went into the woods and said: "We can no longer light a
> fire, nor do we know the secret meditations belonging to

the prayer, but we do know the place in the woods to
which it belongs—and that must be sufficient"; and sufficient it was. But when another generation passed and
Rabbi Israel of Rishin was called upon to perform the
task, he sat down on his golden chair in his castle and said:
"We cannot light the fire, we cannot speak the prayers, we
do not know the place, but we can tell the story of how it
was done." And, the storyteller adds, the story which he
told had the same effect as the other three.[16]

That is the story of tradition, and our capacity to detect it, analyze, it
and interpret it gives us building blocks in arriving at significant historical
insights. Clemens Thoma has done this well and it is good that it go forward.

ENDNOTES

Scripture references are from the *Jerusalem Bible*. New York: Doubleday, 1985.

1   Clemens Thoma and Simon Lauer: *Die Gleichnisse der Rabbiner*. Bern, Peter Lang. 1986.

2.   Babylonian Talmud, *Erubin 13b*.

3.   *The Jewish Anthological Imagination. Part I and II*. Baltimore, Johns Hopkins University Press. January and May 1997.

4.   Gershom Scholem: "Revelation and Tradition As Religious Categories in Judaism," in *The Messianic Idea in Judaism*. New York, Schocken. 1971.

5.   Babylonian Talmud, *Avot d 'Rabbi Nathan 24a and Bava Batra 134a*. The first part of the two passages are the same and read:

> Hillel the Elder had eighty disciples: thirty of them were worthy that the Divine Presence should rest upon them as upon Moses our Teacher, but their generation was not worthy of it; thirty of them were worthy that the intercalation of the years should be determined by them; and twenty were average. The greatest of them was Jonathan ben Uddiel, and the least of them was Johanan ben Zakkai.

6.   *Avot d,Rabbi nathan 24a*

7.   Ibid.

8.   Ibid.

9.   Babylonian Talmud. *Acoda Zara, 16b*.

10.   Babylonian Talmud. *Bava Mezia 59a*.

11.   Ibid.

12.   Ibid.

13.   Ibid.

14. See the Gospel of Mark 15:34.

15. Charles Chavel: *Ramban (Nachmanides) Commentary on the Torah.* New York, Shilo Publishing House. 1971.

16. Gershom Scholem: *Major Trends in Jewish Mysticism.* Jerusalem, Schocken. 1941.

CONVERSATION THREE

ELLIOT R. WOLFSON

LESLIE J. HOPPE, O.F.M.

CONVERSATION THREE

Gazing Beneath the Veil:
Apocalyptic Envisioning the End

ELLIOT R. WOLFSON

He who does not expect will not find out the unexpected. HERACLITUS

Un/veiling the Veil Unveiled

The apocalyptic orientation that evolved in late second Temple Judaism and in the formative stages of Christianity is a highly complex, dense, and multifaceted phenomenon. Following in the footsteps of many, I think it best to begin by focusing on the philological root of the word *apocalypse.* While it would be absurd to think that philology alone determines the meaningfulness of a given phenomenon, it is valid to assume that by heeding the philological resonance of a term, one is in a better position to grasp something of its phenomenological application at a different historical moment.

The Greek *apokalpysis* means unveiling, from the verb *apokalypto,* to uncover, as in stripping the veil to reveal the face of the virgin. To speak meaningfully of the unveiling, one must presume the existence of the veil and what is beneath the veil. Exposing what is hidden—the fundamental turn on the path of secrecy—involves the logical conundrum of removing the veil to recover the originary nakedness. But how does one re/cover the nakedness if not by covering it up? Disclosure of the mystery, therefore, is not discovery of something for the first time, but rather uncovering what had been concealed. As Morton Smith conjectured:

> In the last centuries B.C. ἀποκαλύπτω came to be commonly used of revealing secrets. At about the same time began a great increase of the belief that the god(s) had very important secrets to reveal, secrets about the structure and future of the world that would enable those who knew them to escape impending danger. In the lower-middle

class, Eastern Mediterranean milieu where these ideas
first caught hold, ἀποκαλύπτω was already the common
word for revealing secrets, so it eventually came to be
used for revealing these, and their ultimate success carried
it with them, in spirit of the inappropriateness of its root
meaning for its new role.[1]

In Smith's opinion, the literary form called apocalypse carries that title
for the first time in the late first or early second century A.D. He relates the
fashionableness of the term to the "well-known growth of superstition and of
claims to special revelations and to occult knowledge" in the later Roman
Empire.[2] The roots for this usage, however, are clearly older. The philological
sense of "uncovering" related to the term "apocalypse" is extended to include
the revelation of secrets on the part of God, a motif that is rooted in the unique
blend of ideas characteristic of the Hellenistic syncretism whence the apocalyptic orientation emerged as a distinct phenomenon. By the third century, the
element of secrecy becomes paramount in the minds of those individuals who
apply this term to a distinct genre of Jewish and Christian literature.[3]

The importance of secrecy to apocalyptic has been well noted by many
other scholars. Norman Cohn sums up the matter succinctly: "One feature
common to all the apocalypses is that they purport to unveil to human beings
secrets hitherto known only in heaven."[4] The secrets, as Cohn rightly notes,
refer either to the heavenly world or to events in the mundane realm. In slightly different terminology, John Collins has observed that the content of revelation conveyed in apocalyptic writings embraces "historical and eschatological
events on a temporal axis and otherworldly beings and places on a spatial
axis."[5] In meticulous fashion, Collins has laid out a literary typology of the
apocalyptic phenomenon based on the principal distinction between the "historical view," which emphasizes temporal eschatology, and the "vertical
view," which stresses the spatial symbolism of the heavenly world. For those
experiencing the apocalyptic visions, however, these are not mutually exclusive possibilities; on the contrary, it was presumed that what occurred on earth
reflected what happened in heaven, a point well perceived by Collins himself.

Thus, he notes that the term "apocalypse" refers to a "genre of revelatory liter-ature with a narrative framework, in which a revelation is mediated by an oth-erworldly being to a human recipient, disclosing a transcendent reality which is both temporal, insofar as it envisages eschatological salvation, and spatial, insofar as it involves another, supernatural world."[6]

There are clearly texts that would support the contention that the dis-tinction between the spatial and temporal is problematic. The heavenly abode intersects with the eschatological future in a variety of symbolic ways. One such point of convergence is that secrets pertaining to the end are unveiled in the visionary ascent. The imaginary vision, which facilitates the ecstatic excursion into the celestial realm, yields foresight into the future. The rela-tionship between space and time as sentient coordinates of the imaginal expe-rience demands a comprehensive analysis that lies beyond the scope of this study. Suffice it to say that eschatological salvation and supernatural realm, respectively the temporal and spatial coordinates, are intertwined branches of one hermeneutical tree.

Re/covering the Secret Uncovered

The secret revealed in the apocalyptic vision pertains essentially to the end, which is marked by the expectation of the final judgment of the wicked and the righteous. Even cosmological secrets of nature or mysteries of primeval history revealed in the apocalypses are generally related to the end of the present historical epoch.[7] The intrinsic link between the visionary secret and the end is epitomized in the advice given to Daniel by the angelic voice, "Now you keep the vision a secret, for it pertains to far-off days" (8:26), words that are reinforced by the counsel of God to Daniel: "Keep the words, and seal the book until the time of the end" (12:4).[8] The seer must conceal the secret until the time of the end, for the secret primarily concerns the end of time.[9] The preservation of the secret until the end is accomplished by sealing the secret in a written text. The literary distinction of the apocalypses as com-posed written works has been noted.[10] It should come as no surprise, therefore, that the act of writing is endowed with special significance in the narrative accounts of many of the apocalypses.

It is surely not a coincidence that in 1 Enoch, the oldest extant apocalypse, the seer hides his identity in the enigmatic persona of Enoch the "scribe
of righteousness" (12:4, 15:1). Surely, this title indicates that Enoch's role as
scribe in the heavenly court affords him the opportunity to receive the mysteries.[11] I would go further and suggest that there is an allusion here to the fact
that scribal activity is an essential component of the ecstatic experience of
celestial ascent. Interestingly, in one passage, Enoch instructs his son,
Methuselah, to write in a book that which he will transmit to him so that
knowledge of these matters will be preserved through the generations (82:1).
The ultimate significance of the scribal act is made more explicitly in 2 Enoch
35:1–2, where the divine voice instructs the visionary: "And I will leave a righteous man (a member) of your tribe, together with all his house, who will act in
accordance with my will. And from their seed will arise a generation . . . Then
at the conclusion of that generation the books in your handwriting will be
revealed, and those of your fathers, by means of which the guardians of the
earth will show themselves to the faithful men."[12] In chapter 54 of the same
work, however, we read: "at that time, about this ignorance of ours, so that
they may be for your inheritance of peace. The books which I have given to
you, do not hide them. To all who wish, recite them, so that they may know
about the extremely marvelous works of the Lord."[13] In many passages from
this apocalypse, the reader is informed of the numerous books that Enoch was
to write for his progeny, recording his visionary experiences and the secrets
about God, the cosmos, and human history that were revealed to him (23:6;
33:8–11; 40:1–12; 43:1–2; 47:1–2; 48:6–7; 50:1; 53:2–3; 54:1; 65:5; 68:2).
The demand for secrecy and the more hortatory use of the apocalypse are not
in conflict. The apocalyptic visionary is encouraged to emulate the process
of concealing what had been revealed, for he is instructed to seal up the text
in which the secrets had been written until the eschaton, when they shall be
disclosed.

The centrality of writing the secret is underscored in an interesting way
in the response of the divine voice in 2 Baruch 50:1. "Listen, Baruch, to this
word and write down in the memory of your heart all that you shall learn."[14]
The scribal character of this apocalypse is apparent from the attribution of the

vision to Baruch ben Neriah, the one who committed to writing the words of Jeremiah.[15] The influence of this particular prophetic work in this apocalypse is also evident from the fact that the visionary is asked to write down the content and form of his experience in his heart, an image that reflects Jeremiah's notion of engraving on the tablet of the heart.[16] Inscribing on the heart must be seen as an illustration of the textual nature of visionary experience, a point well attested in apocalyptic sources. To be sure, at a later point in the text (77:11ff.), Baruch is invited to produce a written text to send to the Jewish community in Babylon. It is noteworthy, however, that initially the visionary is requested to inscribe his visions upon the memory of his heart. It is possible that in this context, writing upon the memory of the heart conveys a sense of esoteric writing, that is, to write without writing, to preserve in memory without running the risk of divulging secrets to undeserving recipients.

The emulation of the process of concealing by way of revealing finds its most profound expression in the fact that the apocalyptic visionaries were encouraged to record their experiences in written documents. Perhaps the point is best epitomized in 4 Ezra 12:36–38: "And you alone were worthy to learn this secret of the Most High. Therefore write all these things that you have seen in a book, and put it in a hidden place; and you shall teach them to the wise among your people, whose hearts you know are able to comprehend and keep these secrets."[17] In a second passage from this work, Ezra expresses his concern that the ways of the Lord will be forgotten due to the darkness of the world and the lack of righteousness on the part of its human inhabitants. Thus, he requests of God that he send the Holy Spirit to him so that he may write down "everything that has happened in the world from the beginning, the things which were written in your Law, that men may be able to find the path, and that those who wish to live in the last days may live" (14:22). Ezra receives a positive response to his request, and he is instructed to prepare many writing tablets in order to write everything down with the guidance of divine inspiration (depicted by the image of God illumining the lamp of understanding in the visionary's heart). The concluding remark is particularly instructive: "And when you have finished, some things you shall make public, and some you shall deliver in secret to the wise; tomorrow at this hour you shall begin to write" (14:26).[18] Subsequently, the reader learns that the five men who accompanied Ezra on his sojourn in the field, the place of his ecstatic experience, did the writing (14:37–48).

The narratological details here are crucial. Ezra is beckoned by a voice to drink of a cup filled with "something like water," but whose "color was like fire." As a consequence, his heart poured forth understanding, and wisdom increased in his breath, for "the spirit retained its memory" (39–40). The fiery water opened the path of insight, a retaining of spirit in memory, an effluence of wisdom and understanding. This, in turn, opens Ezra's mouth to speak, and thus he spoke incessantly forty days. In this time, the five men with him composed forty books. Ezra speaks, the others write. God commands Ezra to make twenty-four of these books public and to hide the last seventy of them. Twenty-four of the compositions are fit for the worthy and the unworthy, but seventy are revealed only to the wise, for in these books is the "spring of understanding," the "fountain of wisdom," and the "river of knowledge" (41–47).

On the basis of comparing this text and a passage from the Qumran *Rule of the Community*, Michael Stone raised the question whether we can assume that here is an allusion to an esoteric practice of revealing esoteric texts exclusively to a circle of initiates. He decided against this possibility, for the apocalypses were not esoteric in the sense of being the "inner or secret teaching of a clearly defined group." Stone surmised, moreover, that apocalyptic teachings may have been transmitted in secret, but now that the end was near, they were being exposed. He admits, finally, that even this cannot be maintained consistently in the extant apocalyptic sources.[19] Without challenging Stone's cautionary reluctance to generalize about the nature of esoteric writing in Jewish apocalypticism, I do think there is textual justification for offering another view of 4 Ezra. The aforecited remark in 4 Ezra 14:26 is especially noteworthy, for, according to this text, the demand to write down the secrets is transmitted with the caveat that some of those secrets must remain hidden except for the wise who will receive them "in secret"—a doubling of secrecy, to receive the secret in secret. The reflexive structure of secrecy reflected here, the secret occluding itself as secret to be a secret, brings to mind a salient feature of the hermeneutics of kabbalistic esotericism.[20] More importantly, it does suggest that the author had in mind an esoteric hermeneutics that persists even in the eschaton. The task was to compose an esoteric book, that is, a book that revealed secrets in a manner that they remained concealed from those unworthy to receive them. Even in the eschaton the secrets that were written down can be explicated only to a select group of individuals.[21] Hence, the esoteric manner of recording secret wisdom in a book guaranteed its preservation and eventual dissemination, but it also assured its secrecy.

Reflecting on the depiction of the visionaries mentioned in the Cologne Mani Codex, an account of Mani's early life in the Jewish-Christian Elchasaite sect, William Adler remarked:

> What is notable in the description of their revelations is the overriding importance that is attached to the preservation of their heavenly mysteries in a fixed written form . . . . This fairly fixed description of the archetypal apocalypse suggests that Mani's conception of the apocalypse as "esoteric book wisdom" was firmly embedded in the religious traditions of his community. Indeed, these two features— secret wisdom and the authority of the written text—typify much of the Jewish apocalyptic legacy inherited by early Christianity.[22]

Adler is reluctant to go so far as to say (following Bornkamm) that the "true theme" of Jewish apocalyptic is the disclosure of divine secrets, but he is willing to entertain the possibility that the Christian communities who transmitted and enlarged upon this literature did, in fact, identify the writing of secret wisdom as the defining feature of Jewish apocalypses.

Hermeneutics of Secrecy and Ontology of Time

The end and the secret belong together, for the end tells us something vital about the nature of the secret.[23] From beginning to end, the end is the mystery that marks the horizon of our envisioning and delineates the limit of our language. An echo of this is heard in the prologue to the Book of Revelation:

John receives the revelation of Jesus through the intermediary of an angel. By the written record of the apocalypse, the unveiling of the vision through the multiple veils of the text, John bears witness to the word of God and to the testimony of Jesus. The liturgical blessing that concludes the prologue conveys the nexus of mystery and the end: "Blessed is the one reading and hearing the words of prophecy and keeping the things written therein, for the decisive point of time is near" (Rev 1:3). The expression "decisive point of time" renders the word *kairos*, which no doubt reflects the LXX translation of the biblical *'et*, the appointed time, a term that assumes eschatological significance in the apocalypse attributed to Daniel. In the eschaton, that which was hidden in the text may be disclosed, for the seals of the scroll will be undone and the veil removed from the face unveiled.

The apocalyptic secret orients one to the decisive point of time, the end that is close at hand. But we must suppose that the secret revealed at the end will have been disclosed once before; indeed, in virtue of this alone can the matter be considered a secret. For the secret to be discovered, it must be uncovered, but to be uncovered, it must be recovered. Discovering the secret thus is an act of recovery. The task of reading is given unusual weight in the imagination of apocalyptic visionaries, a point to which I shall momentarily return. What is critical to emphasize here is that Jewish and early Christian apocalyptic texts affirm the notion of an esoteric wisdom openly hidden in a written text.[24] From this perspective, apocalyptic esotericism may be considered a form of envisioned reading or what some scholars have called inspired exegesis.[25]

The phenomenon of apocalyptic secrecy had a profound impact on both Judaism and Christianity, especially the mystical element cultivated by the two religious cultures in late Antiquity and the Middle Ages.[26] By its nature, secrecy entails a fundamental paradox: To endure as a secret, the secret must be withheld in its disclosure.[27] Ingrained in the texture of apocalyptic consciousness is this structure of secrecy, for the mystery is connected to the future that is revealed in the present as not being present. Details about the end are communicated in visionary terms predicated on a symbolic prehension that puts the end forward by holding it back. One might argue that the tension between disclosure and concealment is alleviated to some degree by the temporal deferral of the complete exposure of the secret until the end, *'ad 'et quts*. That is, the revelation of the secret in the present is justified by a sense of the end's imminence, but the secret will be fully disclosed only in the future. However, there remains an aura of secrecy surrounding the secret even as it is unveiled in the eschaton, for not everyone will comprehend the secret of the secret. The point is captured by the observation in 2 Baruch that "those who live on earth in those days will not understand that it is the end of times" (27:15).[28] Even more important is a second passage from this work, "For in that time there will not be found many wise men and there will also be not many intelligent ones, but, in addition, they who know will be silent more and more" (48:33).[29] The end is not marked by an indiscriminate dissemination of secret gnosis; on the contrary, those who know the secret will be more reticent to divulge it. Disclosure of mystery at the end is not a closure of secrecy, but an intensification of the occult mentality that is expressed in the cultivation of a deeper silence to utter the secret more loudly.

In the apocalyptic imagination, the hermeneutics of secrecy and the ontology of time are intertwined. The secret of the end, which is always revealed in the present, is of the future that originates in the past. What is yet to be reverts to what has already been, but what has already been springs forth from what is yet to be.[30] As Catherine Keller perceptively notes, the *eschatos* is the "horizon that always recedes again into a 'not yet' that 'already is.'"[31] The perpetual postponement of the end provides a model of time that is circular in its linearity—what will be has already been for it is what will be. I cannot agree with the claim that the linear eschatology of the apocalyptic texts militates against a cyclic view of time and the eternal recurrence of history.[32] In my judgment, there is no justification for adopting a perspective that pits the cyclical view against the linear as polar opposites. The paradoxical nature of time in apocalyptic symbolism requires one to see that what recurs is precisely what has never been. In this linear circularity, time and eternity converge.[33] The unveiling of the eschatological secret in the present bridges the temporal rupture between past and future by imparting hope in the return of that which has not come. In the words of the prophet, *yesh tiqvah le-'aharitekh,* "there is hope for your future" (Jer 31:17). Hope is linked necessarily to the future, for hope is meaningful only in relation to what is to come. The receding nature of the end as the "not yet" that "already is" preserves the need for hope.

Consider the remark in 2 Baruch 85:10, "For the youth of this world has passed away, and the power of creation is already exhausted, and the coming of times is very near and has passed by." It makes perfectly good sense to speak of the passing of youth and the exhausting of the power of creation, but how can one understand the ostensibly paradoxical claim that the "coming of times" is both "very near" and "has passed by"? If the end is near, it has not arrived and thus could not have passed by; conversely, if the end has passed by, it is no longer yet to come and thus it is not "very near" but "already gone." To grasp this paradox, we must ponder the intricate nexus between hermeneutics and ontology, secrecy and time. Just as there is no unveiling of a secret that is not concomitantly a veiling, so there is no attainment of the end that is not concurrently a deferment. The ecstatic visionary well understands that the coming of the end is "very near" precisely because it has already "passed by." To live in the end is to wait for the beginning. In virtue of this waiting, hope "lasts forever and ever" (2 Baruch 78:6).

Secrecy, Vision, and Interpretation

In the apocalyptic genre, secrecy, vision, and interpretation intersect. The information communicated through visionary and auditory experiences (in some cases connected with a tour of heaven led by an angelic guide) is presumed to be an interpretation of an archaic secret, the clearest explication of which is ultimately attributed to God who alone is the one who reveals hidden mysteries. The interpretation of the secret (designed by the Persian loan word *raz* or by the Hebrew *soc*, which translate into the Greek *mysterion*) is allocated to the spiritual elite to whom God has accorded the wisdom to understand.[34] In this respect, apocalyptic sources have much in common with the sectarian writings of the Qumran community where emphasis is likewise placed on the true interpretation (*pesher*) of divine mysteries (*nistarot*) in Scripture as a sign of religious authority and spiritual nobility (exemplified by the Teacher of Righteousness, *moreh tsedeq*).[35] The interpretative aspect of the apocalyptic vision is well captured by Perrin in his account of the extensive quotation of previous texts: "The apocalyptic writers constantly used and reused, interpreted and reinterpreted, the sacred texts of their tradition, especially earlier apocalyptic texts."[36] The vision, therefore, is a re/vision, a "seeing again" that is informed in great measure by prior textual accounts of visionary experiences.[37] Interpretation is not a layer added onto the vision, but part of the matrix wherein the latter takes shape. Knowledge of the secret, therefore, is a re/covery of an archaic mystery, a hermeneutical re/inscription of the textual opening.

The revelatory nature of interpretation underscores an important dimension of the apocalyptic orientation, which had a profound impact on subsequent stages in the evolution of Jewish and Christian mysticism. These sources render problematic the tendency to posit a rigid dichotomy between textual interpretation and visionary experience. The current scholarly debate regarding the question of the literary versus the experiential nature of the apocalyptic phenomenon misses the point, in my opinion, for there simply is no reason to make such a distinction when evaluating the lived hermeneutical experience of apocalyptic visionaries.[38] For these individuals, reading was an act of envisioning what was described in the text, whether the written text of Scripture, the secret inscribed in the hidden book of heavenly origin, or simply the contents of the dream or vision. In some contexts, such as Daniel 9 and Ezra 12, a mediating angel explains to the visionary the apocalyptic significance of a previous prophetic revelation. The re/vision is precisely what accounts for the notion of an apocalypse, an unveiling of a text that was once opened and subsequently sealed. As a number of scholars have pointed out, the visions were probably received while the author was mediating on a relevant scriptural passage, a kind of prophecy induced by textual interpretation. Summarizing this position, Markus Bockmuehl wrote: "The main paradigm of apocalyptic revelation, therefore, seems to be that of inspired interpretation—i.e., an indirect, 'hermeneutical' revelation. Although this involves prima facie the interpretation not only of biblical passages but of a range of symbolic phenomena in dreams and visions, the substance of apocalyptic discourse does depend most typically on biblical precedents and source materials."[39]

The contours of the apocalyptic vision are shaped by literary and oral traditions; thus the interpretative process is already operative at the level of experience. Naturally, it is reasonable to assume that there can be post-experiential interpretations of the vision that will deviate from the experience of envisioning; however, the envisioning itself arises in part as a result of the interpretation of earlier visions that are recorded in authoritative documents. To polarize revelation and interpretation casts a false impression, for that which is revealed is revealed in the act of interpretation and that which is interpreted is interpreted as a consequence of the revelation. Thus, I would argue that it is of little value to distinguish between one text that conveys a "real" experience and another that is merely a "literary" report of an experience. Such a distinction is predicated on the ability to isolate phenomenologically an experience from its literary context, and that is a questionable presumption inasmuch as all such experiences occur within a textual framework. I do not intend by this to reduce the experiential dimension of the ecstatic experiences by claiming that they are pure literary constructions, that there is, to paraphrase Derrida, nothing outside the text. I simply raise the issue of the mutual interdependence of experience and its report to challenge those who would view some later texts as pure literary constructions in contrast to earlier texts that report actual experiences.

Symbolism, Pseudonymity, and the Imaginal Redemption of History

One of the more intriguing aspects of apocalypticism is the symbolic transformation of language occasioned by the visionary apprehension of the mystery. In apocalyptic writings, the linguistic utterance is manifestly symbolic: Matters pertaining to the upper world are expressed in terms of events in the spatio-temporal plane, but the true meaning of the latter is rendered transparent through the former. Indeed, the sense of historicity itself is transformed by the view that what occurs below is a reflection of the event above. One specific example of the homologizing of the lower and upper realms is evident in the relation that is established between the angelic court above and the earthly community of the righteous below, an orientation already evident in the Book of Daniel. Not only is there an intimate connection between the human and heavenly realms, but also basic to the apocalyptic orientation is the possibility of traversing ontological boundaries. Celestial beings enter the mundane realm in the guise of mortal beings, and mortal beings are translated to and occupy a position within the celestial realm. For the heroic human figure to abide in the heavenly domain, he must divest himself of the earthly garment and put on the cloak of angelic splendor.[40] Such a metamorphosis is related in the celebrated verse in Daniel that describes the wise ones shining like the splendor of the sky, an allusion to the angelification of the enlightened in the eschaton (12:3). Repeatedly in Jewish and Christian apocalypse, the spiritual elite are described in terms of an eschatological transmutation, an apotheosis that is described primarily by the images of donning garments of glory, coronation, and enthronement, images that convey the transformation of mortal flesh into a resplendent and fiery ethereal body.

Knowledge of the apocalyptic secret, therefore, is destabilizing inasmuch as it calls into question the rigidity of the ontological boundaries that determine normal modes of sense perception and rational intellection.[41] The sense of destabilization is commensurate to an awareness repeatedly illustrated in the apocalyptic texts concerning the disjointedness of the world. To cite Collins once more: "Both the temporal eschatology and the otherworldly revelation provide a framework which sets the present time and place of humanity in urgent relief. . . . The transcendent character of the eschatology points to the underlying problem of all the apocalypses—this world is out of joint, one must look beyond it for a solution."[42] In another study, Collins astutely characterized apocalyptic eschatology as the transcendence of death, which signifies the overcoming of the restrictions of the mortal body by the elevation of the human being to the heavenly form of life either already before death or through the resurrection after death. "By its focus on heavenly, supernatural realities," writes Collins, "it provides a possibility that the human life can transcend death, not merely by future generations of the nation but by passing to the higher, heavenly sphere. It is this hope for the transcendence of death which is the distinctive character of apocalyptic over against prophecy."[43]

This shift to transhistorical eschatology with its emphasis on the transcendent signals the major transition from the prophetic sensibility to the apocalyptic orientation. History no longer was viewed as containing within itself the possibility for its own redemption. Apocalyptic salvation is predicated on the recognition of the temporal domain as the great abyss, an awareness that wells from the existentialist encounter of the soul with the looming end of the historical epoch. Some scholars have described the apocalyptic position as historical defeatism, which necessitated an escapist flight from reality, whereas other scholars have countered that despite the somewhat pessimistic portrait of historical reality, the apocalyptic writers were still committed to the prophetic notion that Israel's salvation would be implemented in the spatio-temporal realm.[44] I basically agree with the view expressed by Bockmuehl that the "apocalyptic fascination with the secrets of heaven betrays a significant alienation between present and ultimate reality," although this does not "diminish the writers' deep commitment to the outworking of God's plan of deliverance within history. . . . The apocalyptic view of history thrives on the paradoxical assurance that divine deliverance is guaranteed to take place in defiance of the present historical phenomena."[45] In a similar vein, A. Hilary Armstrong remarked that "the experience of the early Christians" was "like all apocalyptic experiences" insofar as it "could only dominate a small group for a short time in its full and authentic religious intensity. Nonetheless, it transmitted to the soberer Christian reflection on historical experience which inevitably succeeded it, when the Judgment did not occur and the Kingdom did not come, the conviction that it is only in the perspective of the end of the world that human life and history has meaning."[46]

If there is a sense of hope communicated in the apocalyptic visions, then it is a hope that is related dialectically to the sense of utter hopelessness in the mundane course of affairs. The historical crisis can be ameliorated either by a cosmic transformation, which alters the nature of the world in a fundamental way, or by an otherworldly journey, which posits a source of salvation that lies beyond this world. The apocalyptic temperament stems from a keen sense of discomfort with the sensible world, a breach that can only be mended by the mythic reconfiguration of history in terms of the engendering symbol of the end of days. As Gershom Scholem expressed the matter, "the apocalyptists have always cherished a pessimistic view of the world. Their optimism, their hope, is not directed to what history will bring forth, but to that which will arise in its ruin free at last and undisguised."[47]

The pessimistic view regarding the historical process explains the augmented use of symbols on the part of apocalyptic visionaries, a phenomenon that has been well noted and variously explained by scholars. Norman Perrin correctly observed that "symbols were not only used in depicting the End, they were also used in giving an account of the events of past and present that preceded, in the apocalyptic view, the coming of the End."[48] Paul Hanson went so far as to define apocalypticism as "the symbolic universe in which an apocalyptic movement codifies its identity and interpretation of reality."[49] Historical facticity is retold in symbolic terms; that is to say, the seemingly concrete facts of human experience are hermeneutically transmuted into poetic metaphors that recast the mundane reality in mythical images.[50] The line distinguishing myth and history in apocalyptic texts is significantly blurred by the assumption that the imaginal symbol provides the narrative framework to interpret historical events.[51] In some instances, the symbolic orientation implies a degree of dissimilitude, for contemporary events were portrayed in the narrative guise of an older period. For instance, the present form of the Book of Daniel, the last work to be included in the biblical canon, has been described as a product of the Antiochan persecutions even though it is set as the narration of events that took place at the Babylonian court during and after the exile of 586 B.C. While the first six of the twelve chapters may have originated in the Babylonian Diaspora, they were probably redacted during the Antiochan crisis, between 169 and 165 B.C., the time when the last six chapters (containing the four apocalypses) were composed. What is presented as historical drama is fiction. The same may be said for other Jewish apocalyptic works, such as the Book of Enoch, 4 Ezra, and the Apocalypse of Abraham. The symbolic-mythic approach toward history may also shed light on the phenomenon of pseudonym in apocalyptic writings. Needless to say, this phenomenon must be understood in the context of the ancient world: To compose a visionary treatise in the name of a legendary figure is not an act of intellectual dishonesty. On the contrary, hiding one's identity behind the veil of a figure from the past bespeaks an act of utmost piety. Nevertheless, the use of pseudonym may strike the ear as a curious dimension to find in a literary tradition concerned with unveiling secrets hidden beneath the surface. In spite of—or perhaps on account of—the insistence in apocalypticism on seeing what is unseen, there is a tendency to mask, to conceal, the historical moment in the garb of fictional narrative.[52] This does not diminish the sense of history, however, but simply highlights the fact that the latter can only be expressed in symbolic language predicated on the assumption that the value of the historical datum lies in its narratological retelling. Years ago, D.S. Russell observed:

> The apocalyptic books constitute a record . . . not in terms of historical event, but in terms of the response of faith which the nation was called upon to make. They cannot be understood apart from the religious, political and economic circumstances of the times, nor can the times themselves be understood apart from these books whose hopes and fears echo and re-echo the faith of God's chosen people. The allusions which they make to current affairs are frequently concealed beneath the guise of symbol and imagery so that more often than not it is difficult, if not impossible, to give a precise identification of this reference or that character. But they reveal quite clearly the inner side of that conflict which continued almost unceasingly throughout these three centuries; they bring to light the faith and emotions which lie behind the historical events and so make these events more understandable than they otherwise would be.[53]

I would go further than Russell in emphasizing the symbolic as well as the narratological dimension of the historical event. Apocalyptic eschatology does not only imply that history finds "its justification beyond history" in the "unity in which the temporal is taken up into the eternal by means of those moral and spiritual qualities which make up the purpose of God."[54] The very nature of historical events is cast as essentially symbolic, a representation (from the Greek *symbolon*) by a concrete image of an occurrence in the celestial realm. It is not only a matter of the meta-historical frame of reference to endow history with meaning. The apocalyptic orientation is an imaginary thinking, a thinking through symbols, a language that is perceived as symbolic in its very nature. Ultimately, there is nothing real but the symbols. The boundaries of the texts of biblical prophecy are expanded, therefore, as the visions of the past are re/visioned in the name of ancient figures. The phenomenon of pseudepigraphy must be understood as a feature of the symbolic mentality of the apocalyptic seers. This is not to say that every occurrence of false authorship is explicable in terms of what I have called the symbolic mentality, nor is it the case that pseudonymity is a necessary feature of Jewish or Christian apocalypses (the obvious exception that is often noted by scholars is the Book of Revelation, which is attributed in an apparently accurate way to an historical figure whose name is John). Rather, my argument is that in this particular literary genre, the turn to the symbolic occasions a turning away from an empiricist conception of the historical. As Collins put it, "By concealing the historical specificity of the immediate situation beneath the primeval archetype, the apocalyptic symbolism relieves anxiety."[55] In my judgment, the symbolic portrayal of events bespeaks a sense of the irredeemability of history on its own terms.

To underscore the point I am making, it would be useful to recall an essay by W. D. Davies on the parallels between early Christianity and the seventeenth-century pseudo-messianic Sabbatian phenomenon. Davies emphasizes that supporters of Sabbatai Sevi messianic employed apocalyptic terminology to refer symbolically to the supernatural world, but at the same time this terminology referred quite literally to a socio-political reality. Given his insistence on the concurrent affirmation of the symbolic and the historical, Davies maintains that the comparison of early Christianity and Sabbatianism provides a corrective to the tendency in modern scholarship on apocalyptic language to overemphasize the spiritual at the expense of ignoring the "literal dimension," which is characterized further as having a "catastrophic political and social relevance." In particular," writes Davies, "the political and socio-logical implications of early Christianity and their actual impact would be more adequately recognized if this literalism were taken more seriously. This would help us to comprehend that all messianism has a revolutionary, subver-sive potential."[56] Davies does not wish to undermine the symbolic character of apocalypticism, but only to emphasize its political underpinning. I am not convinced of his argument, however, as I believe the apocalyptic tempera-ment expresses a far greater split between the symbolic and the historical. Concern for the inward condition, which in the end is a matter of the imagi-nation, far outweighs concern for how the spiritual ideal would be practically implemented in the socio-political arena. I take this to be the ultimate conse-quence of the symbolic approach to history as it evolved in Jewish and Christian apocalypticism.

Here it would be profitable to consider that Scholem already noted that the shift from the relatively straightforward nationalistic eschatology of the ancient Israelite prophets to the cosmic eschatology of the apocalyptic vision-aries was marked by a dichotomization of experience into polar opposites: This aeon, which is the reign of darkness, is followed by the aeon to come, which is the reign of light; Israel represents the force of holiness set over and against the heathen nations or the force of impurity. In his typical ironic and paradoxical nature, Scholem noted that, on the one hand apocalypticism pro-vided the framework in which the idea of prophetic messianism began to have a historical influence but, on the other, the esoteric form of eschatology in the apocalyptic visions underscored a withdrawal from history, a process that is even more pronounced in the Gnostic-oriented chariot mysticism. In Scholem's own words: "The stronger the loss of historical reality in Judaism during the turmoil surrounding the destruction of the Second Temple and of the ancient world, the more intensive became consciousness of the cryptic character and mystery of the Messianic message, which indeed always referred precisely to the re-establishment of that lost reality although it also went beyond it."[57] Scholem has astutely perceived that the preeminence of secrecy in the phenomenon of apocalypticism is related to an ahistorical eschatological orientation even though he still insists—surely in an ironic way—that apocalypticism provides the historical framework for prophetic messianism.

In conclusion, it might be said that possession of the secret in the apocalyptic texts is not merely a cognitive or epistemological phenomenon; it is decidedly ontological insofar as the mystery relates to the wisdom of God reflected in nature and history. To gain knowledge of the mysteries unveiled in the apocalyptic vision, therefore, is an act of ultimate empowerment, for through such an acquisition one becomes like God or, at the very least, as I noted above, like the angelic beings who surround the throne of glory. This transfiguration, which is most frequently depicted in the images of illumination, is a key feature of the symbolizing tendency of these texts, which squarely locates the apocalyptic temperament in a mode of experience situated in between prophecy and mysticism. The enduring legacy of the apocalyptic sentiment relates to the ability of the symbolic imagination to transform the nature of historical consciousness. What is real is the image, for the latter alone renders transparent the implicit meaning of empirical events, an insight that is at once liberating and restraining, a paradoxical confluence that perhaps best depicts the distinguishing predilection of the apocalyptic cast of mind, which has played such a major role in shaping the attitude towards exile and redemption in the religious history of Judaism and Christianity.

ENDNOTES

Scripture references are from *TANAKH: A New Translation of the Holy Scriptures*. Philadelphia: Jewish Publication Society, 1985.

1. M. Smith, "On the History of ΑΠΟΚΑΛΥΠΩ and ΑΠΟΚΑΛΥΨΕ," in *Apocalypticism in the Mediterranean World and the Near East: Proceedings of the International Colloquium of Apocalypticism, Uppsala, August 12–17, 1979*, edited by D. Hellhom, 2nd edition (Tübingen, 1989), p. 12.

2. Ibid., p. 19.

3. A useful collection of studies examining elements of esotericism in early Christianity is G. Stroumsa, *Hidden Wisdom: Esoteric Traditions and the Roots of Christian Mysticism* (Leiden, 1996).

4. N. Cohn, *Cosmos, Chaos and the World to Come: The Ancient Roots of Apocalyptic Faith* (New Haven and London, Yale University Press, 1993), p. 163.

5. J. J. Collins, "Introduction: Towards the Morphology of a Genre," in *Semeia* 14 (1979): 5.

6. Ibid., p. 9

7. M. Himmelfarb, *Ascent to Heaven in Jewish and Christian Apocalypses* (New York and Oxford, 1993), pp. 72–94.

8. See J. J. Collins, *The Apocalyptic Vision of the Book of Daniel* (Ann Arbor, 1977), pp. 153–179.

9. See D. S. Russell, *The Method and Message of Jewish Apocalyptic* (Philadelphia, 1964), pp. 263–284.

10. M. E. Stone (ed.), *Jewish Writings of the Second Temple Period*, "Jewish Apocalyptic" (Philadelphia, 1974), pp. 432–433.

11. See J. C. Vanderkam, *Enoch and the Growth of an Apocalyptic Tradition* (Washington, 1984), p. 133; Himmelfarb, *Ascent to Heaven*, pp. 23–25.

12. *The Old Testament Pseudepigrapha*, vol. 1: Apocalyptic Literature and Testaments, edited by J. H. Charlesworth (Garden City, 1983), p. 159.

13. Ibid., p. 180.

14. *Old Testament Pseudepigrapha*, pp. 637–638.

15. Jer 32:12–13, 16; 36:4–19; 45:1–2. Himmelfarb, *Ascent to Heaven*, pp. 101–102, suggested that the emphasis on writing in Jeremiah and Ezekiel provided the "necessary conditions for the pseudepigraphy of the apocalypses."

16. Jer 17:1; 31:33. The idiom of writing upon the tablets of the heart is also found in Prov 3:3 and 7:3. On the "secret thoughts" lying in the "inner chambers," see 2 Baruch 83:3.

17. *Old Testament Pseudepigrapha*, pp. 550–551.

18. Ibid., p. 554.

19. Stone, "Apocalyptic Literature," pp. 431–432.

20. "Occultation of the Feminine and the Body of Secrecy in Medieval Kabbalah," in *Rending the Veil: Concealment and Secrecy in the History of Religions*, edited by E. R. Wolfson (New York and London, 1999), pp. 113–154; idem, *Abraham Abulafia Kabbalist and Philosopher: Hermeneutics, Theosophy, Theurgy* (Los Angeles, 1999), pp. 1–38.

21. See I. Gruenwald, *From Apocalypticism to Gnosticism: Studies in Apocalypticism, Merkavah Mysticism and Gnosticism* (Frankfurt am Main, 1988), pp. 71–78.

22. W. Adler, "Introduction," in *The Jewish Apocalyptic Heritage in Early Christianity*, edited by J. C. Vanderkam and W. Adler (Assen and Minneapolis, 1996), pp. 11–12.

23. In Rom 11:25 and 1 Cor 15:51, the word *mystery* is used by Paul as part of his argument about resurrection of the dead and Israel's messianic salvation. This usage clearly reflects Jewish apocalypticism. See M. Bockmuehl, *Revelation and Mystery in Ancient Judaism and Pauline Christianity* (Tübingen, 1990), pp. 170–175. For discussion of Paul's indebtedness to the Jewish apocalyptic orientation, see A. F. Segal, *Paul the Convert: The Apostolate and Apostasy of Saul the Pharisee* (New Haven and London, 1990), pp. 158–166, and the recent survey in M. C. de Boer, "Paul and Apocalyptic Eschatology," in *The Encyclopedia of Apocalypticism*, vol. 1: *The Origins of Apocalypticism in*

Judaism and Christianity, edited by J. J. Collins (New York, 1998), pp. 345–383.

24.   W. Adler, "Introduction," in *The Jewish Apocalyptic Heritage in Early Christianity*, edited by J. C. Vanderkam and W. Adler (Assen and Minneapolis, 1996), pp. 12–16.

25.   On the hermeneutical aspects of apocalyptic visionary literature, see the comprehensive discussion in D. Patte, *Early Jewish Hermeneutic* (Missoula, 1975), pp. 139–208.

26.   The fullest treatment of the impact of apocalypticism on early Jewish mysticism is found in I. Gruenwald, *Apocalyptic and Merkavah Mysticism* (Leiden, 1980). Also see the more recent survey by M. Mach, "From Apocalypticism to Early Jewish Mysticism" in *The Encyclopedia of Apocalypticism*, vol. 1: *The Origins of Apocalypticism in Judaism and Christianity*, pp. 229–264. On the apocalyptic orientation as the "Jewish matrix" for Christian mysticism, see B. McGinn, *The Foundations of Mysticism: Origins to the Fifth Century* (New York, 1991), pp. 9–22. A study of the impact of the apocalyptic imagination on medieval Jewish mysticism remains a scholarly desideratum. On medieval Christian apocalypticism, see the following works by B. McGinn: "Apocalypticism in the Middle Ages: An Historiographical Sketch," in *Medieval Studies* 37 (1975): 155–173; "Awaiting an End: Research in Medieval Apocalypticism 1974-1981," in *Medievalia et Humanistica* N.S. 11 (1982): 263–289; *Apocalyptic Spirituality* (New York, 1979); *Visions of the End: Apocalyptic Traditions in the Middle Ages* (New York, 1979); "Symbols of the Apocalypse in Medieval Culture," in *Michigan Quarterly Review* 22 (1983): 265–283; "Apocalyptic Traditions and Spiritual Identity in Thirteenth-Century Religious Life," in *The Roots of the Modern Christian Tradition*, edited by E. R. Elder (Kalamazoo, 1984), pp. 1–26 and 293–300; *The Calabrian Abbot: Joachim of Fiore in the History of Western Thought* (New York and London, 1985), pp. 74–122, 145–160. See also P. J. Alexander, "Medieval Apocalypses as Historical Sources," in *American Historical Review* 73 (1968): 997–1018; *Prophecy and Millenarianism: Essays in Honour of Marjorie Reeves*,

edited by A. Williams (Essex, 1980); M. Reeves, "The Development of Apocalyptic Thought: Medieval Attitudes," in *The Apocalypse in English Renaissance Thought and Literature*, edited by C. A. Patrides and J. Wittreich (Manchester, 1984), pp. 40–72; R. K. Emmerson, *Antichrist in the Middle Ages: A Study of Medieval Apocalypticism, Art, and Literature* (Seattle, 1981); R. Landes, "Lest the Millennium Be Fulfilled: Apocalyptic Expectations and the Pattern of Western Chronography 100-800 c.e.," in *The Use and Abuse of Eschatology in the Middle Ages*, edited by W. Verbeke, D. Verhelst, and A. Welkenhuysen (Leuven, 1988), pp. 137–211; E. A. Matter, "The Apocalypse in Early Medieval Exegesis," in *The Apocalypse in the Middle Ages*, edited by R. K. Emmerson and B. McGinn (Ithaca, 1992), pp. 38–50, and R. K. Emmerson and R. H. Hertzman, *The Apocalyptic Imagination in Medieval Literature* (Philadelphia, 1992).

27. E. R. Wolfson, "Introduction," in *Rending the Veil: Concealment and Secrecy in the History of Religions*, edited by E. R. Wolfson (New York and London, 1999), p. 3.

28. *Old Testament Pseudepigrapha*, p. 630.

29. Ibid., p. 637

30. My formulation has benefited from the analysis of Heidegger's notion of ecstatic temporality as presented by D. F. Krell, *Of Memory, Reminiscence, and Writing: On the Verge* (Bloomington and Indianapolis, 1990), pp. 244–246.

31. C. Keller, *Apocalypse Now and Then: A Feminist Guide to the End of the World* (Boston, 1996), p. xiii.

32. See Russell, *Method and Message of Jewish Apocalyptic*, pp. 213–217.

33. In this respect, the apocalyptic sense of temporality is similar to the doctrine of eternal return that has been expressed repeatedly in Western philosophy. For an illuminating study of this motif, see N. Lukacher, *Time-Fetishes: The Secret History of Eternal Recurrence* (Durham and London, 1998). On the importance of linear calculations of timetables in apocalyptic writings, see J. Licht, "Time and Eschatology in Apocalyptic Literature and in Qumran," in Journal of Jewish Studies 16

(1965): 177–182, and the extensive discussion of W. Adler, "The Apocalyptic Survey of History Adapted by Christians: Daniel's Prophecy of 70 Weeks," in *The Jewish Apocalyptic Heritage in Early Christianity*, pp. 201–238.

34. On the apocalyptic nexus of mystery and God's hidden wisdom, which is reflected in Paul's comment in 1 Cor 2:6–10, see discussion in Bockmuehl, *Revelation and Mystery*, pp. 157–166.

35. See Russell, *Method and Message of Jewish Apocalyptic*, p. 117; Patte, *Early Jewish Hermeneutic*, pp. 218–227; J. J. Collins, *The Apocalyptic Imagination: An Introduction to the Jewish Matrix of Christianity* (New York, 1989), pp. 120–121. On apocalypticism and the Qumran community, see J. J. Collins, "Patterns of Eschatology at Qumran," in *Traditions and Transformations: Turning Points in Biblical Faith*, edited by B. Halperin and J. D. Levenson (Winona Lake, 1981), pp. 351–375; idem, *Apocalyptic Imagination*, pp. 115–141; idem, "Was the Dead Sea Sect an Apocalyptic Movement?" in *Archaeology and History in the Dead Sea Scrolls: The New York University Conference in Memory of Yigael Yadin*, edited by L. H. Schiffman (Sheffield, 1990), pp. 25–51; idem, *Apocalypticism in the Dead Sea Scrolls* (London, 1997); M. E. Stone, "Apocalyptic Literature," in *Jewish Writings of the Second Temple Period*, edited by M. E. Stone (Philadelphia, 1974), pp. 423–427, 431–432; M. Philonenko, "L'apocalyptique qourânienne," in *Apocalypticism in the Mediterranean World and the Near East*, pp. 211–218; H. Stegemann, "Die Bedeutung der Qumranfunde für die Erforschung der Apokalyptik," op. cit., pp. 495–530; D. Dimant, "Apocalyptic Texts at Qumran," in *The Community of the Renewed Covenant*, edited by E. Ulrich and J. C. Vanderkam (Notre Dame, 1994), pp. 175–191; F. García Martinez, *Qumran and Apocalyptic: Studies on the Aramaic Texts From Qumran* (Leiden, 1992); idem, "Apocalypticism in the Dead Sea Scrolls," in *The Encyclopedia of Apocalypticism*, vol. 1: The Origins of Apocalypticism in Judaism and Christianity, pp. 162–192.

36. Perrin, "Apocalyptic Christianity," in P. D. Hanson (ed.), *Visionaries and Their Apocalypses* (Philadelphia, 1983), p. 126.

37. C. Rowland, "The Visions of God in Apocalyptic Literature," in *Journal for the Study of Judaism* 10 (1979): 152–153; idem, *The Open Heaven: A Study of Apocalyptic in Judaism and Early Christianity* (New York, 1982), pp. 226–227. See also D. G. Meade, *Pseudonymity and Canon: An Investigation into the Relationship of Authorship and Authority in Jewish and Earliest Christian Tradition* (Tübingen, 1986), pp. 73–102; M. E. Stone, "Apocalyptic—Vision or Hallucination?" in *Milla wa-Milla* 14 (1974): 47–56; idem, "Apocalyptic Literature," pp. 430–431; Gruenwald, *From Apocalypticism to Gnosticism*, p. 72.

38. An example of the tendency to reject the assumption that the authors of the apocalypses were themselves visionaries based on a sharp distinction between the realms of practice and literature is found in M. Himmelfarb, "The Practice of Ascent in the Ancient Mediterranean World," in *Death, Ecstasy, and Other Worldly Journeys*, edited by J. J. Collins and M. Fishbane (Albany, 1995), pp. 123–137, and idem, *Ascent to Heaven*, pp. 95–114.

39. Bockmuehl, *Revelation and Mystery*, p. 31.

40. See J. H. Charlesworth, "The Portrayal of the Righteous as an Angel," in *Ideal Figures in Ancient Judaism*, edited by G. W. E. Nickelsburg and J. J. Collins (Chico, 1980), pp. 135–151; D. Dimant, "Men as Angels: The Self-Image of the Qumran Community," in *Religion and Politics in the Ancient Near East*, edited by A. Berlin (Bethesda, 1996), pp. 93–103; W. F. Smelik, "On Mystical Transformation of the Righteous Into Light in Judaism," in *Journal for the Study of Judaism* 26 (1995): 122–144; J. J. Collins, "A Throne in the Heavens: Apotheosis in pre-Christian Judaism," in *Death, Ecstasy, and Other Worldly Journeys*, pp. 43–58, and D. L. Bock, *Blasphemy and Exaltation in Judaism and the Final Examination of Jesus* (Tübingen, 1998), pp. 113–183.

41. It is of interest to consider in this connection the description of the eschaton in 2 Baruch 83:9–21 in terms of the transformation of everything into its opposite. This, too, suggests a destabilizing of boundaries.

42. J. J. Collins, "Jewish Apocalypses," in *Semeia* 14 (1979): 26–27.

43. J. J. Collins, "Apocalyptic Eschatology as the Transcendence of Death," in *Visionaries and Their Apocalypses*, p. 68.

44. Russell, *The Method and Message in Jewish Apocalyptic*, p. 220.

45. Bockmuehl, *Revelation and Mystery*, p. 26. See also Gruenwald, *From Apocalypticism to Gnosticism*, pp. 13–15, 42–49.

46. A. Hilary Armstrong, "The Hidden and the Open in Hellenic Thought," in *Eranos Jahrbuch* 54 (1985): 108.

47. See G. Scholem, *The Messianic Idea in Judaism and Other Essays on Jewish Spirituality* (New York, 1971), p. 10.

48. N. Perrin, "Apocalyptic Christianity," in *Visionaries and Their Apocalypses*, edited by P. D. Hanson (Philadelphia, 1983), p. 126.

49. P. Hanson, "Apocalypticism," in *Interpreter's Dictionary of the Bible Supplementary Volume* (Nashville, 1976), p. 30.

50. See N. Perrin, "Eschatology and Hermeneutics," in *Journal of Biblical Literature* 93 (1974): 1–15.

51. Keller, *Apocalypse Now and Then*, p. 87, thus describes the apocalyptic orientation: "Its own narrative historicity is neither that of a history nor that of modern historicism. Nonetheless, the text is not simply ahistorical. It takes aim at historical events. Its narrative does not mirror facts past or future, but offers an interpretative framework for them." See also H. O. Maier, "Staging the Gaze: Early Christian Apocalypses and Narrative Self-Representation," in *Harvard Theological Review* 90 (1997): 131–154. The interest in history is even more diminished in Gnostic apocalypses wherein the mythopoeic images seem to have overwhelmed the sense of historicity. See Collins, "Introduction," p. 13; F. T. Fallon, "The Gnostic Apocalypses," in *Semeia* 14 (1979): 123–158; G. MacRae, "Apocalyptic Eschatology in Gnosticism," in *Apocalypticism in the Mediterranean World and the Near East*, pp. 317–325.

52. On the phenomenon of pseudonymity in the apocalyptic texts, see Russell, *Method and Message in Jewish Apocalyptic*, pp. 127–139; J. J. Collins, "Pseudonymity, Historical Reviews and the Genre of the Revelation of John," in *Catholic Biblical Quarterly* 39 (1977): 329–343; *idem, Apocalyptic Vision of the Book of Daniel*, pp. 67–74; idem,

Apocalyptic Imagination, pp. 30–31; Himmelfarb, *Ascent to Heaven*, pp. 98–102, and the work of Meade cited above, n. 26.

53. *Method and Message in Jewish Apocalyptic*, p. 16.

54. Ibid., p. 224.

55. *Apocalyptic Imagination*, p. 40.

56. W. D. Davies, *Jewish and Pauline Studies* (Philadelphia, 1984), p. 267.

57. Scholem, *Messianic Idea*, p. 7.

CONVERSATION THREE

Apocalyptic Impulse in Judaism and Christianity: A Response to Elliot R. Wolfson

LESLIE J. HOPPE, O.F.M.

I want to thank my colleagues Hayim Perelmuter and John Pawlikowski for inviting me to offer this response to Professor Wolfson's paper. Responses to academic papers have a form all their own. An indispensable element in that form is for the respondent to thank the person who delivered the paper for a stimulating and learned study. I say this because I want Professor Wolfson and you to know that my comments of appreciation are *not pro forma* but reflect a sincere conviction about the contribution that this paper makes to our understanding of a religious phenomenon that appears to defy understanding. Those who are familiar with the study of apocalyptic know of the association that many scholars make between prophecy and apocalyptic. Professor Wolfson's trajectory of prophecy-apocalyptic-mysticism is an insightful and significant addition to a discussion that is still trying to make sense of the phenomenon of apocalyptic. My comments on Professor Wolfson's paper will begin by quoting the opening sentences of his concluding paragraph. I will then make a few comments on motifs that appear in that sentence.

> [T]he possession of the secret in the apocalyptic texts is
> not merely a cognitive or epistemological phenomenon; it
> is decidedly ontological insofar as the mystery relates to
> the wisdom of God reflected in nature and history. To gain
> knowledge of the mysteries unveiled in the apocalyptic
> vision, therefore, is an act of ultimate empowerment, for
> through such an acquisition one becomes like God . . .

There are three parts of this statement that I would like to comment on: "the secret in apocalyptic texts," the characterization of possessing that secret as something "not merely a cognitive and epistemological phenomenon," and the knowledge apocalyptic imparts as "an act of ultimate empowerment."

Let me begin by commenting on the element of secrecy that is a primary motif in Wolfson's paper. As a literary form, apocalyptic claims to receive and communicate secret knowledge from God. This knowledge is meant for select individuals:

> So during the forty days ninety-four books were written. And when the forty days were ended, the Most High spoke to me, saying, "Make public the twenty-four books that you wrote first and let the worthy and the unworthy read them, but keep the seventy that were written last, in order to give them to the wise among your people. For in them is the spring of understanding, the fountain of wisdom, and the river of knowledge" (4 Ezra 14:44–47).

By learning the secrets, these select individuals possess knowledge which others do not have. This secret information carries with it power—at least from the perspective of those who know the secrets. Thus knowledge differential produces power differential and gives those with the secret knowledge a real social advantage. Dr. Wolfson is correct when he characterizes the gaining of the knowledge imparted by apocalyptic as "an act of ultimate empowerment," though I do not agree that this empowerment means "becoming like God." Rather, knowing what is going to happen allows for the select few to be prepared for what is going to happen. Those without this knowledge cannot not be prepared.

Most of my comments, however, focus on how we ought to understand the possession of the secret itself. Apocalyptic is a literature of desperation— desperation that results from a perception of powerlessness. It reflects the belief that it is impossible to effect change from within. It gives up on the present and seeks to give meaning to the life of the powerless through its rhetoric. It is a rhetoric characterized by stinging condemnations of the social, economic, political, and religious status quo. But apocalyptic is not simply a rhetoric of condemnation, it is a rhetoric of violence and a rhetoric of power:

> I came to bring fire to the earth and how I wish it were already kindled . . . . Do you think that I have come to bring peace to the earth? No, I tell you, but rather division. From now on five in one household will be divided, three against two and two against three; they will be divided: father against son and son against father, mother against daughter and daughter against mother, mother-in-law against her daughter-in-law and daughter-in-law against mother-in-law (Luke 12:49–53).

As a rhetoric of violence, it calls for God's intervention to reorganize society and considers it impossible that current leadership can be a partner in the new world envisioned by the apocalypticists: "God has brought down the powerful from their throne, and lifted up the lowly; God has filled the hungry with good things and sent the rich away empty" (Luke 1:52–53). Apocalyptic is not a rhetoric of persuasion. It awaits God's soon to come intervention to destroy the enemy.

Apocalyptic claims God's own intervention, not for the ontological transformation of the individual but for the reorganization of society. Unlike the prophets, who believed that it was possible for the people of Israel and Judah to rethink their social and religious systems so as to effect necessary change, the apocalypticists offer only one hope: that God will intervene directly to change the system. What human beings can do is merely prepare themselves for this divine intervention. Apocalyptic holds that human beings cannot solve their problems. Only God can solve them through destructive intervention. Consider the Book of Daniel as an example. Daniel was co-opted for the service of an evil empire. He, however, refuses to be totally co-opted and remains faithful to God. Working within the system, Daniel is able to make some minor changes, but as a whole Daniel is ineffective in changing the system. This is the story of chapters 1–6. In chapters 7–12, Daniel receives visions about God's intervention that will change the system through destruction.

Apocalyptic emerged as ancient Israelite religion with its concern for the survival of the nation in this world was undergoing a transformation into what eventually became rabbinic Judaism with its concern for the survival of the individual in the world to come. Daniel asserts that "those who are wise shall shine like the brightness of the firmament; and those who turn many to righteousness, like the stars for ever and ever" (12:3). This may sound like the second century B.C.E. version of "ontological transformation," but it is hardly that.

The religious establishment in both Judaism and Christianity recognized apocalyptic as dangerous. Apocalyptic texts can and have been used to challenge the authority of the religious establishment. That may be one reason why both Judaism and Christianity have almost entirely abandoned it and its rhetoric. Some forms of evangelical Christianity, in particular Fundamentalism, still use apocalyptic rhetoric as they await Armageddon. They pour over texts from both Testaments that they call "biblical prophecy" to glean from them the secrets about the end of this age. Their knowledge of the end gives them power: "I have read the end of the book and we win." This secret knowledge gives Fundamentalists the power to challenge what they consider illegitimate forms of religion with the assurance that their rhetoric of violence is justified.

Dr. Wolfson may be right about the apocalyptic impulse in Judaism leading to mysticism, but I do not think that the same may be said of Christianity. For better or for worse, Christians who continue to use apocalyptic rhetoric do so as their early Jewish predecessors did—as an act of desperation against a system that was perceived as oppressive, in order to assert that the soon-to-come end will bring the destruction of evil powers and a creation of a new world.

ENDNOTES

Scripture references are from the *New Revised Standard Version*. Nashville: Thomas Nelson, Inc., 1990.

CONVERSATION FOUR

ALAN F. SEGAL

CELIA DEUTSCH

CONVERSATION FOUR

*One Covenant or Two: Paul and Early Christianity on
Universalism and Cultural Pluralism*

ALAN F. SEGAL

A fter two millennia of mostly hostile relations between Judaism and Christianity, the second half of the twentieth century called forth the agenda of a Christian view of Judaism. Unfortunately, the Holocaust was the major factor in the renewed interest in the subject. To be sure, Nazism was an anti-Christian movement; yet it relied heavily on a history of Christian anti-Jewish sentiment to promulgate and gain acceptance for its anti-Semitic policies.

Life rarely presents us with true symmetries: Judaism does not owe a similar debt to Christianity. For one thing, Christian anti-Semitism is, intellectually, a Christian problem, however tragic its consequences for Jews. Secondly, while Christians have always viewed Judaism as parochial, modern Western Jews have no similar sense of themselves as intolerant. Indeed, the sophisticated Jewish intellectuals of European life in the last two centuries have viewed themselves as universalists and, more recently, as pioneers in cultural pluralism. There is vibrant history of Jewish intellectual accommodation to, toleration of, and occasionally appreciation of Christianity.

Possibly this is in part due to the rabbinic formulations for dealing with Christianity. Traditionally within rabbinic Judaism, the righteous of all nations have a place in the world to come; so righteous Christians are the equivalent of the most moral Jews. On the other hand, Judaism has often considered Christianity, as a religion, to be a partial and garbled truth. It granted to Islam far greater praise for its strict, simple, and elegant monotheism. To the extent that it improves behavior, Christianity was tolerated, but theologically it was a kind of idolatry at best. Theoretically, Christianity and Islam provide their adherents with the instruction necessary for them to be righteous and hence "eligible for the world to come."

On the other hand, what was granted to the category of Christians was not automatically granted to each individual. For good reasons, Jews had very low moral expectations of the gentiles around them. In a sentence that summons a whole vanished world of Eastern European Jewish struggle, Elie Wiesel has said that where he grew up, he had low expectations of what non-Jews might do. His despair at the Holocaust came from what God had allowed to happen. For all these reasons, we need to reconsider the theological underpinnings of our thinking.

One major theological thrust for Christianity has been to discuss the possibility that God intended there to be two covenants rather than a single one. This notion is implicit within the Christian designation of the Bible into two volumes, as it were, the Old Testament and the New Testament. But equally part of that notion is the assumption that the Old Testament has been partly surpassed, superseded, and rendered obsolete.

A new theological start might be made if the notion of two covenants were renovated by considering that they are both still in effect. Logically, this might serve to put the two religions on an even footing and eliminate much of the arguments between them. Alternatively, a degree of autonomy might be gained if we, like Rosenzweig, consider ourselves to be both part of the same covenant, albeit in very different ways. Franz Rosenzweig's pre-World War II theology of Judaism, *The Star of Redemption*, was based on the notion that two religions are true—Judaism and Christianity. He both exemplifies the privileged position which Jews in Europe gave to Christianity and the way in which Jews tried to pioneer notions of cultural pluralism, especially in Germany which was already split into Catholic and Protestant factions. In a sense, German Jews were arguing to be equal Germans, differing only in their religious commitments.

But Rosenzweig did not see a contemporary historically meaningful Islam. Turkey was the "sick man of Europe." So, if we use Rosenzweig's model, we must also recognize the need to modify it to encompass the other faiths of people of good will. Of course, the model for Judaism can continue to be: "The righteous of all nations have a place in the world to come." Either picture—righteousness, one covenant or two—might yield more understanding and mutual tolerance for the religious communities of Judaism and Christianity. The problem is to discover which is likely to be the best formulation and which is most in line with traditional thinking in Judaism and Christianity.

The Problem in Acts

What I propose to do today is to look at how these attitudes developed in the first and second century to see how the historical record might correspond with our current theological possibilities. In the first centuries of the Common Era, the mature rabbinic doctrine that the righteous of all nations have a place in the world to come was still in its development. There was not a single answer to the question "What was the Jewish view of the place of the gentiles in God's scheme?" That is to say, "Judaism" did not have a single policy on the status of the gentiles; there was no single Judaism of the day. Jews did have opinions about gentiles, and various Jewish sects had policies or theologies that involved gentiles in some way. And most Jewish sects had ambivalent opinions. This paper will attempt to address the ambivalence and show how various communities dealt with it.

A major point of this paper is to show that incipient Christianity, at the same time as it deals with its universal mission, shows the same difficulties and tensions in holding its own group definition in mind as do the other Jewish sects of the first century. We will see that Christianity resolves the dilemma, not because it takes seriously the lessons of Paul, but when it no longer has a significant Jewish population. Indeed, in very important ways, early Christianity ignored the position of Paul, forcing him to counsel his gentile churches to compromise. Perhaps that is the path which will be most fruitful to Christian theology in the future. In any event, the easy contrasts made between the New Testament and other varieties of Judaism just do not work. It is not just a question of Jewish parochialism being replaced by Christian universalism. Each community was involved in the discussion about universalism and answered the question in a different but similar way and resolved that quandary in a similar but unique way.

Let us take the Christian community first, because Christian history on this issue is actually clearer than the rabbinic one. According to Acts 15 the issue arises at Antioch before the Jerusalem council, because emissaries from Jerusalem maintain that one cannot be saved unless one is circumcised after the custom of Moses: "Then certain individuals came down from Judaea and were teaching the brothers, 'Unless you are circumcised according to the customs of Moses, you cannot be saved'" (Acts 15:1). Sometimes this is taken by a Christian readership to show the beginning of the process by which Christianity rid itself of painfully parochial ideas in Judaism. Yet, even leaving aside the issue of dating in rabbinic Judaism, this report is at odds with normative rabbinic thought, which feels that the righteous of all nations have a place in the world to come. How do we understand this difference in perspective on Jewish life?

Of course, there are several grounds for distrusting Luke. Almost all NT critics distrust Luke's chronology of the events of Paul's life for several reasons, not least of all that he is a very tendentious writer separated by at least two generations from Paul. When it comes to issues of historical interpretation, the situation is more subtle and less satisfying. As I will show, there were Jews who refused to accept any gentiles into the faith. So it is entirely possible that the conservative members of the church did not go along with the Jerusalem church's decision. The restrictive understanding of salvation is characteristic of some kinds of apocalyptic Judaism. But we shall see that it is certainly not a universal doctrine within the Jewish community. Paul will help us solve this dilemma, because Paul is the only Pharisee who ever gave us his personal writings.[1]

At any rate, I take it to be established and completely certain from the Epistle to the Galatians that Paul's opinion is that gentiles do not need to be circumcised to be saved, as he says so clearly. It is also the position of the church council, evidently also of Petrine Christianity. It may even have been the position of James, but it clearly is not the position of all Christians and Jews, else who are the opponents of Paul in Galatia?

This range of opinion is, in turn, not uniquely characteristic of Christianity. Although there is no evidence that Jews accepted converts without circumcision, there is some evidence that some did not demand conversion of all who wanted to gain the benefits of God's favor. This more tolerant view of gentile behavior is characteristic of some Pharisaic and later rabbinic Judaism but emphatically not true of apocalypticism. A stronger statement attributable to Paul—namely, that no one needs to be circumcised to be saved—also appears to have some precedent within the Jewish community, but it is a very minority position, limited to that class of Jews represented by the "radical allegorizers" mentioned by Philo (Migr. Abr. 89–94), who apparently identify as Jews but do not perform the rituals. Thus, Luke and Paul taken together witness some of the rough spectrum of Jewish opinions as well as the early Christian opinions on that issue. What differs is the relative weight to be given to the various positions in the opinion of the church writers.

Luke equates the idea that there is no *salvation* without circumcision with the position of the party of the Pharisees who say, "It is necessary to circumcise them, and to charge them to keep the law of Moses" (15:5). The two questions which Luke mentions in this passage are hardly identical. In the first instance (Acts 15:1), we are talking about salvation; in the second (Acts 15:5), we need only be talking about proper conversion, whether Christians should also be good Jews.

Normative rabbinic Judaism distinguishes radically between conversion and salvation. It does say all Israel will be saved in Sanhedrin 10, using Isaiah as a prooftext, a statement mirrored by Paul, who quotes first Joel 2:32 to the effect that: "Everyone who calls upon the name of the Lord will be saved" (Rom 10:13).[2] Later on Paul goes on to say that all Israel will be saved: "And so all Israel will be saved," (Rom 11:26), which more or less mirrors the rabbinic notion. It is worthwhile to trace how Paul means these two notions to be put together.

More specifically, rabbinic Judaism says that all Israel will be saved except heinous and unrepentant sinners, since it subsequently suggests that several groups of heretics will be excluded along with various sinners in the Bible. But rabbinic Judaism allows that some gentiles can be saved *qua* gentiles without conversion. On the other hand, rabbinic Judaism requires that all converts to Judaism be strictly charged to keep the law of Moses: No doubt this is something that Paul had in mind when he says: "Now I, Paul, say to you that if you receive circumcision, Christ will be of no advantage to you. I testify again to every man who receives circumcision that he is bound to keep the whole law" (Gal 5:2–3). Indeed, I will show that even Paul tells us that the later rabbinic notion that gentiles can be saved without conversion was already well discussed in the first century (Rom 2).

Paul shows us that the following, possibly later rabbinic discussion, already has a first century milieu. Rabbinic writings debate the issue of the salvation of the gentiles, as they debate most every issue.

> Rabbi Eliezer said: "All the nations will have no share in the world to come even as it is said, 'the wicked shall go into Sheol, and all the nations that forget God' (Ps. 9:17). The wicked shall go into Sheol—these are the wicked among Israel." Rabbi Joshua said to him: "If the verse had said, 'The wicked shall go into Sheol with all the nations,' and had stopped there, I should have agreed with you, but as it goes on to say 'who forget God,' it means there are righteous men among the nations who have a share in the world to come" (Tosefta Sanhedrin 13:2).[3]

According to the rabbinic writings, Luke is half right. Some Pharisees (let us for argument's sake identify Pharisees and Tannaim, even though the two are not exactly coterminous), represented by Rabbi Eliezer, said that only Israel will be saved. Others, represented by Rabbi Joshua, said that the righteous gentiles would be saved as well. Would that we could trust that these were the actual positions of those rabbis! We cannot anymore, given our natural skepticism about the value of oral reports. Yet, doubt is not the same as error. The midrash is not necessarily at error, even if we must be skeptical of its accuracy unless we can find some grounds for believing it. We do note that the Mishnah and midrash are at least consistent on this issue. The positions attributed to Rabbis Eliezer and Joshua b. Hananiah are typical of other remarks that rabbinic literature has attributed to them. Rabbi Eliezer is a severe critic of gentiles. Rabbi Joshua b. Hananiah is more liberal. He removes all distinctions between Jew and gentile in attaining salvation through the doing of good deeds. He says: "Everyone who walks in blamelessness before his Creator in this world will escape the judgment of hell in the world to come." He even disagrees with the usually more tolerant Rabbi Gamaliel by maintaining that the blameless children of wicked heathen will also have a share in the world to come. Though Rabbi Joshua probably does not allow conversion without circumcision, he at least looks at the positive side of the issue, saying: "Baptism without circumcision makes one a ger, (that is, a proselyte, a person in the process of converting)" (b. Yeb. 46a).

If these statements were historical, then they would be directly coterminous with the first generations of Christians. And they are to be found in early rabbinic sources—the Tosefta is as important as the Mishnah in terms of authority and dating. But if the early third century is our *ad quem*, the attribution to the first century is the very thing which we must question unless one has a good reason to establish it. Furthermore, the rabbinic discussions are certainly not *ipsissima verba* of the rabbis, just as Luke's statements are likely not the exact words of the conservative party of Jews within the Christian movement. But the midrash does leave us with the impression that the same issues which were debated in the Church in the first century were also being debated by the rabbis as early as the second, and perhaps even earlier.

It is possible that all the Christian Pharisees were of the most conservative persuasion, and that some more liberal ones show up in rabbinic Judaism. However, that seems statistically unlikely. Note, too, that this issue is crucial for understanding Paul's program for Christianity, which I need to discuss as least briefly at the end of this chapter.

But before we come to Paul directly we have to look at the wider context of these ideas, at least briefly. And the wider context includes some sociological observations about the nascent Christian and Jewish communities.

The Jewish Environment

The status of the gentiles is discussed in later rabbinic Judaism through at least two different rubrics—the resident alien and the doctrine of the

"Noahide Commandments." We shall see that they make different assumptions about the purpose of the gentiles, and they sometimes imply conflicting approaches which, as it turns out, need to be systematically worked out both in Christianity and in rabbinic Judaism.

The issue of the resident alien derived from the biblical rules incumbent upon "the stranger in your gates."[4] Resident aliens were obliged to abstain from offering sacrifices to strange gods (Lev 17:7–9), from eating blood in any form (Lev 17:10ff), from incest (Lev 18:6–26), from work on the Sabbath (Ex 20:10f), and from eating leavened bread during the Passover (Ex 12:18f).[5] Closely allied with this issue is the rabbinic doctrine of the "Noahide Commandments." This rabbinic doctrine is derived from a sophisticated and theological formulation that some legal enactments were given before Sinai, during the primeval history, to all human beings. Furthermore, the sign of the Noahide covenant, the rainbow, is available to all humanity to symbolize God's promise of safety. And it is completely outside of the special covenant with Abraham and his descendants. The covenant with Noah is expanded to the entire primeval period, encompassing all the revealed commandments preceding Sinai. The Noahide Commandments (e. g., T. AZ 8.4 and more fully in b. Sanhedrin 56b) function somewhat like a concept of "natural law," which any just person can be expected to follow by observation and reason. In more Christian theological language, it is available by God's grace to all humanity. Here is the earliest version, as stated in the Tosefta to Avodah Zarah:

> Seven commandments were the sons of Noah commanded:
> (1) concerning adjudication (*dinim*), (2) and concerning
> idolatry (*abodah zarah*), (3) and concerning blasphemy
> (*qilelat hashem*), (4) and concerning sexual immorality
> (*giluy arayot*), (5) and concerning bloodshed (*shefikhut
> damim*), (6) and concerning robbery (*hagezet*), (7) and con-
> cerning a limb torn from a living animal (*eber min hahayy*).

In the basic version, nothing is mentioned which crosses the border of specific Jewish law because all these things are strictly forbidden for Jews *ab initio.* The rabbis immediately bring up more questionable ordinances, presumably asking whether a particular rule is specifically Jewish or should apply to all humanity. For instance, the rabbis mention cross-breeding (*Kilayim*), castration (*sirus*), eating blood from a living animal (*Dam min hahayy*), and witchcraft (*kishuf*). To these is sometimes added in later discussions the recognition that YHWH, the God of Israel, is the one true God. Other tannaim limit the Noahide laws to the prohibition of idolatry or those concerned with idolatry, blasphemy, and adjudication (See j. Kilayyim 2.7). As David Novak says in his discussion of the Noahide laws: "What emerges from all of this discussion is that in the Tannaitic period, there was a debate over the number and content of the Noahide laws. We have no record, however, that any authority in that period rejected the doctrine *per se*."[6]

Of course, the minute we mention a rabbinic doctrine from a third century text we risk anachronism in assuming that it comes from the first century. To find out what was practiced in first century Judaism, we have to consult other varieties of Judaism. Another close parallel to the Noahide Commandments can found in the Book of Jubilees 7:20–21, which is pre-Christian:[7]

> And in the twenty-eighth jubilee Noah began to command
> his grandsons with ordinances and commandments and all
> of the judgments which he knew. And he bore witness to
> his sons so that they might do justice and cover the shame
> of their flesh and bless the one who created them and
> honor father and mother, and each one love his neighbor
> and preserve themselves from fornication and pollution
> and from all injustice.

The particular ordinances thought to be universally humane by Jubilees are establishing justice, eschewing incest, honoring parents, loving neighbors, and prohibiting adultery, promiscuity, and *pollution* from injustice.[8] In Jubilees, this short lawcode forms the basis of the judgment against the giants, which brings on the flood and sets the scene for the myths contained in the book of Enoch.

It would be unwise, however, to assume that Jubilees is promulgating such ideas in order to find a basis for humane universalism—which is more or less what the rabbis and Christians do with it. Quite the contrary, Jubilees has a strictly dualistic view of the world, both on the divine and human level, in consonance with the ideas of Qumran sectarians in whose library it figured prominently. Israel is identified as a good kingdom. God selected it as special and above all other peoples (2:21) to be marked by circumcision (15:11). It alone can participate in the sabbath and the other God-ordained festivals. The other nations are condemned and God has placed spirits in authority over them to lead them astray. Jubilees 22:16 warns Jews not to eat with a gentile. Jubilees forcefully says that there is no salvation without circumcision on the eighth day (15:26–27). That virtually means that conversion of the gentiles is impossible. Even a charitable reading supposes that only the children of converts can enter the community:

> And anyone who is born whose own flesh is not circumcised on the eighth day is not from the sons of the covenant which the Lord made for Abraham, since (he is) from the children of destruction. And there is therefore no sign upon him so that he might belong to the Lord because (he is destined) to be destroyed and annihilated from the earth and to be uprooted from the earth because he has broken the covenant of the Lord our God. Because the nature of all of the angels of the presence and all of the angels of sanctification he sanctified Israel so that they might be with him and with his holy angels.[9]

The obvious reason for the inclusion of the Noahide Commandments at this place is to provide Jubilees with a legal warrant for condemning the gentiles. God would not consign most of humanity to destruction without reason; the gentiles know His law and spurn it. This is entirely appropriate to a sectarian position, where all the gentiles and all but a saving remnant of Israel are scheduled for divine destruction. We know from this evidence that there were sects within Judaism which did not subscribe to any liberal ideas about the capabilities of gentiles. [10]

This issue had already surfaced in the lives of sectarian Jews, as Jubilees had made clear. So, too, in the first century, in Diaspora Judaism the Jewish Sibylline Oracles specified those rules incumbent upon righteous gentiles:

> Happy will be those of mankind of earth who will love the great God, blessing him before drinking and eating, putting their trust in piety. They will reject all temples when they see them, altars too, useless foundations of dumb stones (and stone statues and handmade images) defiled with blood of animate creatures, and sacrifices of four-footed animals. They will look to the great glory of the one God and commit no wicked murder, no deal in dishonest gain, which are most horrible things. Neither have they disgraceful desire for another's spouse or for hateful and repulsive abuse of a male. Other men will never imitate their way or piety or customs, because they desire shamelessness. On the contrary, they deride them with mockery and laughter Infantile in their foolishness, they will falsely attribute to those what wicked and evil deeds they themselves commit (Sybilline Oracles 4:24–39). [11]

Here again murder, theft, and other specifics are mentioned as primary prohibitions for all humanity to observe. Sacrifice is entirely forbidden.

Pseudo-Phocylides also mentions the general principles of Jewish ethics without mentioning the ceremonial Torah. One of the witnesses of this poem reports that it ended with the exhortation that "purifications are for the purity of the soul, not of the body" (11. 228–230, *Charlesworth* 2, p. 582). Aristeas likewise says: "Honoring God is done not with gifts or sacrifices but with purity of soul." [12] These sentiments come from the prophets who rebuked the misuse of the cult. But they are used in Hellenistic Judaism to argue against the necessity of temple worship, both for Jews in diaspora and gentiles.

It is also part of a proselyte literature designed to convince pagans of the inherent morality of Judaism and to bring them to the status of God-fearers, in the first instance, but apparently not closer to God than that. If they later chose to join Judaism, that was their own decision.

Once the social significance of the different formulations is outlined, the reasons for the ambiguity become clear. The difference between the Noahide Commandments and the Rules for the Sojourner is clear from a social point of view. The resident alien must, because of his close association with Israelites, observe some of the laws of Judaism, while the Noahide commandments refer to the ultimate disposition of gentiles and thus entirely to gentiles who are not observant. The resident sojourners may be ethical or not; the issue is irrelevant. The law is there for the benefit of the Israelites who need not tolerate certain impieties within their own territory. With the Noahide Commandments the gentiles need not observe any Jewish law at all. The sole question is whether they can be righteous, hence worthy to inherit the world to come.[13]

This corresponds to the two different but related social situations of Jews in the Roman Empire. The first, that of the resident alien, refers to a situation where Jews are in the majority and have political power. In that situation they can maintain that gentiles ought to do a certain amount of Jewish ritual—such as circumcision if they want to live under Jewish rule. The issue is ritual or cultic, although it later becomes the legal basis for discussions of conversion in Judaism. In the second situation, Jews are understood as a minority living amongst gentiles and the question arises what God has in store for them. The issue is therefore strictly moral, as the requirements for gentile performance of Jewish law is not at issue.

The second situation, in which Jews are not the majority of the population and have very limited abilities to affect or control their neighbors, is a common diaspora condition; there is even a danger of gentile backlash in being too open to mission. We have ample evidence of the concern of the pagan community that the Jews and Christians are stealing their children from them. In these situations, the concept of a righteous gentile, who eschewed sin but did not explicitly take up the special rules of Judaism, would have a positive value. So before the third century, when the mature doctrine is being voiced in rabbinic Judaism, certain ambiguities would naturally obtain. In areas around Palestine with a Jewish majority and certain rights of self-rule, one set of procedures would be more relevant. In other areas, different procedures might prevail. During the hostilities with Rome when circumcision was forbidden, the only alternative for an interested gentile would have been becoming a "God-fearer." So, too, in mature Christianity and Judaism, both of which work with a gentile majority as the given, the concept of righteous gentile is much more important. In the first and early second century, before the situation clarified, it was more fluid, as the Christian evidence shows us. The ambiguity of the Christian formulation of the Apostolic Decree merely underlines the imprecision of the earliest discussions of the issues.

The Apostolic Decree

Luke tells us something about the status of the discussion about the Noahide Commandments in first century Judaism. Acts 15:19, 20, 15:29, and 21:24, 25 describe an Apostolic Decree defining a minimum of practice for the new gentile Christians:

> Therefore my judgment is that we should not trouble those of the Gentiles who turn to God, but should write to them to abstain from the pollutions of idols and from unchastity and from what is strangled and from blood. For from early generations Moses has had in every city those who preach him, for he is read every sabbath in the synagogues. (15:19, 20)
>
> That you abstain from what has been sacrificed to idols and from blood and from what is strangled, and from unchastity. (15:29)
>
> Thus all will know that there is nothing in what they have been told about you but that you yourself live in observance of the law. But as for the gentiles who have

> believed, we have sent a letter with our judgment that they
> should abstain from what has been sacrificed to idols and
> from blood and from what is strangled and from
> unchastity. (21:24, 25)

In other words, the Christian discussion of gentiles is evidence that such ideas were being debated in Judaism too, even if the argument had special constraints within the Christian community. The Christian Decree is neither exactly the resident alien nor the Noahide commandments, but it is a peculiar, ambiguous melange, perhaps even a combination of both. The new Christian "God-fearers" (*sebomenoi* or *phoboumenoi*), as such gentiles had been called in Judaism, had to abstain from idol sacrifices (*eidolothuton*), from blood (*haimatos*) likely, as we shall see, and from meat with blood in it. They must also stay away from another completely opaque term (*pnikton*), as I shall show, from animals which had been throttled and killed—hence a translation of the Hebrew term *trefah*.[14] Furthermore, they should stay away from forbidden marriages, incest, and unchastity (*porneias*).[15]

The question is: what kind of a code is the Apostolic Decree? Is it moral or cultic? Even such terms are not easy to use because they contain some ambiguities as well. The Apostolic Decree can hardly be a complete moral code, because such obvious sins as theft are entirely missing, although it is present in the rabbinic formulation of the Noahide laws. Thus, it is not exactly what the Noahide Laws is supposed to be. The question here is only the rules specifically appropriate for those gentiles who want to live amongst a predominantly Jewish-Christian community if they do not convert to Judaism. Thus, these laws are not exactly the Noahide laws, because they assume a social situation where the Christians are subject to other moral standards as well. But they are not exactly the rules for resident sojourners either, since they are not necessarily within the borders of the land of Israel. Obviously, the Apostolic Decree is another formulation of the same type as both of them, but for a unique purpose: just rules for Jewish Christians and gentile Christians living together. In other words, in the Apostolic Decree, some moral issues were taken for granted as resolved because they were obviously eschewed by all Christians.[16]

Steve Wilson has demonstrated in his book *Luke and the Law*[17] that the Apostolic Decree in Luke's formulation is closer to the Noahide laws than to the laws of the resident alien, which are outlined in Leviticus 17 and 18, because the term *haima* in Acts appears to refer to bloodshed in general rather than to the kosher laws. And one can see here that bloodshed is most often mentioned as one of the gentile sins in this Jewish apologetic literature. Furthermore, a minority Western reading of the text omits *pniktos* and adds a negative form of the golden rule, which is a hallmark of rabbinic Judaism as well as of Christianity. Thus, in the Western text, the reading clearly implies a moral code—hence Luke appears to have something like the "Noahide Commandments" in mind. Wilson seems to be correct about Luke's understanding, but is this the genesis of the law? He asks this question and we need to answer it. The answer appears to be negative. The original context of the rules appears to be cultic or ceremonial, hence closer to the rules for resident aliens. Why else would one adopt such ambiguous categories and not adopt a straightforwardly moral system, much closer to the "Noahide Laws"? Whether Luke was the first to see the regulations as basically moral is also doubtful, but it is clear that the moral interpretation has great advantages for Luke's overriding historical purposes.

There is likely a cultic interpretation underlying Luke's narrative—a cultic interpretation that continues even after Luke. If so, there is a level of tradition that precedes Luke's interpretation. It had to deal with the issue of Jewish law because of the particularly difficult issue of gentiles and Jews not only worshipping together but eating together and marrying. More importantly, it appears to be an early and different solution to the same problem that Paul was addressing. The rule against strangled food in the Apostolic Decree appears to be a reference to the Jewish concept of *trefah*, improperly killed food, which may not be eaten. Thus, in this early version the Christian Church was saying that the gentiles could be accepted into their community if they did not violate their most basic Jewish sensibilities. It is the later Fathers who link it with a specific form of cooking because they cannot conceive of a time before the abrogation of all the Jewish laws. Thus, the Christian community is not entirely basing its legislation on "Noahide" laws but on the resident alien rules as well.

The original Christian version of the rules which Luke records is stricter than other Jewish versions of the laws of the sojourner, probably because Christian Jews and gentiles came into more intimate contact—a large section of the Church was allowed to remain uncircumcised, thus bringing possible sources of pollution much closer to home, as it were. Thus it really is closer in spirit to the Levitical rules about the resident alien. The rabbis, conversely, did not expect Jews and gentiles to eat together, much less to marry.

Steve Wilson suggests that Luke understands the Apostolic Decree as a kind of Noahide Commandments because he already knows that the food laws and ceremonial laws of Judaism are now suspended. But Wilson also suggests that this is not necessarily what the original law meant to do. It may have come from the actual time of Paul, a time when Paul's solution to the issue of Jewish law for gentiles was provocative and not widely accepted, and certainly a time before Luke's summary historical theology had not yet penetrated, a time which Luke has no ability to detail accurately. Thus, the history of the Apostolic Decree is incomplete in Christian sources as well.

Just as there are problems reading the history of the Noahide Commandments in Jewish documents, so, too, there are insoluble problems in tracing the history of the Apostolic Decree in Christian documents, a history which is, indeed, known to us in far more detail than rabbinic history. But it will turn out that these two documents should be seen as the same history, and when they are, the same social problems and the same tendencies towards universalization are evident in both communities.

In some sense, it is virtually impossible to say for sure whether the Christian decree, and indeed even the nonrabbinic Jewish parallels, should be seen within the discussion of resident aliens or the Noahide commandments. I will try to show that they both go over a long time period when both precedents were individually seen as relevant. All of them are dealing with the same issue from a variety of different sociological situations.

Thus the Christian evidence which is conflicted as to whether the term *haima* refers to a Jewish rule of slaughter or bloodshed, should be interpreted to mean that the ambiguity was consistent in early Christianity. Whether *haima* refers to a moral action or a ritual one is not entirely clear in Church tradition, which has taken it in both ways. Traces of the decree appear in Revelations 2:14,20,24; Didache 6:3; Justin, *Dial.* 34–35; Tertullian, *Apol.*; Eusebios, *H. E.* 5.1.26, in a letter dated 177 c. e., from Lyons; Minucius Felix, *Octavius* 30; Sibylline Oracles, 2.93; *Pseudo-Clementine* Homily 7.8.1. The early Christians more closely approximate the ordinances of Jubilees than did the third-century rabbis. See John Hurd, *The Origin of I Corinthians* (New York: Seabury Press), 1965, pp. 250–253 for the basic bibliography.

In this regard, the interpretation of the Greek words *haima*, *eidolothuta*, and *pniktos* is crucial for understanding the intent of the Apostolic Decree. They are ambiguous words because they can be seen in either a cultic or a moral setting.

In the same way, *eidolothuta* can be meat sacrificed to idols, as it means in Paul, or it would be better construed in this context as all forms of idolatry. If the term were *eidolatria*, we might have assumed that this was merely a moral law. But it is clear that the context here is cultic because *eidolothuta* appears to mean all idolatrous practices, not merely meat sacrificed to idols. The original context for the rules appears to be cultic, at least in some places. But, of course, that does not mean that Luke was the first to take them in a moral sense, as referring to gentile salvation. Probably there was real ambiguity between various sorts of Christian communities right from the start.

In short, it is interesting that the Christian community was not entirely clear at the beginning as to whether it meant its gentile participants to be converts or resident aliens, or merely righteous gentiles. It depended on whose writings one followed. Paul was clearly a proponent of conversion status in a spiritual sense, but he appears to think that the Christians are righteous gentiles—needing to observe no special rules. Peter and James appear to have favored resident alien status.

It occurs to me that this ambiguity has a positive social function. Sometimes ambiguity is a positive literary device, not just lack of clarity. There is a very important secondary benefit for the ambiguity in the question of blood-shed being ethical or ritual. In the Jewish case, gentile godfearers did not have to be integrated into the same community. But this is precisely what Paul insisted on. On the other hand, other Christians insisted on gentiles observing at least some of the laws; not being Pharisees, they may have assumed this was enough to become one community with Jews. Or they may have assumed, as Paul did when he was a Pharisee, that converts must accept all the laws. So a variety of perspectives is protected by a certain ambiguity in the Apostolic Decree. That ambiguity is resolved by Luke who has already decided based on his view of the culmination of history in a single community of Jew and gentile, though his way of achieving this vision appears to be slightly different from Paul's. But we can ask whether the specifics of Jew-ish-Christian interaction must not have been the original problem, since the possibility is not logical.

This is precisely the same history of tradition that we see within the Jewish community as well. Though both issues are present in the Jewish com-munity—both the Levitical laws of the resident alien and the universalization problem of the Noahide commandments—it is the latter problem that comes to predominate in Jewish tradition. The former ceases to be a large historical problem after the nation state is destroyed.

Even the later, rabbinic discussion, which has satisfactorily resolved all the ambiguities between converts and gentiles, is not entirely unambiguous in dividing the issues into ethical versus ceremonial laws. Although the basic seven Noahide Commandments are purely ethical for the rabbis, in the sense that they do not obligate anyone to the laws of Judaism, the subsequent dis-cussion of the rabbis clouds the issue a bit. The rabbis debate a number of other ordinances as to whether they should be considered Noahide. And it is not clear how they understood them. Perhaps witchcraft, castration, drinking the blood of a living animal could be understood as universal laws. But cross-breeding is not at all clear.[18]

Rabbinic tradition has also suffered from a certain amount of ambiguity, especially in regard to the development of legal terminology. This ambiguity makes it possible to conflate the theological doctrine of universalism with the desire for converts. The terms for a convert to Judaism come from the biblical rules concerning resident alien. Because the term *ger*, which means resident alien in the Bible, was taken by the rabbis to mean a convert or proselyte (someone in the process of converting), they found the need to distinguish between a *ger toshava*, resident alien, and a *ger tsedek*, an actual convert:

> Ger denotes a full proselyte (*ger tsedeq*). *Toshab* denotes
> a ger who eats nonkosher meat *(nevelot)*. The family of a
> ger denotes it is gentile. The offshoot of a ger's family
> denotes one sold to an idolatrous cult (Sifra Behar 1 lOa).

This is, of course, a later summary and a solution to an exegetical problem which perplexed the rabbis for some time. But it points out that before this distinction there was some ambiguity in everyone's mind about the differences between resident aliens and proselytes. Since the same term could refer to either, sometimes one needed to have a distinction between them and sometimes it was convenient not to make a distinction. Apparently, however, they were clearly not separable at the beginning. So it appears that during the early period there was some confusion between what standards righteous gentiles ought to maintain and what proselytes ought to maintain before they converted completely to Judaism. The first would be entirely ethical, but the latter might include also some of the ritual of Judaism. It is not surprising that it is the Christian record, with its extremely important but special circumstance of a community containing both gentiles and Jews, that shows us so clearly that such an issue was being discussed. And it also shows us that the confusion was present in the first century.

In order to see the tradition fully, we must look into both the Christian community and the Jewish community. Neither gives us the whole picture. Nor is it clear that in all cases that both Judaism and Christianity will always develop the same theological doctrines to face parallel problems. But in this case they did. Furthermore, neither community gives us enough information to discover the history by itself. We need the witness of both to understand either.

Romans 9–11

Paul obviously stands in opposition to the way these issues were resolved by the Apostolic Decree. He believes that Christ is the end of the Law, meaning that none of the special laws of Judaism are definitive for salvation. Yet, I have demonstrated in *Paul the Convert*, that Paul does not stick to his ideological position. Instead, he goes along with the apostolic decree in the name of Church unity: "Do not for the sake of food laws destroy the work of God" (Rom 14:20). In other words, in order that his Gospel be understood and his gentile Christians be accepted, Paul himself counsels caution. One need not exercise the freedom which one has gained in Christ.

Paul considers himself among the strong (cf. "we who are the strong" Rom 15:1). He can confidently say that no food is unclean of itself, only to him who thinks it unclean (Rom 14:14). But in his capacity as apostle he is prepared to make an accommodation. It is possible to call this strategy a compromise, though Paul does not have to compromise his position to carry it out; rather, he again simply refrains from the freedom that he has preached is available to his gentile churches.

Dietary laws of the new community should unify it, not separate it. In 1 Corinthians Paul cautions against giving offense to either Jews or Greeks. Neither should offend the other in the interest of Christian unity. His personal behavior is the pattern for all to follow:

> So, whether you eat or drink, or whatever you do, do all to the glory of God. Give no offense to Jews or to Greeks or to the church of God, just as I try to please all men in everything I do, not seeking my own advantage, but that of many, that they may be saved. Be imitators of me, as I am of Christ (1 Cor 10:31–11:1).

In Romans 11:1 Paul returns to the issue of the salvation of Israel. Some Israelites are to be saved as he has been, since he too is an Israelite, of the seed of Abraham, of the tribe of Benjamin. The hardening of heart of most of the Jews is not incompatible with God's promises in the Bible, because the number of faithful is always small, according to Scripture. Though Israel has not retained the prize, they are not disqualified forever. Through their intransigence, the Jews seem to have forfeited their reserved first place, and gentiles will be saved before them. As opposed to his statement in Romans 1 and Galatians, his opinion here is that salvation will come to the gentiles first and then to the Jews.

Paul begins his last argument in this section by emphasizing that he is speaking to gentiles, because he is the apostle of the gentiles. But he is speaking to the Christian community, not to the Jews or the unconverted gentiles. Paul says that God's promise is not removed from the Israelites; rather, the order in which salvation is brought has been reversed. It is possible to interpret this passage as a statement of double salvation, Jews by Torah, gentiles by faith. Since the passage is meant for gentile ears, it emphasizes faith as the path of salvation for gentiles by saying that it is the equivalent of Torah, hence Torah does continue to save.

A double plan for salvation, however, does not seem to be the point here, as Paul's lament for the stubbornness of the Jews shows. The figure of the wild olive illustrates his hope that some Jews will be saved by the provocation of the inclusion of the gentiles and follow the gentiles into the Church. Some of the olive branches are broken off, and a wild olive is grafted on. The broken branches represent the unconverted part of Israel, whereas the root must be the Israelites. One wonders whether Paul would not have excluded many Jewish Christians, who upheld the cultic differences between gentiles and Jews, for they demonstrated lack of faith as well. Only the faithful will inherit the promises. The faithful acknowledge the special process of transformation beginning in the world. It is to them that the gentiles will be grafted and they should not boast of their understanding of faith. Faith in the Mosaic legislation is not the equal of faith in Christ. Paul only equates the faithful in Christ who observe Torah with the faithful in Christ who do not observe Torah. Paul argues that Jewish Christians (with faith) and gentile Christians (with faith) are equal, not that Jews and Christians are equal. This is the meaning of his statement in Romans 10:12–13, "For there is no distinction between Jew and Greek; the same Lord is Lord of all who bestows His riches upon all who call upon Him. For 'everyone who calls upon the name of the Lord shall be saved.'"

At the moment that he states that all Israel will be saved, he uses Isaiah 59:15–21 as his prooftext: "Out of Zion will come the Deliverer; he will banish ungodliness from Jacob" (Rom 11:26). The context shows precisely what he has in mind in the Isaiah text:

> Truth is lacking, and he who departs from evil makes himself a prey. The LORD saw it, and it displeased him that there was no justice.

> He saw that there was no man, and wondered that there was no one to intervene; then his own arm brought him victory, and his righteousness upheld him.

> He put on righteousness as a breastplate, and a helmet of salvation upon his head; he put on garments of vengeance for clothing, and wrapped himself in fury as a mantle.

> According to their deeds, so will he repay, wrath to his adversaries, requital to his enemies; to the coastlands he will render requital.

> So they shall fear the name of the LORD from the west, and his glory from the rising of the sun; for he will come like a rushing stream, which the wind of the LORD drives.

> "And he will come to Zion as Redeemer, to those in Jacob who turn from transgression, says the LORD.

> "And as for me, this is my covenant with them, says the LORD: my spirit which is upon you, and my words which I have put in your mouth, shall not depart out of your

mouth, or out of the mouth of your children, or out of the
mouth of your children's children, says the LORD, from
this time forth and for evermore."

This is a markedly apocalyptic passage in which the Glory of the Lord
serves as vindicator. Those who call upon the name of the Lord, who grant
that he is to come back soon and bring judgment, will be those who receive
the Spirit forever.

Paul implies that only those who accept Christ will be saved, a momen-
tous statement about the future of Israel but, strangely, he does not actually
state it. Paul's refusal to spell out the implications of his reasoning is
extremely important. Having possibly committed himself to the proposition
that only a remnant of Israel will be retained, the standard apocalyptic notion,
he then surprisingly asserts the rabbinic notion that all Israel will be saved. At
this point, such a statement adds mystery (Rom 11:25) but not logical clarity
to Paul's discussion: "I want you to understand this mystery: a hardening has
come upon part of Israel, until the full number of the gentiles has come in."
He is puzzled, indeed angered, by the Jewish lack of interest in the Gospel.
This implies that he had expected the Jews will precede gentiles into the
Gospel community and, indeed, in larger numbers. He still thinks that they
will come, after they are made jealous by the faith of the gentiles. But he does
not spell that out in detail. Rather, Paul says that God's promises are still
intact: "For the gifts and the call of God are irrevocable" (11:29). Of course,
it is clear that he hopes the remaining Jews will come to Christ as he did,
freely and without coercion. Though the mission to the Jews has been a failure,
God will eventually reveal the reason. Therefore, there need not be a continuing Christian mission to the Jews.

Paul does not state exactly how the process of redemption for Jews will
come about. The ambiguity appears deliberate and truthful, in line with Paul's
respect for the sovereignty of God. Paul evidently had received no direct revelation specifying how the future would unfold; his visions of the Christ did
not specify exactly what the future would bring. Thus, he does not offer a

forecast. Instead, Paul tries to answer the question, as the rabbis might, by pondering the meaning of Scripture.

One thing is clear. Paul warns his gentile converts not to boast about their status, for God's judgment is unsearchable and God's ways are inscrutable:

> O the depth of the riches and wisdom and knowledge of
> God! How unsearchable are his judgments and how
> inscrutable his ways!
>
> "For who has known the mind of the Lord, or who has
> been his counselor?"
>
> "Or who has given a gift to him that he might be repaid?"
> (Rom 11:33–35 quoting Isa 40:13 and Job 35:7).

Though Paul anticipates the conclusion and is convinced of its speedy arrival, he does not state it explicitly, because to do so would presume to know God's actions, which would be boastful pride exceeding human ken. He does not know exactly what God intends to do and admits as much. Thus it is clear that Paul is not laying down what the future of Jewish and Christian history *will be or ought to be or specifying what Christians ought to believe about Jews.* He is only explaining for his embattled minority in his own day why they should persevere in spite of rejection by the Jewish community and perhaps even by some of their own brothers and sisters in Christ, who have not accepted them as full members of the faithful community. Paul's discussion was never meant as a statement of surety; it was a consolation in time of despair.

What does that mean in regard to our problem of whether there are two covenants or one? Paul speaks of the covenant coming through Christ's blood in 1 Corinthians 11:24, where he writes about the Lord's supper. So it is clear that the covenant for Christians is ratified and enacted through their liturgical life, as it is for Jews. It is also true that especially in 2 Corinthians 3 Paul speaks disparagingly against the covenant of law, proposing in its stead a covenant of Spirit in 2 Corinthians 3:6. But it seems clear that this statement is a further statement of consolation.

Paul's statements about universalism mean that Paul's otherwise somewhat parochial statements ought to be seen in a wider perspective. Paul seems to believe in several covenants, yet they are not the same covenants that we moderns would like to outline for best intergroup relationships. He may believe that there is a Noahide Covenant under which the gentiles stand, as he seems to feel that his gentile congregations have the same rights as righteous gentiles. He certainly acknowledges the Mosaic covenant under which those stand who are circumcised according to the custom of Moses. Both are part of God's ultimate providence and guidance for humanity, though there is no doubt that he sees a better way. Neither is exactly the separate covenant for Jews and gentiles that is implicit in the notion of a New and an Old Testament, for they are meant to supplement each other. Indeed there was no New Testament in Paul's day, and it is entirely clear that he did not anticipate one. Yet, for Paul, the major covenant by which his congregations should learn to guide their lives was the covenant of Abraham, for Abraham preceded the Mosaic covenant and yet he had faith in God's promises. This is the clear pattern he picks for Christians to follow. Yet he acknowledges the validity of each covenant, for to do less would be to say that God forswore himself. Although it is dangerous to try to synthesize all of Paul's writing into one single systematic theology, it seems clear that his critiques of Jewish law must stand secondary to his confidence in God's promises. For him, it was a question of successive revelations of God's promises, none of which undid the previous ones.

It thus seems to me that those who use the arguments of Paul or the Church to exclude Jews from God's plan, or who claim to know what God has in mind for Jew or gentile, are falling victim to the kind of pride against which Paul warns. The best plan for us all is the plan that treats all persons of righteousness, good will, and honest faith as equals, no matter whether they be Jew or gentile, Christian, Muslim, or even Hindu, Buddhist, or anyone else. If they are striving to bring God's kingdom to earth, they must be working to achieve God's plan.

ENDNOTES

Scripture references are from the *Revised Standard Version*. Nashville: Thomas Nelson, 1952.

1.   In my estimation, Josephus was never a Pharisee; he only styled his life as one in order to pursue his political career. See Steve Mason, *Flavius Josephus on the Pharisees: A Composition-Critical Study* (Leiden: Brill, 1991) and *Josephus and the New Testament* (Peabody Mass.: Hendrickson, 1992), p. 40.

2.   "Then everyone who calls on the name of the Lord shall be saved; for in Mount Zion and in Jerusalem there shall be those who escape, as the Lord has said, and among the survivors shall be those the Lord calls" (Joel 2:32).

3.   Mishnah Sanhedrin 10, Tosefta Sanhedrin 13:2, Sanhedrin 105a, Sifra 86b, b. Baba Kamma 38a.

4.   David Novak, *The Image of the Non-Jew in Judaism: An Historical and Construtive Study of the Noahide Laws*, Toronto Studies in Theology Volume 14 (Toronto: The Edwin Mellen Press, 1983), p. 6.

5.   See Steven Wilson, *The Gentiles and the Gentile Mission* (Cambridge: Cambridge University Press, 1974). My interpretation softens Wilson's arguments a bit.

6.   Novak, op.cit., p.6.

7.   Ibid., pp 3–35. Novak dates the laws to Maccabean times, albeit with no textual support, because it seems to him to be appropriate to the time of forced conversions. Then he discounts the witness of Jubilees. Neither hypothesis convinces me. But Novak's main emphasis is on the later discussion of these rules in talmudic and posttalmudic times, which is more convincing.

8.   Notice that by Paul and other apocalyptic groups especially, but in line with Judaism generally, pollution can be used as a metaphor for unrighteousness.

9. So translates O. S. Wintermute in James Charlesworth (ed), *The Old Testament Pseudepigrapha* (Garden City, NY: Doubleday, 1983) vol. 2, p.107.

10. The rabbis also clarified that when a child is not circumcised, his future reward is not automatically imperiled. Such a lack is, in the opinion of the later rabbis at least, a sin of his father (*Shulhan Arukh, "Yoreh Dea" 260.1*). Sabbath laws took precedence over circumcision laws for children born by caesarean section. So for later rabbinic tradition, it was not even necessary to be circumcised on the eighth day to be Jewish, to be part of Israel, or to be deserving of the world to come.

11. Note that blood here refers to the blood of any sacrifice.

12. Raeissaenen, *Law*, pp. 36, 38.

13. See, for example, H. Waitz, "Das Problem des sog. Aposteldecrets," *Zeitschrift für Kirchengeschichte* 55 (1936) pp. 227–263.

14. The later Church sometimes interpreted *pnikton* to mean to abstain from animals killed and prepared by stewing or boiling—what the French and especially the Cajuns would call *la viande étouffée*—perhaps a remembrance of the rule against meat and milk but, in any case, mistaken.

15. Wilson, *The Law in Acts*, pp. 87–100. In the Christian case, the issue is inherent to any discussion about how Jewish Christians and gentile Christians can interact as a single community.

16. See the helpful articles of Kirsopp Lake, "The Apostolic Council of Jerusalem," and "Paul's controversies," in *The Beginnings of Christianity: The Acts of the Apostles* (Grand Rapids: Baker, 1979) vol. 5, *Additional Notes*, pp. 195–211 and 212–223.

17. Cambridge: Cambridge University Press, 1983, see pages 84–102.

18. Perhaps it means lewd human sexual practices with animals, but usually in rabbinic writings it appears merely to mean cross-breeding of animal species. But the implication is clearly to define a minimum moral and ethical standard for all human conduct, not to specify the complete moral code. This can be seen even in the Jubilees account, which does not mention any specifically ceremonial or cultic laws, though it is quite concerned with them.

CONVERSATION FOUR

The Apostolic Decree in Acts:
A Response to Alan F. Segal

CELIA DEUTSCH

Professor Segal's paper demonstrates the ambiguity surrounding the stipulations found in Acts 15. Do these requirements function analogously to the laws for the resident alien, or to the Noahide commandments?[1] Do they, in other words, indicate proselytes who are on their way to full conversion, resident aliens living in the land of Israel, or do they indicate righteous gentiles? Are the rules cultic or ethical? Both? Is the ambivalence intentional?

Whether or not Acts 15 records an "actual" Jerusalem council is a question for another study.[2] Professor Segal has used the material with reference to Paul. However, I would like to examine more closely *Luke*'s use of this material.[3] What does the Apostolic Decree signify in its literary context in Acts? How does it serve Luke's rhetorical strategies? And what is at stake for the writer, given his social context in the Roman empire in the last quarter of the first century of the Common Era?

In Acts 15, Luke describes the convening of leaders in Jerusalem to address the issue of halachic requirements for gentile members. The participants decide that gentile converts should "abstain only from things polluted by idols and from fornication and from whatever has been strangled and from blood" (*apechesthai ton alisgematon ton eidolon kai tes porneias kai tou pniktou kai tou haimatos*, vs. 20).[4] The "letter" sent out at the end of the conference is worded in a slightly different manner: "abstain from what has been sacrificed to idols and from blood and from what is strangled and from fornication" (*apechesthai eidolothyton kai haimatos kai pnikton kai porneias*, vs. 29).[5] Acts 15: 29 may actually represent the more original wording, with 15:20 representing Luke's interpretation.[6]

The author places the Apostolic Decree midway through his second volume.[7] The Way has begun to spread out to the Diaspora.[8] Paul has already made his first missionary journey (13:1–14:25) and returned to Antioch (14:26). Luke is well on his way towards demonstrating how the Gospel reached Rome.

The immediate context of the Decree represents a chiasm in which the principal terms are geographical.[9] Chapter 15 begins in Antioch, with a delegation coming down from Jerusalem (vs. 1). *Stasis* (conflict) occurs, with the Jerusalem delegation on the one side, and Paul and Barnabas on the other. Paul, Barnabas, and some others are delegated by the Antioch community to go to Jerusalem to discuss the necessity of circumcision for salvation (vv. 2–4), and the correlative question of halachic observance (vs. 5), which is raised there by Pharisee "believers" (*pepisteukotes*). Discussions occur in Jerusalem; a decision is reached, and a delegation sent with Paul and Barnabas to Antioch (vv. 5–29). The delegation returns to Antioch and reads the letter containing the Decree to the assembled community which receives it with joy (vv. 30–35). Paul and Barnabas remain in Antioch and "there with many others, they taught and proclaimed the word of the Lord" (vs. 35).

Crucial to the text are two related statements: "Unless you are circumcised according to the custom of Moses, you cannot be saved" (vs. 1) declared in Antioch by the delegation from Jerusalem, and "It is necessary for them to be circumcised and ordered to keep the law of Moses," asserted by Pharisee believers in Jerusalem (vs. 5). There are, then, among other issues, assumptions regarding requirements for salvation, halakhic requirements of gentile members/proselytes, and the relationship of diaspora communities to that in Jerusalem. The dispute involving diaspora and Jerusalem is resolved in Jerusalem by James' decision. The decision is legitimated by the presence of Peter and James, as well as by that of Paul and Barnabas and of the apostles and elders.

I would suggest that the stipulations of Acts 15, while certainly similar and probably related to both the rules for resident aliens of Lev 17–18[10] and the Noahide commands, also function differently from either of these. As Professor Segal observes, the rules for resident aliens are for gentiles living in the land of Israel where Jews are, of course, in the majority. Resident aliens are not proselytes in the biblical texts, although the LXX uses *proselytos* to translate *ger* in Lev 17–18, and the rabbis will use *ger* to designate proselytes. In Acts 15, however, gentile members of a diaspora community which was at most only partially Jewish—Luke's community, not the early Jerusalem community—are required to abstain from idolatry, certain foods, and illicit sexual unions.

The Noahide laws answer a question about salvation of gentiles. They do not presume a change of community. Gentiles remain gentiles. Certainly, the issue of the salvation of gentiles is posed in Acts 15:2. But the gentiles of Acts 15 have changed community. They are now members of the Way. One might rephrase the matter as being a question of requirements of gentile members of the community of salvation. The stipulations of Acts 15 are boundary markers, setting forth a minimum for those belonging to the Way, to the community of those who are saved. They are directed specifically at gentiles entering the community, people who will enjoy full membership in the new community without, however, first becoming proselytes, i.e., converts to Judaism. Luke has Peter say:

> And God, who knows the human heart, testified to them
> by giving them the Holy Spirit, just as he did to us; and in
> cleansing their hearts by faith he has made no distinction
> between them and us (15:8–9).

And shortly after, James says, "Simeon has related how God first looked favorably on the gentiles, to take from among them a people for his name" (vs. 14).

The Apostolic Decree, with its smooth resolution to a difficult situation, a resolution indeed greeted with joy (*ekare san epi te paraklesei*, 15:31), is coherent with the Lukan redactional project of showing a community in harmony with itself (never mind, for the present, texts where evidence of tension belies such an endeavor!).[11] According to Luke, Jewish—even Pharisee—and gentile members are given a means of coexisting in equality, and the great figures of the early communities (Peter, Paul, James) are in accord. All of this agrees nicely with early statements concerning community harmony and growth such as those found in 2:43–47 and 4:32–35.[12]

Luke, as others in the emerging communities, is articulating a process of self-definition. He is careful to note that his community is not the same thing as the Jewish community.[13] In the immediate context, he uses Amos 9:11f. to say that God's calling together a people from the gentiles is in accord with prophetic inspiration (vv.14–17). Peter, of course, has been made "the one through whom the gentiles would hear the message of the good news and become believers" (vs. 7). Gentile members are not to be charged with the yoke of Torah (15:10). The Lukan community is not the Jewish community, but the community of "believers."[14]

Why, then, the stipulations? Luke's community, as did so many early Christian communities, included Jews as well as gentiles. The Apostolic Decree represents at least one group's struggle to accommodate a mixed membership. But there are other reasons as well. While Luke's community is not the "same thing" as the Jewish community, neither is it altogether other.[15] In the first volume, Luke's carefully constructed infancy narratives demonstrate that the circle into which Jesus is born and welcomed constitutes the best of Israel, its true heirs. And Acts opens with scenes set in pious Jewish contexts.[16] The stipulations of the Decree suggest conditions of some minimal degree of halachic observance for *gentiles*.[17] And they insure modes of behavior which honor the sensibilities of Jewish members. Luke thus suggests a kind of continuity between the Jewish tradition and the Way. He also makes provision for a community made up of Jewish and gentile members to live in some kind of peace.

What does all of this mean in terms of the Lukan project? Luke conducts a conversation not only with his own community but also with the gentile non-Christian society in which he finds himself, a society in which the Roman empire is the ruling power.[18] Thus, to his community Luke presents the ideal of concord and the means necessary to effect and maintain it, among other things the Apostolic Decree of Acts 15. And he attempts to remind his community and to reassure the imperial authorities that the new community is *ordered*. It does not represent an upstart religion, a new religion, but is, rather, in continuity with the ancestral religion and its ways.

This is crucial not only from a theological point of view, but from a sociopolitical perspective as well. In traditional societies, the new is suspect because it is perceived as disrupting the order of things. Imperial Rome was no exception. The new had no authority, because it represented a break with ancestral ways.[19] Innovations were thus legitimated by demonstrating their continuity with established tradition.[20]

This was true in a general sense; it was also true from the point of view of religion. The state cult was a matter not necessarily of personal piety in relation to a particular deity, but of participating in a strategy of maintaining the social order. Failure to execute the cult properly threatened the order of things.[21]

While conquered peoples were expected to participate in the state cult, they were also allowed, even expected, to retain their ancestral religions (*ta patria*).[22] Jews, exempted from actual worship (although obligated to say prayers for the emperor and, late in the first century, to pay a tax to the emperor rather than to the Temple)[23] were allowed to retain their religion precisely because it was an ancestral religion and bore the authority of demonstrable antiquity.[24] With Julius Caesar, Judaism became in effect a *religio licita*, "an incorporated body with an authorized cult."[25]

Luke describes the Way as an ancestral religion. He does this by implying that it is the legitimate heir of Judaism. And he does it more explicitly. For example, Luke places the word "ancestral" (patrōs) on Paul's lips on three occasions. In his speech on the steps of the Jerusalem barracks, Paul says that he has been "educated strictly according to our ancestral law" (22:3). In the speech before the governor Felix, Paul says: ". . . according to the Way, which they call a sect, I worship the God of our ancestors, believing everything laid down according to the law or written in the prophets" (24:14). And in Rome, he tells the local Jewish leaders that he has "done nothing against our people or the customs of our ancestors" (28:17). Luke appears to use this word to suggest an accusation that members of the Way have broken with ancestral ways and worship a new God, i.e., a divinity that is not an ancestral god.

Thus, the Way would represent a *new* religion. Luke is careful to show that, on the contrary, it is ancestral. The Apostolic Decree suggests a legal and ritual framework for maintaining contact with the earlier tradition of origin.

All of this is confirmed by Lukan use of *ethos*.[26] This term represents timehonored law and practice, whether Roman or Jewish.[27] With the exception of 25:16, all of the occurrences in Acts indicate a suspicion that the Way represents a threat to custom.

Luke demonstrates that not even Paul is a threat to custom. In Acts 16:1–5, immediately following Paul's return to Antioch and departure on a new missionary journey, Luke has Paul see to it that Timothy is circumcised. Then, in 21:21–24 he has James and the elders urge Paul to undergo the rite of purification with those who are under a vow in order to assure Jewish believers that he is not trying to persuade diaspora Jews not to "circumcise their children or observe the customs." Paul complies. In the closing chapter, Paul tells the leaders of the Roman Jewish community that he has "done nothing against our people or the customs of our ancestors" (*tois ethesi tois patroois*).

All of this is significant for understanding Acts 15. We reread the opening verse:

> Then certain individuals came down from Judea and were
> teaching the brothers, Unless you are circumcised accord-
> ing to the custom of Moses, you cannot be saved.

Those who come to Antioch and the Jerusalem Pharisee believers represent the concern for ancestral custom. Those represented by Paul and others in the Antioch community symbolize a threat to the order of ancestral custom. In this context, the Apostolic Decree might display to the outside world, the Roman world, a relationship of continuity between the Way and the parent, established ancestral tradition. It serves other socio-rhetorical purposes as well.

Romans feared rioting and civil disorder, and with good reason.[28] Revolts and civil wars shook Rome through the second and first centuries

B.C.E.[29] *Collegia*, cells of social life which emerged in the Augustan era as trade associations, burial societies, and cult groups, were often a perceived source of unrest.[30] *Collegia* dedicated to cult claimed the Senate's attention as early as the second century B.C.E., for religious disorder "could easily be transformed into social revolution."[31]

Luke's description of a closely knit association, which incorporated people of lower classes, shared a common chest and gathered for worship, resembled that of the *collegium* (also called *thiasos*, *hetaeria*).[32] Indeed, Pliny, writing in the early second century, will call the Christians *hetaeria*.[33] And, by the end of that century, Tertullian is using this terminology in his *Apologeticum*, 38.1–3.

We noted that *collegia* were frequent sources of civil disorder in the Roman Empire. If we read Acts carefully, we can discern voices accusing Christians of a variety of offenses against the Empire. Rome was frequently nervous about rioting.[34] Acts 15 opens with *stasis* between the Jerusalem delegation and Paul and Barnabas over the issue of requirements for gentile members.

Stasis signifies more than "dissension."[35] It implies conflict, even violence, in short, civil disorder.[36] It occurs elsewhere in Acts, always in situations involving Paul. In 19:40, the town clerk (*grammateus*) pleads for order in the wake of the silversmiths' riot at Ephesus. Demetrius the silversmith had instigated the demonstration by recalling that "this Paul has persuaded and drawn away a considerable number of people by saying that gods made with hands are not gods" (19:26). In 23:7, 10 *stasis* breaks out in the Sanhedrin during Paul's trial. The ferocity of the conflict is indicated in vs. 10 where the tribune orders troops to take Paul, fearful that members of the Sanhedrin would "tear Paul to pieces" (*me diaspasthe*). And in 24:5, Tertullus, the prosecuting attorney, accuses Paul before Felix the governor of arousing to *stasis* Jews "throughout the world."

Other texts in Acts also suggest Roman association of rioting with the Way, particularly with Paul. In 17:6f Jews in Thessalonica, jealous of Paul's success, hire a gang of ruffians to start an "uproar" (*ethoruboun ten polin*) and, unable to find Paul and Silas, drag Jason and some believers (*adelphous*)

before the city authorities and accuse them of "turning the world upside own
. . . They are all acting contrary to the decrees of the emperor, saying that
there is another king named Jesus" (17:7).[37] The accusation specified the
kind of offense—treason.[38] Luke takes care to note that it is *Jews* who have
made the accusation—and started the disturbance, as they will in the following incident in Beroea. Luke emphasizes his reassurance by telling us that
in Beroea high-born Greek women and men, as well as Jews, believe it is
Jews from Thessalonika who start the disturbance in Beroea (17:10–15).

Paul is associated with rioting in 21:27–38, even confused with "the
Egyptian who recently stirred up a revolt and led the four thousand assassins
out into the wilderness" (vs. 38). In the trial before Felix the governor, the
prosecuting attorney Tertullus calls him a "pestilent fellow, and agitator among
all the Jews throughout the world, and a ringleader of the sect of the
Nazarenes" (24:5, *loimon, kinounta*). Luke tells us, though, that it was the Jews
from Asia who were responsible for the riot, not Paul (21:27f; 24:19). And he
has Paul declare his innocence of any part in the disturbance, first before the
governor Felix (21:1021), and then before Festus his successor (25:8).

While Jews, specifically Jews from Asia, are behind the riots associated
with Paul, Roman officials, on the contrary, treat Paul fairly and courteously.[39]
Sergius Paulus, the Roman proconsul, is favorably impressed with his striking temporarily blind the magician Bar-Jesus; he believes (13:7, 12). Gallio,
the anonymous Jerusalem tribune, Felix, Festus, King Agrippa and Queen
Bernice—all give Paul a gracious hearing. On several occasions Roman officials find him innocent vis-à-vis Roman law.[40] This, despite the fact that Felix
does seem to expect a bribe (24:26).[41] Such treatment on the part of the
authorities suggests the respectability of the Way.

Romans appear to have associated the Way with magic, an accusation
which would imply at the very least the suspicion of threat to civil order. In
Acts 8:9–13, Simon, a magician practicing in Samaria, is bested by Philip and
even baptized, and in 13:4–12, Paul defeats the magician (also called a "Jewish false prophet") Bar-Jesus. And in chapter 19 magicians who came to
believe burned their books in public (19:19; cf. vv. 13–19). While Simon is
presumably a Samaritan, the latter two are *Jewish* magicians.[42]

Romans during the Republic as well as during the Empire exhibited an ambivalent attitude towards magic.[43] Indeed, there is a certain lack of consistency about just what the Romans (as well as Greeks) considered to be "magic."[44] One author would define magic in classical antiquity as a form of "unsanctioned religious activity."[45] Another author would call it that form of religious deviance whereby individual or social goals are sought by means alternate to those normally sanctioned by the dominant religious institution.[46] He would further qualify this:

> [G]oals sought within the context of religious deviance are magical when attained through the management of supernatural powers in such a way that results are virtually guaranteed.[47]

I would simply note, with Professor Segal, the polemical function of the term "magic." It is not so much a matter of *objective* dominance and deviance as it is a matter of perception. Usually the term "magic" is a charge made by detractors of those whom they perceive to be engaged in incorrect or dangerous praxis.[48]

Greeks and Romans were ambivalent towards activity we would term "magic" or "unsanctioned religious activity" or "alternative religious practice." On the one hand, Roman officials sometimes included wonderworkers in their retinues. The story about Sergius Paulus would appear to reflect such practice (Acts 13:4–12).[49] On the other hand, the Romans feared magic, and prohibited it at times.[50] Indeed, it was forbidden in some forms by the law of the Twelve Tables.[51] Foreign religions (*externa religio*) were suspected of "black magic and conspiracy against the state."[52]

Magic is a term for the other in the attempt to influence the divine. It is a category which "serves to differentiate between the person(s) labeling and the person(s) so labelled."[53] Luke's narrative suggests to the knowing reader that Christians, particularly their leaders, are associated with magic by non-Christians. [54] Luke would have us know that Philip and Paul, emissaries of the

Way, are not magicians—the magicians are Samaritans and Jews and cause disorder—but rather exercise power over them.[55] In this they are like Jesus who had been accused of exorcising by the power of Beelzebul, but who instead exercises power over the prince of demons.[56] Luke uses the stories about Sergius Paulus and Bar-Jesus, as well as the sons of Sceva, to distance himself and his community from the Jewish community, implying that the Jews are actually "in bondage to the devil."[57]

Luke uses other characters to suggest that the Way is acceptable to the establishment. In Beroea, Paul's preaching attracts "not a few Greek women and men of high standing" who become believers (17:12). Lydia, a "worshiper of God" (*sebomene ton theon*), as a merchant in purple cloth, would be affluent (16:14), even though not necessarily of high social standing. Apollos' learning would possibly suggest someone of relatively high social standing, or at least relative economic means (18:24–28).[58] Cornelius is a centurion (10:1), and Paul himself is a Roman citizen (16:377 22:22–29; 23:27). Indeed, his citizenship is through birthright and not purchase (22:22–29). Moreover, he is learned (26:24) and a Pharisee (23:6–7; 26:5–8). That is, he is a member of the group entrusted by Rome with managing the bureaucracy of the land of Israel in the post-destruction era.

Participation as well as conversation within the broader Roman context by members of the establishment not only gives the Way a certain respectability but also reassures the leaders that its adherents are no threat to civil order. It is an important component in the task of constructing a self-image by a relatively new movement[59] in a period certainly following Nero's reign, and possibly the reigns of Domitian and even Trajan as well.

The stipulations of Acts 15, then, must be seen in the context of an implied, and sometimes overt, accusation that the Way is a vehicle of social disorder. They demonstrate that the *ekklesia* of the Way is able to resolve *stasis* to the satisfaction of all parties, unlike the Sanhedrin which requires Roman intervention (23:10).

The stipulations in Acts 15 are meant only for Gentile believers (it is presumed by the text that Jewish believers are Torah observant). As we noted earlier, in the LXX ger becomes *proselytos*, but "inasmuch as Luke thinks of the Gentile church as being the proper continuation of 'biblical' Israel, he may very well think of Gentile Christians as being similar to proselytes."[60] The Apostolic Decree, with its echoes of the Hebrew Bible, particularly the Torah, insures that a necessary minimum of ancestral law is maintained in the community (dare we say "new"?) composed of Jews and Gentiles. It functions to demonstrate that gentile Christianity is faithful to the Law of Moses, yet freed "from any need to be converted to Judaism, especially from the need to be circumcised."[61]

This in turn suggests that Christianity is, as heir to Judaism, worthy at least of the toleration which characterized much of the way in which Rome related to Judaism.[62] As converts who had left their ancestral religions for a "deadly superstition,"[63] Christians were vulnerable. They, like the Jewish proselyte, had no "recognized status in society."[64] Luke's description of them as adherents of an ancestral religion and heirs to Judaism, a religion with state recognition, may represent an attempt to alleviate that anomalous situation.

But why the specific items in the Decree—abstinence from meat sacrificed to idols (*eidolothuton*), from blood (*haimatos*), from what is strangled (*pnikton*) and from unlawful sexual intercourse (*porneias*) (15:29; 21:25)?[65] These prohibitions are linked by a resonance with the requirements of the resident aliens and the Noahide commands in their various forms, as Professor Segal has noted. I believe, moreover, that these prohibitions were observed literally in Luke's community, as well as elsewhere.

Canonical as well as patristic evidence suggests that the prohibitions were significant for many early communities and, whatever the moral interpretation given them, were observed quite literally. In many communities, meat offered to idols was forbidden.[66] In some it was forbidden to eat meat with blood in it.[67] And some of these materials forbid that which is strangled.[68]

The sources cited here link the first three prohibitions to idolatry in various ways. Certain of these texts offer a possibility for the problematic inclusion of *pniktos* in the list. Idolatry was associated with demons as early as the middle of the first century C.E.[69] Furthermore, Origen tells us that things strangled are forbidden because the blood is still in them, and that the odor which arises from blood "is said to be the food of demons" (*Contra Celsum* 8:30).

Thus, anything associated with idolatry, specifically with things strangled, is related not only to idolatry, but to sorcery.[70] While the patristic evidence is at least several decades—and possibly as much as a century—later than Luke, it does suggest that Luke included *pniktos* as much for its association with idolatry, demonic cults, and magic as for its resonance with Leviticus 17–18.

With regard to *porneia*, it had been a metaphor for idolatry since the prophets.[71] The author of Revelation, possibly contemporaneous with Luke, links them as well, also associating them with sorcery (*pharmakeia, pharmakoi*).[72] In the following century, Tertullian associates food laws with Christian marital fidelity.[73] Moreover, idolatry is associated with adultery and other forms of sexual transgression in most of the early patristic sources we have cited.[74] The dietary prescriptions of Acts 15 thus signal that gentile members of the Way have crossed the boundary which separates them from idolaters, as well as from those involved in demonic cults and magical practices.

Earlier in this response I noted that Luke's community is engaged in a process of self-definition. Boundary setting is one of the strategies in that process. In other words, making a statement about who is in and who is outside the community. Meals present an important vehicle for this process, encoding messages "about different degrees of hierarchy, inclusion and exclusion, boundaries and transactions across the boundaries."[75] The first three prohibitions apply to food laws—to the source of meat (hence, not sacrificial meat) and to properly slaughtered meat. The last applies not simply to sexual practice, but to family law, forbidding illicit sexual relations.[76] While the prohibitions of Acts 15 might be construed to refer to attendance in cultic activities at temples, several of the later sources we cited suggest that they refer to non-cultic meals held in homes as well.[77] Table and household are thus included in the prohibitions of the Apostolic Decree.

Note the ways in which this eliminates certain important social contacts between members of the Way and outsiders—and outsiders might include friends, business contacts, patrons and clients, and members of one's family. Exclusion from meat sacrificed to idols excluded the member of the Way from the sacrificial meals so common and so important in the Greco-Roman world.[78] The fact that meat in the market was often left over from sacrifices would mean that Christians would have a hard time in attending dinner parties in the homes of non-Christians. They would have to avoid such occasions as weddings, funerals, birthday celebrations of non-Christian relatives, friends, clients, and patrons.[79] And because meat for sale in the markets was often sacrificial meat, even the poor would have difficulty on the rare occasions they might have sought meat for celebrations.[80]

The stipulations of Acts 15, while far from the full requirements of *kashruth*, serve as a way of enacting and encoding the boundaries of the emerging social structure of the Lukan community. [81] This functions vis-à-vis the Lukan community itself, reminding it of its separation from the idolaters, as well as its relation to and distinction from the parent religion. The stipulations serve as dietary practices for a new people (*laos*) drawn from Jews and gentiles. Moreover, while promulgated in an effort not to "bother" gentile converts, the prescriptions of the Apostolic Decree actually exact a price, especially from more affluent members. And this serves, in turn, to further socialize the members in the emerging identity of the community.

The stipulations also suggest to the surrounding context of the Mediterranean world a proper way of understanding the identity of the Way.[82] On the one hand, the Way is not Judaism, but rather its proper heir. As such it can claim to be an ancestral religion. Even its dietary regulations confirm this. On the other hand, it is distinct from other Greco-Roman associations; its members are not idolaters and have no association with magic. They are an ordered community who can so manage conflict that harmony is ultimately restored and maintained.

The Apostolic Decree is so effective that the stipulations occur in a number of texts until well into the Byzantine era. As late as 692 a church synod reiterates the prohibition against blood.[83] The evidence represents a broad variety of literary genres as well as geographical and social contexts. Professor Segal's presentation invites us to explore the Apostolic Decree and these later materials in relation to questions of intergroup relations in the Roman Empire. What, in other words, can this array of evidence tell us about the ways in which followers of the Way, early Christians, related in their specific contexts to Jews (both Christian and otherwise) and to the Roman imperial social order in which they all lived?

ENDNOTES

Scripture references are from the *New Revised Standard Version*. Nashville: Thomas Nelson, Inc. 1990.

1.   For bibliography, see R. Pesch, *Die Apostelgeschichte*: vol. 2 (Apg 13–28), Evangelischer Katholischer Kommentar zum Neuen Testament (Zürich: Benziger and Neukirchen-Vluyn: Neukirchener Verlag, 1986), p. 68f. For more recent bibliography, see A. J. M. Wedderburn, "The 'Apostolic Decree': Tradition and Redaction," *NovT* 35(1993), p. 363, note 2. Those who believe that the stipulations of Acts 15 reflect the laws for the Israelite and resident alien in Lev 17–18 include P.J. Achtemeier, "An Elusive Unity: Paul, Acts, and the Early Church," in *Catholic Biblical Quarterly* 48 (1986), p. 23; T. Callan, "The Background of the Apostolic Decree (Acts 15:29, 29; 21:25)," CBQ 55 (1993), pp. 284–97; E. Haenchen, *The Acts of the Apostles: a Commentary*, trans. by B. Noble, G. Shinn, H. Anderson, R. McL. Wilson (Philadelphia: Westminster, 1971), p. 449; J. C. Hurd, *The Origin of 1 Corinthians* (1965; reprint ed., Macon, GA: Mercer University, 1983), p. 252f. As Callan notes (p. 284), this has been the common position since the publication of the article by H. Waitz, "Das Problem des sogenannten Aposteldekrets und die damit zusammenhängenden literarischen und geschichtlichen Probleme des apostolischen Zeitalters," in *ZKG* 55 (1936), pp. 227–63. Those who believe that Acts 15 reflects some form of the Noahide commands include S. G. Wilson, *Luke and the Law*, SNTSMS 50 (Cambridge: Cambridge University, 1983), p. 100. Sanders believes that Acts 15 reflects the Noahide commands: J. T. Sanders, *The Jews in Luke-Acts* (Philadelphia: Fortress, 1987), p. 122. However, his remarks elsewhere suggest that he believes that Acts 15 also reflects Lev 17–18 (p. 115f).

2.   Others raise the question of the historicity of the Jerusalem council, e.g. Sanders, *Jews in Luke-Acts*, p. 121; Wilson, *Luke and the Law*, p. 76f.

3. On the Apostolic Decree and Lukan redaction, see Wedderburn, "The 'Apostolic Decree.'"

4. All English translations are from the *NRSV* unless otherwise noted.

5. Later, in Acts 21:25, James in conversation with Paul refers back to the letter. The same four terms are used as in 15:29. As Prof. Segal has noted, the question of the terms of the Jerusalem decree presents numerous text-critical problems. For examples of scholarly discussion, see B. M. Metzger, *A Textual Commentary on the Greek New Testament*, 3rd ed. (United Bible Societies, 1971), pp. 429–35, 437f. See also Haenchen, *Acts*, p.449f; Hurd, *The Origin of 1 Corinthians*, pp. 246–50; Wilson, Luke and the Law, pp. 78–84.

6. Cf. Wedderburn, "The 'Apostolic Decree,'" p. 377f.

7. On the literary context of Acts 15, see M. E. Boismard, "Le 'Concile' de Jerusalem (Acts 15, 1–33)," *ETL* 64 (1988), pp. 433–40.

8. *Ho hodos* ("the Way") is a circumlocution for the message of Jesus in Acts 9:2; 16:17; 18:25, 26; 19:9, 23; 22:4; 24:14, 22.

9. Cf. E. Richard, "The Divine Purpose: the Jews and the Gentile Mission (Acts 15)," in *Luke-Acts: New Perspectives from the Society of Biblical Literature Seminar*, ed. C. H. Talbert (New York: Crossroad, 1984), pp. 189–92.

10. Terrance Callan includes other material: Deut 29:10–11; 31:12; 5:14; 16:11, 14; 26:11; Ex 12:48–49; 20:10; Num 9:14; 15:14–16, 26, 29–30; 19:10; 35:15; Lev 20:2–3; 22:18–19; Josh 20:9; Ezek 14:7–8; 47:22–23. See "The Background," p. 285f.

11. Cf. P. J. Achtemeier, "An Elusive Unity," pp. 1–26. Luke has a particular affinity for the verb *kairo*. He uses it in the gospel twelve times. Of these, only one is taken from a non-Lukan source—22:5 (Mk 14:11). The others come from special L (1:14, 28; 13:17; 15:32; 19:6; 23:8), or are redactional in origin (2:23; 10:20; 19:37). The verb occurs in Acts 5:41; 8:39; 11:23; 13:48; 15:23, 31; 23:26. In 15:23 and 23:26 it designates "greetings."

12. B. Witherington III notes the rhetorical function of the speeches in Acts 15 in overcoming *stasis* and achieving harmony: *The Acts of the*

Apostles: A Socio-Rhetorical Commentary (Grand Rapids, MI/Cambridge, U.K.: William B. Eerdmans, 1998), p. 450.

13. Cf. Sanders, *The Jews in Luke-Acts*, p. 128 and passim.

14. Sanders notes that "belief" is "Luke's normal word for conversion": *The Jews*, p. 112. *Pisteuo*: Acts 4:4; 5:14; 8:12, 13, 37; 9:42; 10:43; 11:17, 21; 13:12, 39; 14:1, 23; 15:7; 16:31, 34; 17:12, 34; 18:8; 19:2, 4, 18; 21:20, 25. The verb and its cognates also refers to membership in the community: 2:44; 4:32; 13:48; 14:1;15:5, 7; 16:34; 17:34; 18:27; 19:2, 18; 21:20, 25; 22:19. Luke uses the perfect participle *pepisteukotes* in 15:5. He uses the perfect participle elsewhere in 16:34; 18:27; 19:18; 21:20, 25. It designates membership in the Lucan community. It is not clear why Luke has used this form. In general it designates a "condition or state as the result of a past action." F. Blass and A. Debrunner, *A Greek Grammar of the New Testament and Other Early Christian Literature: A Translation and Revision of the Ninth-Tenth German Edition Incorporating Supplementary Notes of A. Debrunner*, ed. by R. W. Funk (Chicago: University of Chicago, 1961), p. 318.

15. Cf. M. J. Cook, "The Mission to the Jews in Acts: Unraveling Luke's 'Myth of the "Myriads"'," in *Luke-Acts and the Jewish People: Eight Critical Perspectives*, ed by. J. B. Tyson (Minneapolis: Augsburg, 1988), pp. 102–23; S. G. Wilson, *Related Strangers: Jews and Christians 70–170 C.E.* (Minneapolis: Fortress, 1995), p. 64.

16. Cf. Sanders, *The Jews*, p. 126f.

17. Cf. Sanders, *Jews in Luke-Acts*, p. 122. Certainly Acts 10–11 would suggest that all ritual food laws are abolished where gentiles are concerned. This would lead some to believe that the "Apostolic Decree" refers to an ethical analogue to the Noahide commands, or that all of the prohibitions refer to idolatry. The Western text, which does not have *pniktos* and which includes a negative version of the "golden rule" would lend support to an "ethical" interpretation. However, Lev 17:13 refers to hunting and thus, as Philo (*Spec Leg* 4:122) seems to infer, yields meat which has not been properly drained of blood "and might thus not be fitting for an Israelite, or for a Gentile associated with Israel,

to eat" (Sanders, *The Jews*, p. 115). I have not read any truly satisfactory resolution to the question of the relationship between Acts 10–11 and 15. Perhaps Sanders offers a possibility when he notes that Peter's dream justifies Gentile mission (p. 139). In the dream vision Peter is told "What God has made clean, you must not call profane (*koinos*), but Peter later tells Cornelius and his household "God has shown me that I should not call anyone profane or unclean" (*koinon e akatharton*, 10:28). The food in the dream is a metaphor for persons.

18. Sanders notes that Luke-Acts is written after the Neronian persecution and perhaps even after the more widespread persecutions of Domitian and Trajan: "Yet one gets not the slightest hint in Luke-Acts that Christianity faced any difficulty from the Roman authorities" (*The Jews*, p. 313). However, he does not pursue the question of the relationship between the geopolitical context of the Roman empire and Luke's portrayal of the Jews. Wilson explores somewhat more fully the relationship between Luke-Acts, Judaism, and the Roman imperial context (*Related Strangers*, pp. 56–71).

19. Cf. R. MacMullen, *Paganism in the Roman Empire* (New Haven: Yale University, 1981), p. 3.

20. For a discussion of this process in the early part of the first century C.E., see K. Galinsky, *Augustan Culture: An Interpretive Introduction* (Princeton: Princeton University, 1996), pp. 288–331. I am grateful to my colleague Prof. Elizabeth Castelli (Barnard College, N.Y.C.) for drawing this material to my attention.

21. Cf. Galinsky, *Augustan Culture*, pp. 288f, 291. R. MacMullen questions the usefulness of the category "state cult" (cf. *Paganism in the Roman Empire*, pp. 102–104). However, as Galinsky demonstrates, imperial authority sanctioned certain religious practices and institutions even prior to the widespread observance of the ruler cult.

22. Cf. MacMullen, *Paganism in the Roman Empire*, p. 2–4. "The normal Roman attitude towards foreign religions was one of toleration, provided that they appeared to be both morally unobjectionable and politically innocuous," in E. Mary Smallwood, *The Jews Under Roman Rule from*

Pompey to Diocletian, Studies in Judaism in Late Antiquity 20 (Leiden: E. J. Brill, 1976), p. 124.

23.   Philo, Lea. 1S2–58, 311–20; Josephus, AP. 2.77; BJ 2.197, 409; Suetonius, *Dom.* 12, 2; cf. Smallwood, *The Jews*, pp. 137, 148, 376–81.

24.   See L. H. Feldman, *Jew and Gentile in the Ancient World: Attitudes and Interactions from Alexander to Justinian* (Princeton: Princeton University, 1993): 177–200.

25.   Smallwood, *The Jews*, p. 135f. As Frend notes, "A *religio* was *licita* for a particular group on the basis of tribe or nationality and traditional practices, coupled with the proviso that its rites were not offensive to the Roman people or their gods," in *Martyrdom and Persecution in the Early Church: A Study of a Conflict from the Maccabees to Donatus* (1965; reprint ed. Grand Rapids, MI: Baker, 1981), p. 106. Wilson notes that "*religio licita*" is a Christian, rather than Roman, concept (*Related Strangers*, p. 68. The phrase is Tertullian's, *Apol.* 21,1). Conzelmann would oppose use of the phrase in relation to Luke-Acts; cf. *Die Apostelgeschichte*, HNT 7 (Tübingen: J. C. B. Mohr [Paul Siebeck], 1963), p. 10.

26.   Acts 6:14; 15:1; 16:21; 21:21; 25:16; 26:3; 28:17. See also Lk 1:9; 2:42; 22:39. It occurs elsewhere in the NT only in Jn 19:40 and Heb 10:25.

27.   Regarding Roman custom, see Acts 16:21; 25:16; regarding Jewish custom, see 6:14; 21:21; 26:3; 28:17. Cf. Wilson, *Luke and the Law*, pp. 3–11.

28.   Cf. Frend, *Martyrdom*, p. 167. On riots among the poor, see C. R. Whittaker, "The Poor," in *The Romans*, ed. A. Giardina, trans. L. Cochrane (Chicago: University of Chicago, 1993), pp. 287–99.

29.   Cf. K. Christ, *The Romans*, trans. C. Holme (Berkeley, CA: University of California, 1984), pp. 45–8.

30.   For a brief description of the *collegia*, see Christ, *The Romans*, p. 77; J. P. Morel, "The Craftsman," in Giardina, *The Romans*, p. 240f. On the collegia and civil unrest, see Whittaker, "The Poor," in Giardina, *The Romans*, p. 287f.

31.   Frend, *Martyrdom*, p. 109. On the synagogue as a *collegium*, see Small-
       wood, *The Jews*, pp. 133–135.

32.   Cf. Acts 2:42–47; 4:32–35; 6:16. See R. L. Wilken, *The Christians As
       the Romans Saw Them* (New Haven: Yale University, 1984), pp. 31–47.
       W. Meeks comments on the limitations of the *collegium* as an analogy;
       see *The First Urban Christians: The Social World of the Apostle Paul*
       (New Haven: Yale University, 1983): pp. 77–80.

33.   Ep. 10.96.

34.   In relation to Acts, see R. F. Stoops, Jr., "Riot and Assembly: The Social
       Context of Acts 19:23–41," in *JBL* 108 (1989), pp. 73–91; L. M. Wills,
       "The Depiction of the Jews in Acts," in *JBL* 110 (1991), pp. 631–54,
       especially 634–47.

35.   Cf. NRSV.

36.   Cf. Lk 23:19, 25; Acts 19:40; 23:;7, 10; 24:5. See Witherington, *Acts*,
       p. 450.

37.   Cf. Wills, "The Depiction," p. 652f.

38.   Both Jews and early Christians were vulnerable to the charge of *maiestas*
       (treason). Cf. Smallwood, *The Jews*, p. 379f; Frend, *Martyrdom*, p. 167f.

39.   The riot of the silversmiths, in Acts 19:23–40, is only tangentially relat-
       ed to Paul (vs.26). The only reference to Jewish presence is in vs. 33f,
       in the unexplained appearance of Alexander. Here, as in the accusations
       against Paul, it will be a Roman official (the town clerk, *grammateus*)
       who will be the voice of reason and justice (35–40); cf. Stoops, "Riot
       and Assembly," p. 87.

40.   18: 12–17; 22:30; 25:19–27; 26:30–32; 28:18f.

41.   Wills notes that Roman officials viewed positively by Romans are sim-
       ilarly viewed in Acts, and those viewed negatively in Roman sources
       are likewise described in Acts. Wills cites the example of Felix, con-
       demned by Tacitus for his lowly birth and abuse of office; see "The
       Depiction," p. 651f.

42.   On the reputation of Jews as magicians in the Roman empire, see Feld-
       man, *Jew and Gentile*, pp. 379–81.

43. For examples of new approaches to the question of magic in the Mediterranean world of the Hellenistic era and late antiquity, see P. Brown, "Sorcery, Demons, and the Rise of Christianity from Late Antiquity into the Middle Ages," in *Witchcraft: Confessions and Accusations*, ed. M. Douglas (London: Tavistock, 1970), pp. 17–45; J. Z. Smith, "Towards Interpreting Demonic Powers in Hellenistic and Roman Antiquity," in *ANRW*, 2.16.1 (1978), pp. 425–39; A. F. Segal, "Hellenistic Magic: Some Questions of Definition," in *Studies in Gnosticism and Hellenistic Religion Presented to Gilles Quispel on the Occasion of His 65th Birthday*, ed. R. van der Broek and M. J. Vermaseren (Leiden: E. J. Brill, 1981), pp. 349–75.

44. For examples, see F. Graf, *Magic in the Ancient World*, trans. F. Philip (Cambridge, Mass: Harvard University, 1997), pp. 61–88.

45. C. R. Phillips III, *"Nullum Crimen sine Lege: Socio-religious Sanctions on Magic,"* in *Magika Hiera; Ancient Greek Magic and Religion*, ed. C. A. Faraone and D. Obbink (New York: Oxford University, 1991), pp. 260.

46. D. Aune, "Magic in Early Christianity," *ANRW* II.16.2 (1978), 1515.

47. Ibid.

48. "Hellenistic Magic," p. 368. Segal, however, observes the notable exception of the magical papyri in which practitioners sometimes call themselves *magoi*; p. 351.

49. See the evidence collected by James Rives, "The Religion of Sergius Paulus (Acts 13:6–12)," unpublished paper, given to the New Testament Seminar, Union Theological Seminary (N.Y.C.), April 14, 1998. Such evidence would call into question J. Z. Smith's position regarding the illegality of magic, or at the very least require a qualifying of that position. See J. Z. Smith, "Good News is No News: Aretalogy and Gospel" in *Christianity, Judaism and Other Greco-Roman Cults,* ed. J. Neusner (Leiden: E. J. Brill, 1975), 1–23.

50. Cf. S. Benko, *Pagan Rome and the Early Christians* (Bloomington, IN: Indiana University, 1984), pp. 128–30.

51.   Cf. Graf, *Magic in the Ancient World*, pp. 41–43; Segal, "Hellenistic Magic," p. 356f.

52.   Frend, *Martyrdom*, p. 117.

53.   S. R. Garrett, *The Demise of the Devil: Magic and the Demonic in Luke's Writings* (Minneapolis: Fortress, 1989), p. 4.

54.   Ibid., pp. 2–5.

55.   On the association of magic with Christians in this period, see Benko, *Pagan Rome*, pp. 103–39. Wilson believes that Luke is describing a conflict between Jewish and Christian miracle workers, and trying to demonstrate the superiority of Christian magic; *Related Strangers*, p. 66f. However, given the generally pejorative nature of the category "magic," and the ambivalence with which it was regarded by the governing powers, it is doubtful that Luke would have claimed that Jesus or his disciples were magicians. It is more likely that Luke would have been trying to establish that they were miracle workers rather than magicians. Cf. Segal, "Hellenistic Magic," p. 368.

56.   Lk 11:14–23; Mk 3:22–27; Mt12:22–30. The accusation occurs in Q (Lk 11:19–20; Mt12:27–29), as well as Mk (3:22–27). On the association of Jesus with magic, see Morton Smith, *Jesus the Magician* (San Francisco: Harper and Row, 1978).

57.   Garrett, *The Demise of the Devil*, p. 101; see also p. 104f.

58.   Brown notes that learning allows people to cross lines of status; "Sorcery," p. 24f.

59.   Cf. Wills, "The Depiction," p. 652.

60.   Sanders, *The Jews*, p. 116.

61.   Ibid.

62.   While Stoops acknowledges the questions raised regarding the apologetic function of Acts, he would recognize Luke's work, at least in part, as an argument for toleration by Rome and the granting of a measure of autonomy ("Riot and Assembly," pp. 89–91). See Feldman for evidence of both toleration and discrimination (*Jew and Gentile*, pp. 92–106).

63. *Exitiabilis superstitio*, in Tacitus, *Annals*, XV.44.4; "new and wicked superstition" (*superstitio nova et malefica*) in Suetonius, *Nero*, XVI.2. Cf. Frend, *Martyrdom*, p. 162f.

64. Frend, *Martyrdom*, p. 169.

65. Acts 15:20 has *alisgematon ton eidolon* for the first time. As we have already observed, most believe that 15:29 is the original reading.

66. Cf. 1 Cor 8:1,4, 10; 10:14–22; Rev 2:20; 21:8; *Did* 6:2; Justin, *Dial.* 34–35; Minucius Felix, *Oct.* 38; Clement, *Paed.* 2.1.17; Origen, *Contra Celsum* 8:29–30.

67. Cf. Minucius Felix, *Oct.* 30; Tertullian, Apol. 9.13; Origen, *Contra Celsum*, 8:29–30; Pseudo-Clem. *Homs.* 7.4.2; Eusebius, *Hist. Eccl.* 5.1.

68. Tertullian, Anol. 9.13; Origen, Contra Celsum 8:29–30. Tertullian adds animals which die a natural death and says that both animals strangled and those which die a natural death contain blood. See also Pseudo-Clem. *Homs.* 7.4.2, which also includes a reference to ritual washings.

69. E.g., 1 Cor 10:20; Clement, Paed. 2.1.17.2; Origen, *Contra Celsum* 8:30; Minucius Felix, *Oct.* 38.

70. On the relation of things strangled to demons, idolatry, and magic, see Wedderburn, "The 'Apostolic Decree'," pp. 384–89; Wilson, *Luke and the Law*, pp. 96–99.

71. E.g., Hos 1:2; 2:2,4; 4:11–12; 5:4; Jer 2:20; 3:2, 9.

72. Rev 2:20–25; 21:8; 22:15.

73. Apol. 9. While there is no explicit link between food laws and marital fidelity, Tertullian discusses them in the same literary context. On the relationship between pollution rules and moral codes, see M. Douglas, *Purity and Danger: an Analysis of the Concepts of Pollution and Taboo* (London: Ark, 1985), pp. 129–39.

74. See Witherington, Acts, pp. 461–463; also S. Benko, *Pagan Rome and the Early Christians*, pp. 54–78.

75. M. Douglas, "Deciphering a Meal," in *Implicit Meanings: Essays in Anthropology* (London: Routledge and Kegan Paul, 1975), p. 249; quoted by J. H. Neyrey, "Ceremonies in Luke-Acts: the Case of Meals and Table Fellowship," in *The Social World of Luke-Acts: Models for*

Interpretation (Peabody, Mass: Hendrikson, 1991), p. 361. See also P. L. Berger and T. Luckmann, *The Social Construction of Reality: A Treatise in the Sociology of Knowledge* (New York: Doubleday/Anchor Books, 1966), pp. 180–83.

76. Cf. J. A. Fitzmyer, S.J., "The Matthean Divorce Texts and Some New Palestinian Evidence," in *To Advance the Gospel; New Testament Studies* (New York: Crossroad, 1981), p. 88f.

77. Did. 6:2; Minucius Felix, Oct. 30; Tertullian, Apol. 9.13; Origen, *Contra Celsum* 8:29.

78. Cf. MacMullen, *Paganism in the Roman World*, pp. 37, 41, 46. Cf. 1 Cor 8:10f.

79. Cf. P. D. Gooch, *Dangerous Food; 1 Corinthians 8–10 in Its Context*, Studies in Christianity and Judaism 5 (Waterloo, Ont.: Canadian Corporation for Studies in Religion/Corporation Canadienne des Sciences Religieuses, 1993), p. 38.

80. On the ways in which Christians of different social classes would have been affected by the prohibition against meat offered to idols, see W. Meeks, *The First Urban Christians: The Social World of the Apostle Paul* (New Haven: Yale University, 1983), p. 98.

81. Clement's remark is particularly interesting in this regard: "the food of those who are saved and those who perish is separate" (Peed. 2.1.17.2).

82. Douglas remarks, "It would seem that whenever a people are aware of encroachment and danger, dietary rules controlling what goes into the body would serve as a vivid analogy of the corpus of their cultural categories at risk," in "Deciphering a Meal," p. 272.

83. See M. Simon, *Verus Israel: A Study of the Relations between Christians and Jews in the Roman Empire 135-425*, trans. H. McKeating (reprinted; London: Littman Library/Oxford University 1986), p. 336.

CONVERSATION FIVE

LOUIS H. FELDMAN

KEVIN MADIGAN

CONVERSATION FIVE

Hatred for and Attraction to Jews
in Classical Antiquity

LOUIS H. FELDMAN

Everyone who deals with the subject of anti-Semitism (an inappropriate term, of course, since it refers to families of languages rather than attitudes toward people) must approach it with a combination of humility and chutzpah—particularly humility, because we have such a small percentage of what was actually written (almost certainly not more than one per cent, and who knows whether what was written was really representative of what people thought, especially since the rate of literacy in classical antiquity apparently did not exceed ten per cent). Nonetheless, we dare to generalize on the basis of such a small sample. What I propose to do here is to examine the subject especially in the light of what a very important writer in a very important recent work does with this evidence. I am referring to Peter Schäfer's *Judeo-phobia: Attitudes toward the Jews in the Ancient World* (Cambridge, Mass.: Harvard University Press, 1997). People often tend to be wary about books concerning anti-Semitism written by Jews. Well, here is a book by a non-Jew, a German at that, and a highly respected and prolific writer on all aspects of ancient Judaism, particularly, of course, rabbinic literature.

The book by Professor Schäfer is extremely important not only because of what it says but also because of the identity of the author. It is the first comprehensive study of ancient anti-Semitism written by a German scholar since the Holocaust; and the fact that it is written by a non-Jew who is clearly the outstanding German scholar in the field of rabbinic and allied literature makes it particularly significant. That it is critical, intellectually honest, and refreshing makes for extremely stimulating reading. One has learned to expect no less from Peter Schäfer.

It seems to me that it is well for us to begin, as Professor Schäfer does not, with some general considerations about the ancient world which distinguish it from our modern world. In the first place, the ancients could not have conceived of what we would call a separation of church and state. Even if we find individuals such as Caesar and Cicero whose adherence to traditional religious beliefs is questionable, as we may see in Cicero's *De Divinatione* for example, officially, when they are part of the government or commenting on political issues, they say the "right things" so far as religious matters are concerned. The close of Cicero's first oration against Catiline, which he delivered in the Senate, will illustrate this: Once Catiline has left, he says, "You, great Jupiter, who were established with the same rites as this city, whom we name rightly the establisher of this city and empire," will protect us. In any codification of laws, stretching from the Twelve Tables to the Corpus of Justinian, there is no separation of civil from religious law.

On the other hand, polytheism is, by definition, liberal and pluralistic, inasmuch as no pagan religion asserts that other religions and other gods are false. Less powerful yes, but not false. Though one could insist that the gods of one's own nation had fostered the growth and success of one's nation, so that, as the revered Ennius put it, "*Moribus antiquis res stat Romana viresque*," there was always room in the pantheon for another god. Judaism, however, insisted, at least officially in the Torah, that all other religions and all other gods were false and, in fact, at least in the oral tradition, that the pagans, as children of Noah, were forbidden to worship idols. Hence, in the absence of a separation of church and state, Jews, themselves constituting a state, by definition would seem to have, as their goal, the destruction of all other states. Therefore, Apion would seem to be right in asking, in effect, why, if the Jews wish to become Alexandrian citizens, they don't worship the Alexandrian gods. One can go even further and ask how one can trust the Jews if their goal is to destroy the religious basis of the state. Intellectuals and philosophers can and do ask such questions. They are logical. Fortunately, politicians then and now are not. The Hellenistic and Roman rulers, with rare exceptions, such as Antiochus Epiphanes, Caligula, and Hadrian, gave special permission to the Jews to observe their religious beliefs and practices. All the rulers of the Hellenistic and Roman world, from Alexander through his successors and through the Romans, with the exceptions named above, realized that the people from whom they came were a minority in their realm and, realizing how numerous and economically important the Jews were, granted them special privileges. And the intellectuals and philosophers and theologians remained with their logical arguments, wrote books, most of which fortunately have been lost (since we would otherwise have to read them), and gained promotions and tenure in the equivalent of our universities.

As for the Jews, they managed, or at least some of them managed, to interpret the Torah rather liberally. In the first place, the author (who, to be sure, is represented as a non-Jew) of the *Letter of Aristeas*, which tells the story of the translation of the Torah into Greek, speaking to King Ptolemy Philadelphus (15–16) equates the God of the Jews with Zeus. "The same God who has given them their law," he says, "guides your kingdom also, as I have learned in my researches. God, the overseer and creator of all things, whom they worship, is He whom all men worship, and we too, Your Majesty, though we address Him differently, as Zeus and Dis." The key passage is Exodus 22:28, which the Septuagint translates as, "Thou shalt not curse gods," which is then explained by both Philo (*De Vita Mosis* 2.26.205 and *De Specialibus Legibus* 1.7.52) and Josephus (*Against Apion* 2.237) to mean that one is forbidden to speak ill of other peoples' gods. Both Philo and Josephus, significantly, give the same reason for this tolerance, namely, out of reverence to the very word "God."

As for Professor Schäfer's book, let us start with his field of expertise, rabbinic literature. The rabbis, of course, have a good deal to say about the attitude of non-Jews toward Jews, but, *mirabile dictu*, you will find none of it in this book. In fact, the only reference to rabbinic literature appears in a single footnote (p. 252, n. 84), where, discussing the evidence for Hadrian's ban on circumcision, he remarks that the only proof for this ban is the short note in the *Historia Augusta* (*Hadrianus* 14.2), whereupon he adds in the footnote: "Apart from rabbinic sources which are difficult to date and which for the most part refer to the period after the Bar Kochba war." Similarly, in his recent monumental survey, *The Roman Near East 31 BC–AD 337* (Cambridge,

Mass.: Harvard University Press, 1993), Fergus Millar, surely not an anti-
Semite, deliberately and almost totally disregards rabbinic evidence, and this
despite the fact that the rabbis have so much to say about the period that he
covers. In another recent book, Jonathan Price (*Jerusalem under Siege: The
Collapse of the Jewish State 6670 C.E.* Leiden: Brill, 1992, p. 264) actually
states that any rabbinic story unconfirmed by outside sources is to be treated
as fiction. Are all of these people Sadducean sympathizers in their disregard
of the reliability of the Talmudic corpus for historical data? Granted that the
earliest of the midrashim dates from no earlier than 400 C.E., that the codification of the Jerusalem Talmud dates from about the same time, that the codification of the Babylonian Talmud dates from about a century later, that the
rabbinic documents cover a period of several centuries, that the rabbis are
constantly quoting other rabbis who are citing other rabbis, and granted that
the rabbinic documents are concerned with history in only the most incidental way and that we do not know how broad were the circles which they
reflect, are the other sources that much more reliable? In at least some
respects the rabbinic literature is perhaps more reliable: the Talmudic corpus
is a book of debate, with rabbis constantly challenging one another; and how
often do the rabbis admit that they do not know? Indeed, unlike the other
sources, the rabbis are sharply divided in their attitude toward the Romans
(see my "Some Observations on Rabbinic Reaction to Roman Rule to Third
Century Palestine," in *Hebrew Union College Annual* [1992] 39–81). Moreover, precisely because the Talmud is not a history book, the remarks of rabbis
concerning historical details should be of particular value, inasmuch as they
are usually said incidentally, casually, and in passing. As to the gap in time
between the events and the time that they are recorded, is the rabbinic literature necessarily worth less than, say, Arrian's account of Alexander, written
half a millennium after the events?

   As for the inscriptions, at least those in the Diaspora, somewhat over a
thousand deal with Jews. But this is a thousand out of approximately 200,000.
Moreover, they cover a period of hundreds of years and in many countries.
Finally, almost half of the Diaspora inscriptions come from a single community, Rome, which contained perhaps one per cent of the Jews of the Diaspora,

and apparently date from the third century and later. But most important of all, since the great majority of them are inscriptions on tombstones, none of them indicates that the Jews who are memorialized had suffered from any kind of anti-Semitism, let alone that they had been killed in the course of an anti-Semitic outbreak.

As to the papyri, Tcherikover and his colleagues have collected 520, but they cover almost a millennium, and only thirteen allude to anti-Semitism. As to archaeological findings, none of them refers to anti-Semitic attitudes or outbreaks.

Let us examine some actual outbreaks against Jews in antiquity. The most striking case of what we would call a pogrom occurred in Alexandria, the most populous of the Jewish communities, with perhaps as many as 180,000 Jews, in the year 38 C.E. Philo (*Legatio ad Gaium* 18.120) reports that the hatred of the masses toward the Jews had been smoldering for some time. When a pretext was offered on the Jews' refusal to obey the decree of Emperor Gaius Caligula that he be worshipped as a god, the promiscuous mob, carried away with itself, let loose. The order of events was, first, long-standing resentment at the privileged position and influence of the Jews, whether political or economic; second, and more immediate, the accusation that the Jews were unpatriotic, inasmuch as they refused to participate in the state cults which, like a flag, united all the diverse peoples of the empire; third, the rousing of the passions of the mob by professional agitators (though this appears to be exceptional); and fourth, the intervention of the government to preserve order while blaming the Jews for causing the riot. What determined the course of events in this instance was the behavior of Flaccus, the Roman governor of Egypt. During the first five of the six years of his administration, Flaccus (Philo, *In Flaccum* 1.2–3) had shown no signs of anti-Jewish animus and indeed was a model administrator. The change of attitude in Flaccus, and consequently the breakdown of the vertical alliance with the Roman administration, was due to the death of the Emperor Tiberius, who had appointed him and whose close friend he had been, and to the fear that, because Tiberius' successor Caligula had put to death Flaccus' friend Macro, his own position would deteriorate. In desperation, therefore, Flaccus, presumably assuming that the Jews would in their usual fashion remain loyal to the emperor, sought allies among his former enemies.

The immediate pretext for the riot was the visit of Agrippa I to Alexandria and his ostentatious display of his bodyguard of spearmen decked in armor overlaid with gold and silver. The mob responded to Agrippa's majestic appearance by dressing up a lunatic named Carabas in mock-royal apparel with a crown and bodyguards and saluting him as Marin, the Aramaic word for "lord." The implied charge clearly was that the Alexandrian Jews, in giving homage to Agrippa as a king, were guilty of dual loyalty and of constituting themselves, in effect, as a state within a state. The use of the Aramaic word would seem to be intended to emphasize the allegation that the Jews' first loyalty was to the Aramaic-speaking ruler of Palestine. Flaccus, according to Philo (*Legatio ad Gaium* 20.132), could have halted the riot in an hour if he had desired, but did nothing. The scenario is rather strikingly similar to what occurred in our own day in Crown Heights in Brooklyn. That the Jew-baiters decried not merely the alleged lack of patriotism but also, rather simply, the fact of Jewishness can be seen in the treatment of the women, whom they seized and forced to eat pork (Philo, *In Flaccum* 11.96) rather than to worship the image of the emperor. In the end, however, what must have seemed to the opponents of the Jews like an instance of "international Jewish power" asserted itself: Flaccus was recalled in disgrace, banished, and eventually executed.

The next major eruption of anti-Jewish violence coincided, significantly, with the outbreak of the Jewish rebellion against the Romans in 66 C.E., not unconnected, we may guess, with the charge of dual loyalty. Not unexpectedly, this most violent of all the outbreaks against the Jews occurred in Alexandria. Our only source, Josephus, is hardly an impartial witness, especially because he had such an antipathy for Jewish revolutionaries. Yet, his account should be given serious weight, inasmuch as it is far from a whitewash of the murderous actions of the troops sent by the authorities. In recounting the event, Josephus (*War* 2.487) reminds us, as we had already seen in Philo, that there had always been strife between the native inhabitants and the Jewish settlers ever since the time when Alexander the Great, as a reward for the support that the Jews had given him against the Egyptians, had granted them *isonomia*, that is, rights equal to those of the Greeks. Presumably, the Jew-baiters felt assured that the authorities would favor their cause against people who would now be perceived as unpatriotic rebels. The uprising was put down ruthlessly by the Roman governor, Tiberius Julius Alexander (Philo's nephew); and, according to Josephus (*War* 2.497), no fewer than 50,000 Jews were slain. Finally, Alexander gave the signal to his soldiers to cease; but so great, says Josephus (*War* 2.498), was the intensity of the hatred of the Alexandrians that it was only with difficulty that they were torn away from the very corpses.

Most of those who deal with this subject, including Schäfer, concentrate on what the Greek and Roman writers say about the Jews. But aside from the fact that the citations in Stern's collection cover a period of a thousand years, to what degree do we get a representative picture? What percentage of what the Greeks and Romans actually wrote has come down to us? Surely, as we have suggested, no more than one per cent. It is not until Herodotus in the fifth century B.C.E. that any extant Greek writer alludes to the Jews at all; and even he refers to them only obliquely, if at all, when he discusses circumcision. Ezra is a contemporary of Herodotus, or perhaps of Plato, but neither of them as much as mentions him; and the first and only pagan writer who does mention him is Porphyry (*Adversus Christianos* [ap. Macarius Magnes 3.3]) at the end of the third century C.E. Indeed, one of the most important points to be made is the degree to which the Jews are simply ignored. A writer such as Cicero who, to be sure, knew about Jews and refers to them in his oration *Pro Flacco*, ignores them completely in a work such as *De Natura Deorum*, where he deals at length with various theories concerning theology and where we might have expected some mention of them, inasmuch as the Jewish view of deity is, from a pagan point of view, so unusual. Stern's monumental three-volume collection of testimonials seems large; but I have found a total of only 3372 lines of actual text in Greek or Latin in volume 1 (covering from Herodotus through Plutarch in the first century C.E.); and this includes a good deal of information that is only peripheral to anything Jewish. In volume 2, covering through the sixth century, there are 5006 lines. This comes to approximately 204 1/3 pages, and a good deal of this consists of passages about the properties of the Dead Sea. When we consider that in the first century the Jews comprised perhaps as much as ten per cent of the population of the Roman Empire, what surely must strike us, at least on the basis of what literature has come down to us, is that non-Jewish writers have little interest in the Jews; and it cannot be merely that the Jews were not in contact with non-Jews, since in Alexandria, at least, Philo was hardly unique in his knowledge of Greek literature and in his interest in attending sporting events and theaters. If anti-Semitism was more of an issue one would expect a lot more attention.

Another indication of this lack of interest in the Jews on the part of non-Jewish writers is the degree to which they cite Jewish writers or writings. So far as we can tell, though, there are a very few writers, notably Alexander Polyhistor in the first century B.C.E., who seems to have been acquainted with the Bible. Only one writer, Pseudo-Longinus (9.9), in the first half of the first century C.E., quotes, or rather closely paraphrases, a very brief passage from the Bible (Genesis 1:3, 9–10), and some think that he himself was a Jew. Moreover, though Philo writes voluminously in excellent Greek and lived in the greatest cultural center of his era, Alexandria, he is never quoted as such by any extant pagan writer. Alexandria was the center of great scholarship, having the Museum, the equivalent of the Institute for Advanced Study in Princeton, yet neither do any of the scholars of the Museum mention the Jews, let alone make any anti-Semitic comments, at least in the fragments that have come down to us, nor do Jewish writers such as Philo mention them or try to refute them. Indeed, there is only one passage in a pagan author that we can definitively say shows that the author, the third-century Heliodorus, in his novel *Aethiopica* (9.9.3), appropriates language taken from Philo (*De Vita Mosis* 2.36.195), yet it contains nothing that is either for or against the Jews. Otherwise, Philo's writings apparently had little or no impact upon later pagan Graeco-Roman thought or literature, with the possible exception of Numenius and Plotinus. It is not until early in the third century that we find a Christian writer, Clement of Alexandria, who definitely has read Philo.

As for Josephus, the only passages in pagan writers which cite Josephus as a writer are to be found in a fragment (no. 17) in the second-century

Appian, referring to the prophecy that someone from Judaea would become ruler of the world, and at the beginning of the fourth century in Porphyry (*De Abstinentia* 4.11–13), who paraphrases at some length Josephus' description of the Essenes (*War* 2.119–161). Among Christian writers he is not cited until the end of the second century by Theophilus of Antioch (*Ad Autolycum* 3.20–23), and not at length until the third-century Hippolytus (for the list of citations see Heinz Schreckenberg, *Die Flavius Josephus Tradition in Antike und Mittelalter* [Leiden: Brill, 1972], p. 72). That only a single papyrus fragment (*War* 2.576–79, 582–84; in Papyrus Graeca Vindobonensis 29810) from any of Josephus' works has thus far been found would seem to indicate that he was not much read in antiquity, at least in Egypt, though we must be very careful about generalizing from the papyri that have been found, since almost all of them come from one country, Egypt, and so large a percentage comes from one little town, Oxyrhynchus.

If anti-Semitism was a burning issue, one would have thought that attempts would have been made by pagans to answer the one work devoted to refuting anti-Semites and which contains many debatable points and had the sponsorship of the great bibliophile Epaphroditus and of the emperor Domitian, namely Josephus' essay *Against Apion*. Yet, there is no such mention of the essay, let alone a refutation. If there had been a widespread outcry of anti-Semitic comments among ancient intellectuals, we would have expected that some indication of this would have been discovered among the thousands of scraps of literary papyri that have been found among all of the papyri, but not a single such scrap has yet emerged. We would have expected to find at least some of the anti-Semitic statements of Manetho, Chaeremon, Lysimachus, Apion, or Apollonius Molon, and while it is true that we have uncovered fragments of Apion, for example, none of the anti-Semitic comments have been found. We have fragments of the essay *Against Apion*; and in contrast to the fact that we have 53 manuscripts of the *Jewish War*, 33 of the first ten books of the *Antiquities*, and 44 of the second half of the Antiquities, we have only eight of the essay *Against Apion*, and for part of it no Greek manuscripts exist at all, and we have to rely upon the Latin translation that was done under the leadership of Cassiodorus.

Moreover, though the *argumentum ex silentio* must be used with caution, if, indeed, anti-Semitism was rife among pagan intellectuals, we would have expected Philo, who was the head of what was, in effect, the Anti-defamation League of Alexandria and who headed a delegation to the Roman Emperor Gaius Caligula no less, to have replied to their writings, and he does not. As to other Jewish writers (and there is some doubt as to whether they are Jewish) such as Demetrius, Eupolemus, Pseudo-Eupolemus, Artapanus, Cleodemus-Malchus, Aristeas, Philo the Epic Poet, and Ezekiel the dramatist—none of them replies to anti-Semitic comments, and none of them is quoted by a pagan writer. But, in all fairness, we must note that we know of at least seven writers—Alexander Polyhistor, Apollonius Molon, and Teucer of Cyzicus in the first century B.C.E., Apion of Alexandria, Damocritus, and Nicarchus in the first century C.E., and Herennius Philo of Byblus in the second century—who are said to have written whole monographs on the Jews. Teucer's work, in particular, seems to have been very extensive, consisting, as it did, of six books. There may well be significance in the fact that none of these works has survived. Is this another indication of lack of interest in the Jews? Or is this a case of deliberate suppression by later Christian writers and bibliophiles who found these works too pro-Jewish for their tastes? If we had these works, how different would our picture be of the attitude of Graeco-Roman intellectuals toward the Jews?

Schäfer concludes his book with the view that the only crucial question is what the Greco-Egyptian and Greek authors made out of Jewish separateness. "They turned Jewish separateness into a monstrous conspiracy against humankind and the values shared by all civilized human beings, and it is therefore their attitude which determines anti-Semitism" (p. 210).

But we must make one additional comment with regard to the attitude of pagan intellectuals toward the Jews, and that is that, unlike the influence of modern intellectuals, especially since the Age of the Enlightenment in the eighteenth century, pagan intellectuals seem to have had little influence upon public policy or upon mass movements in antiquity. How much influence did Alexander the Great's tutor, Aristotle, who had such a negative view of barbarians, have upon Alexander? Did Cicero, for example, who speaks in a very nasty way of the Jews as a pressure group in his speech *Pro Flacco* (28.66), despite his extremely important position in the Roman republic, have any influence on the republic's attitude toward the Jews? Did Seneca, who refers to the Jews as a most accursed race (*sceleratissimae gentis*) have any influence on the policy toward the Jews of Nero, with whom, according to Tacitus (*Annals* 13.2), he had paramount influence and who is defended by Josephus (*Antiquities* 20.154–155) against his detractors? How much influence did Tacitus, who was the soninlaw of the powerful Agricola and who authored the most extensive tirade against Jews that has come down to us, have upon public policy? What the Graeco-Egyptian and Greek authors made out of Jewish separateness, in point of fact, is mere rhetoric and quite unimportant. How much of a role did intellectuals play in inciting the rioters and justifying the pogrom in the year 38? Did they produce anything like a *Protocols of the Elders of Zion* to set forth their theory of a monstrous conspiracy against all humanity, and did such a work play any role in outbreaks against Jews?

Among the chief contentions of Professor Schäfer's book are the following: (1) Whereas others, notably Isaak Heinemann, have emphasized the importance of second century B.C.E. Syria-Palestine as the origin of anti-Semitism, Schäfer finds its origin in Hellenistic Egypt ca. 300 B.C.E., but argues that it actually goes back even further to the destruction of the Elephantine Jewish military community in Egypt in the fifth century B.C.E.; (2) though the ancients are critical of other peoples besides the Jews, the charges of xenophobia and misanthropy are leveled against the Jews alone; (3) the peculiarity of the Roman attitude toward the Jews is best expressed by the term "Judeophobia" in its ambivalent combination of fear and hatred of the Jews, occasioned by Jewish success in winning converts. How valid are these contentions?

As for the first of these contentions, tracing back anti-Semitism to the experience of the Jews in Elephantine, Schäfer may well be right in concluding that there was a fundamental conflict between the Jews of Elephantine and the Egyptian priests nearby. But is this anti-Semitism? Or is this, rather, an attack upon the soldiers in Elephantine who were the agents of the Persian government in keeping the native Egyptians under subjection and who happened to be Jewish? Would the Egyptian priests, in principle, have destroyed all Jewish temples simply because they were Jewish? The situation of the Jews in Alexandria, as Schäfer notes, was actually very similar to that of the Jews in Elephantine in that they were the supporters of a hated foreign rule; but was the opposition to them due to their being Jewish or to their being foreign occupiers of Egyptian soil?

Schäfer rightly objects to the view expressed by Heinemann, Bickerman, and especially Habicht that ancient anti-Semitism began in the second century B.C.E. when the Hasmoneans created a new Jewish state and violently expanded its borders in all directions at the expense of their neighbors and forced conversion of those who held different beliefs. But if this were so, we would have expected anti-Jewish texts to stress this aggressive expansion, and we do not find such.

Most of Schäfer's discussions are based on what extant passages in Greek and Roman writers have to say. In dealing with this evidence, however, we should heed several caveats: (1) most of the passages come from fragments, and thus we are generally not in a position to know the occasion and original context of the remarks; (2) many of the passages occur in Josephus, particularly in his essay *Against Apion*, or in Church Fathers, where there is often a question of their authenticity and, in any case, where the polemical nature of the work in which they are embedded is clear; (3) many passages come from rhetorical historians or satirists, where the references are clearly colored and exaggerated; (4) we may note the patterns of ethnographical treatises which, especially under the influence of the Aristotelian Peripatetic school, had developed an interest in strange, foreign peoples and in their historical origins or in geographical oddities, as we see particularly in the large number of references to the properties of the Dead Sea.

In any case, the anti-Jewish remarks are to be seen in the context of their appearance. Thus, the anti-Jewish outburst in Cicero's *Pro Flacco*, which Schäfer cites at some length, is to be explained, at least in part, by the fact that he was defending a client who had been accused of pocketing money which the Jews had collected for transmission to the Temple in Jerusalem. Cicero himself points out the difference between his true opinions and those that he uttered as a lawyer (*Pro Cluentio* 139). Moreover, the charge made against Jews that they are lazy (Seneca, ap. Augustine, *City of God* 6.11) is also made against the Egyptians by Polybius and against the Germans by Tacitus. The charge that the Jews are superstitious (Agatharchides, ap. Josephus, *Against Apion* 1.205–211; Plutarch, *De Superstitione* 8.169C: they allowed the enemy to capture Jerusalem on the Sabbath because they refused to fight on that day) is also made by Tacitus against the Germans and by Lucian against the Egyptians.

As for the charge that the Jews hate humankind and that they refuse to mingle with others, this, I should like to suggest, is not unconnected with the fact, noted by Josephus (*Antiquities* 20.264), that the Jews in his day did not favor those who have learned foreign languages (the chief of which, of course, would be Greek), let alone those who master them. Such skill, he notes, is characteristic of ordinary freemen and even slaves. Many Jews, to be sure, did acquire a smattering of Greek; but since language is the key to culture, and especially so in antiquity, the Jews, it is not surprising, were regarded by some non-Jewish intellectuals as obscurantists in their opposition to acquiring a good knowledge of Greek. In this connection we may note that Cleomenes, the author of an astronomical work (*De Motu Circulari* 2.1.91) in the first or second century C.E., in viciously attacking the vulgar language of Epicurus, remarks that the latter's expressions "derive in part from brothels, . . . and in part they issue from the midst of the synagogue and the beggars in its courtyards." His utter contempt is manifest when he states that these expressions are "Jewish and debased and much lower than reptiles." In an era when language and rhetoric were the *sine qua non* of an intellectual, this disregard for the niceties of Greek style would make the Jews guilty of xenophobia. Indeed, as Saul Lieberman (*Greek in Jewish Palestine* (New York: Jewish Theological Seminary, 1942, p. 30) has stressed, one cannot avoid noting the poverty and vulgarity of the Greek inscriptions of ordinary Jews buried in Palestine. The rabbis (*Megillah* 9b), to be sure, recognized the beauty of the Greek language; but what is important in showing their strongly negative attitude toward Greek culture is that they are said, during the civil war between Hyrcanus II and Aristobulus II in 65 B.C.E., to have placed a curse upon the man who teaches his son Greek *wisdom* (*Sotah* 49b, *Baba Qamma* 82b, *Menahoth* 64b).

As to the alleged xenophobia of the Jews, we may note the statement, quoted in the name of the advisers to the Syrian king Antiochus VII Sidetes in the first century B.C.E. (Diodorus 34.1.1), that the Jews should be wiped out completely "since they alone of all nations avoided dealings with any other people and looked upon all men as their enemies." Even Hecataeus of Abdera (ap. Diodorus 40.3.4), in a passage that is otherwise very favorable toward the Jews, asserts that Moses introduced a certain misanthropic (*apanthropon tina*) and xenophobic (*misoxenon*) way of life. Polytheism is, by definition, pluralistic in its attitude toward other religious beliefs, and though earlier, as we see in such writers as Plato and Aristotle, the Greeks had looked down upon non-Greeks, whom they called barbarians, certainly after Alexander the liberalism and tolerance in religion extended to other peoples and other ways of life. And yet, there were those such as Hecataeus and especially the influential Strabo who praised the Jews as a civilized people, with a lawgiver comparable to the great and much admired Spartan Lycurgus and a laudable code of law.

However, is this negative attitude on the part of the Jews toward other peoples' culture really so very different from what Herodotus (2.35) says about the Egyptians: "As the Egyptians have a climate peculiar to themselves, and their river is different in its nature from all other rivers, so have they made all their customs and laws of a kind contrary for the most part to those of all other men. Among them, the women buy and sell, the men abide at home and weave; and whereas in weaving all others push the woof upwards, the Egyptians push it downwards . . . ." As to Schäfer 's claim that the charge of xenophobia is particularly made against the Jews, Herodotus (2.41) says that "no Egyptian man or woman will kiss a Greek man, or use a knife, or a spit, or a caldron belonging to a Greek, or taste the flesh of an unblemished ox that has been cut up with a Greek knife." Plato (*Laws* 12.953E) says that foreigners are expelled from Egypt for participating at meals and sacrifices.

Likewise, Juvenal, in his third satire, bitterly complains (60–61) that Rome has become a Greek city, so large has the Greek portion of the population, which he refers to as the Achaean dregs, become. The crimes of the

Greeks are said to include seductions and even murders (Juvenal 3.109–125). In the same satire he asserts that the Syrian Orontes river has flowed into the Tiber, that is, Syrians have come to Rome in such large numbers. He devotes the entire fifteenth satire to a fierce attack on the atrocities practiced by the Egyptians in their religious worship.

Furthermore, we see that Jews are not the only ones whose rites are proscribed, since we find that in the year 19 C.E. (Tacitus, *Annals* 2.85.4; Suetonius, *Tiberius* 36) the Egyptian rites are likewise abolished by the Roman authorities. But it is only the Jews who are expelled, as we see in Suetonius (ibid.), and we may conclude that just as the expulsion of the Jews from Rome in 139 B.C.E. (Valerius Maximus 1.3.3) occurred because they had "attempted to transmit their sacred rites to the Romans," that is, to convert them to Judaism, so in 19 C.E. the reason for the expulsion, as we see in Dio Cassius (57.18.5a), was the alleged missionary activities of the Jews. The same conclusion can be drawn from Josephus' account (*Ant.* 18.169–179) that the cause of the expulsion was the fact that a woman of high rank who had become a proselyte had been cheated by some Jews who took for themselves the gifts that they had urged her to send to the Temple in Jerusalem. A third expulsion of the Jews from Rome, which took place during the reign of the Emperor Claudius (Suetonius, *Claudius* 25.4, Acts 18:2) occurred because the Jews were alleged to have been constantly making disturbances at the instigation of a certain Chrestus. Significantly, Dio Cassius (60.6.6), immediately after commenting on the vast increase in the number of Jews in Rome, presumably, at least in part, through proselytism, explicitly declares that Claudius did not drive them out—the clear implication being that on other occasions the Jews had been expelled. We may make five comments about these expulsions: 1) In no case are the Jews expelled simply because they are Jews; 2) so far as we know, the Jews are expelled only from Rome, not from Alexandria or any other city or area; 3) the common denominator of these expulsions, as we can see in one case with the coupling with the Egyptians, were attempts to convert Romans to Judaism; 4) the fact that the Jews are expelled over and over again indicates that they were permitted to return, presumably not long after they had been expelled; 5) we hear of no pogroms in connection with—either before, during, or after—these expulsions. Where we again hear of pogroms, these are all just prior to the outbreak of the war against the Romans in 66, hence connected with a political factor. In that year 66 C.E., we hear that in Caesarea the non-Jewish inhabitants slaughtered the Jews residing in the city (Josephus, *War* 2.457). The popular resentment against the Jews was deep-seated and long-smoldering, though not because they were Jews but rather because of the long-standing quarrel of the Jews and non-Jews, as in Alexandria, over the *civic rights* of the Jews (Ant 20.184). Years later, in 74 C.E., Eleazar ben Jair at Masada (*War* 7.363) recalls that the non-Jews had always been quarreling with the Jewish inhabitants of Caesarea, presumably over this issue. Josephus gives no specific motive, alleged or actual, on the part of the attackers in the assault on Jews in other cities in 66 C.E., as if it were obvious or usual, but significantly Josephus (*War* 2.463) cites the presence of "Judaizers" in each city in Syria who aroused suspicion. And we may guess that one of the causes of the Jew-hatred was precisely the Jewish success not only in winning converts but also in gaining "sympathizers."

As to the motives of the Jew-baiters in these pogroms, Josephus lists three (*War* 2.464, 478): hatred, fear, and greed for plunder—apparently a combination of economic jealousy and fear of Jewish power and expansionism. It is, moreover, revealing to note that in Caesarea, the chief point of conflict, Josephus declares (*War* 2.268, *Ant.* 20.175) that the Jews were superior in wealth—another indication of the importance of the economic factor in explaining the hatred of the Jew-baiters toward the Jews, though we may remark that, generally speaking, ancient historians downplay the economic factor in their view of causality of events but rather highlight personality and military factors. Baron cites Josephus' extra-biblical comment (*Ant.* 2.201–2), in his paraphrase of the Bible, that the oppression of the ancient Israelites by the Egyptians was due to the Egyptians' envy of the Israelites' abundant wealth and, most appropriately, suggests that this reflects contemporary realities with respect to the masses of the Egyptian peasants. In this connection, we may cite a papyrus dated in 41 C.E., in which the author, a wholesale dealer in need of money, warns the recipient that if he fails to obtain a loan from the sources the author recommends, "like everyone else, do you, too, beware of the Jews" (CPJ no. 152). The fact that the writer of the papyrus adds the gratuitous phrase, "like everyone else," would seem to emphasize that, in his eyes, the warning to beware of *the* Jews is a general one, shared by the Gentile population at large, and that seeking loans from Jews was apparently customary.

That there was an economic factor, based on Jewish prominence in trade, in popular prejudice against Jews would seem to be indicated by the remark of Claudius Ptolemy, the noted second century C.E. Alexandrian astronomer, who is convinced that national characteristics are conditioned by the geographical and astronomical situation. His list of those people who are more gifted in trade than others starts with Idumaea, Coele-Syria, and Judaea, and he remarks that they are more unscrupulous, despicable cowards, treacherous, servile, and in general fickle. These people, he adds, are, in general, bold, godless, and treacherous. In referring to the inhabitants of these countries, he really has in mind only the Jews, because all three of these geographical areas are frequently identified with each other (so Stern 2.163). Another economic factor may be seen in Tacitus' bitter remark (*Histories* 5.5.1), alluding to the success of the Jews in winning others to convert to Judaism, that "the worst rascals among other peoples, renouncing their ancestral religions, always kept sending tribute and contributing to Jerusalem, thereby increasing the wealth of the Jews." Hence, it was not merely that Romans were abandoning their ancestral gods, who, in the view of writers such as Ennius and Livy, had enabled the Romans to build their great empire, but they were even contributing monetarily to alien gods, who, in principle, found no place in their pantheon for the Roman gods. Hence, we see the combination of the economic factor and the alleged expansionism of the Jews as factors in Judaeophobia.

On the other hand, if, at a later date, under Domitian, we hear of the expulsion of a group other than the Jews, namely the philosophers (Dio 65 (66) 13.1a), it is apparent, as we can see in the generally mild and eventempered Cassius Dio (ibid.), that these intellectuals had irritated Romans intensely since they "are full of empty boasting . . . and look down on everyone."

What contributed to the suspicion of the Jews was their secrecy in refusing to allow non-Jews to enter the precincts of their great Temple in Jerusalem. Indeed, this seems to have been a factor in bringing about the very first pogrom of which we hear, namely the one in which Ptolemy IV Philopator (3 Macc 5–6) in 217 B.C.E. ordered the Jews to be massacred in Alexandria by a horde of elephants, because upon visiting Jerusalem, when he wanted to enter the Temple, he was mysteriously felled to the ground. Inasmuch as the Ptolemies were themselves a minority in their own empire in Egypt and were regarded as interlopers by the native Egyptians, who were so proud of their long history, and inasmuch as Palestine was a constant battleground between the Ptolemies and the Syrian Seleucids during the third century B.C.E., Philopator may well have wondered what the Jews were hiding in the Temple when they excluded him. Added to the secrecy of the Temple was the secret book (*arcano . . . volumine*) to which Juvenal refers (*Satires* 14.102), the Torah. And when the elephants (it was apparently Greek to them) whom Philopator had lined up to trample upon the Jews disobeyed his order and trampled upon those providing them, Philopator reversed himself, released the Jews, and returned to the previous policy of toleration.

The fact that Roman citizens of Jewish origin were exempted from military service (for religious reasons, notably observance of the Sabbath and dietary laws) from the time of Julius Caesar onwards (*Ant.* 14.226) may have seemed to the Romans an indication that the Jews were not fully loyal to the Romans, especially since the Jews had a state of their own, Judaea, and, as we see from Agrippa I's triumphal march in Alexandria, were loyal to that state. Tacitus (*Histories* 5.13.2), Suetonius (*Vespasian* 4.5), and Josephus (*War* 6.312) mention a belief that someone from Judaea would become ruler of the world. This was interpreted by the Jewish revolutionaries, says Josephus, to refer to someone, presumably a messianic figure, from their own people and would *ipso facto* require a revolution against the Roman Empire. If someone such as Tiberius Julius Alexander did become part of the Roman military and political establishment, he was a renegade to his faith (*Ant.* 20.100), since, with Church and state never being separated, this required worshipping the Roman gods.

Gavin Langmuir, in his already extremely influential book, *Toward a Definition of Antisemitism* (Berkeley: University of California Press, 1990), distinguishes three kinds of hostile assertions: realistic hostility, where there is some basis in fact for the hostility toward the group; xenophobia, where the conduct of a minority of the members of a group is said to be true of all members of the group; and chimeria, where characteristics attributed to the group have never been empirically observed. On this basis he concludes that chimerical (or irrational) anti-Semitism does not arise until about 1150 C.E. In his long and incisive dialogue with Langmuir, Schäfer notes that the most salient example of chimerical anti-Semitism cited by Langmuir is the alleged Jewish custom of human sacrifice. Schäfer objects that a similar charge is made by Apion and Damocritus against the Jews, but, we may object, in any case, such a charge is not uniquely anti-Jewish, since we hear of other cannibalistic conspiracies, the most famous being that connected with Catiline. Since such a charge is made against so many peoples, it hardly indicates that the Jews are to be regarded as a menace to society, especially since, as we see in Cicero, for example, it was understood in those days that rhetoricians were granted the license to exaggerate and, indeed, to do so even wildly. However, the main point to be made is that the charges made by Apion and Damocritus—and we may add that even Theophrastus (ap. Porphyry, *De Abstinentia* 2.26), in an otherwise very favorable notice about the Jews, says that the Jews were the first to institute sacrifices both of other living beings and of themselves—did not lead to outbreaks against the Jews, as did those in the Middle Ages. Are we justified in using Langmuir's terminology in viewing Apion's and Damocritus' charges as chimerical? Yes, they are chimerical, but they are not part and parcel of ancient hostility, so far as we can tell. In all the cases of overt hostility, such as pogroms, we never hear the charge that Jews fatten up and kill non-Jews. We hear of expulsions of the Jews from Rome in 139 B.C.E. and in 19 C.E. and perhaps again during the reign of Claudius, but these are provoked not by harangues or comments of intellectuals but rather by the success of the Jews in winning converts. Indeed, in each case, the Jews apparently return to Rome shortly after their expulsion despite the threat of Jewish proselytizing to the Roman way of life.

Professor Schäfer remarks that the picture of anti-Semitism in Rome "is more complex than in Egypt and Greece. Beginning with Cicero and Seneca, and reaching its climax with Juvenal and Tacitus, there is an ambivalence between dislike and fear, criticism and respect, attraction and repulsion, which responds to the peculiar combination of exclusiveness and yet success that characterizes Judaism in the eyes of the Roman authors." But Cicero, as we know, is a lawyer who argued diametrically opposed points of view. In any case, his anti-Semitic comments, such as his reference to the Jews as a pressure group, is never cited by any other extant author—or, one might add, by the later Church Fathers—despite Cicero's unchallenged position as Rome's greatest orator, and, so far as we can tell, had no influence on Roman governmental policy or the Roman masses. Seneca may have written bitter and nasty comments about the Jews, but though he was for a time the right-hand man of the Emperor Nero (Tacitus, *Annals* 13.2), he apparently had no influence on Nero's policy toward the Jews, if we may judge from Josephus. Juvenal was a professor of rhetoric, and fortunately in those days as in ours, professors were generally regarded as *Luftmenschen*, a source of good jokes, and with little or sharply exaggerated understanding of reality. Though he has some incisive comments, his influence on public policy or the masses was nil. Tacitus may have held office under three emperors, may have been consul under Nerva, and may have been governor of the province of Asia under Trajan, but we know of no evidence that he carried his anti-Semitic views into practice in any of those positions.

If fear of the Jews because of their success in winning converts is seen solely in Roman literature, why are there no riots in Rome but rather, most notably, in Alexandria against the Jews? Indeed, according to Suetonius (*Claudius* 25.4) it is the Jews who are alleged to have made constant disturbances (*assidue tumultuantis*) in Rome, at the instigation of Chrestus, and these are said by Suetonius to have led the Emperor Claudius to expel the Jews from Rome. But we do not hear in Suetonius or in any other Roman source, or in Josephus, who was a contemporary, of popular riots by non-Jews against Jews at that time. It is furthermore significant that though we hear of cities in Asia Minor and Libya that did not honor the privileges that had been granted to the Jews by previous rulers and even confiscated money that the Jews had collected for transmittal to the Temple in Jerusalem, the Jews had their rights reaffirmed by Roman authorities. In any case, we do not hear of any riots or pogroms. Rather, the anti-Semitism manifested itself in such acts as stealing money (Ant. 16.45) which the Jews had collected in Asia Minor for transmittal to Jerusalem—acts which the civic magistrates apparently ignored. Since the Romans were themselves a minority in their own empire, and since the Jews constituted, as we have noted, as much as ten per cent of the population of the Roman Empire and as much as twenty per cent in the eastern portion of it, the Roman policy of tolerance, even from a purely political point of view, made much sense. The attempt of the Emperor Gaius Caligula to impose the imperial cult upon the Jews, since he hoped that this would be the one common denominator that would unite all the people of the Empire, was the exception; the norm was the decree of his successor, the Emperor Claudius, reaffirming the privileges of the Jews everywhere. Even the massacres of Jews in Damascus and other cities in Syria (*War* 2.559–561, 2.461–465) are isolated events, coinciding with the beginning of the Jewish war against the Romans. Another factor here appears to have been the success of the Jews in converting, in a city such as Antioch, a great number of Greeks "perpetually," to quote the words of Josephus (*War* 7,45), who generally is careful to soft-pedal the conversion activities of Jews because he realized how sensitive the Romans were to such acts. In Damascus, we read (*War* 2.560) that the inhabitants "distrusted their wives, who were almost all addicted to the Jewish religion." Significantly, when the revolt of 66–74 C.E. ended and the people of Antioch (*War* 7.103–111) petitioned the commander-in-chief of the Roman army, Titus, when he visited the city, to expel the Jews, he refused; and when they asked that the privileges previously enjoyed by the Jews in Antioch should be rescinded, he likewise refused, and this after four years of bloody war with the Jews. It is surely remarkable that, on the whole, after three great rebellions against the Romans, against Nero, Trajan, and Hadrian (the last, that of Bar Kochba, tied up a seventh of the entire Roman army in the tiny area of Judaea), the Roman government reaffirmed its policy of protecting the privileges of the Jews. This eventually became the policy inherited even by Constantine and the Christian emperors who succeeded him.

Langmuir views the Graeco-Roman attitude toward the Jews as devoid of any sense of threat; hence, Greeks and Romans are the prime example of an in-group with "realistic" assertions about the Jews. Schäfer correctly challenges this and insists, as we have seen, that it is precisely the feeling of being threatened by the Jews which informs many, if not most, anti-Jewish statements in antiquity. Moreover, to assert, as does Langmuir, that xenophobic assertions on the part of Greeks and Romans originate from the conduct of a minority among the Jews and that this is then attributed to all Jews is not borne out by the data, since the anti-Semitic statements are almost always made about *the* Jews.

According to Langmuir, the essential inferiority and powerlessness of the out-group, that is the Jews, are a crucial factor in turning anti-Judaism into anti-Semitism. Schäfer correctly insists that this does not apply to the Jews of antiquity. A people that produced a Herod, as well as four commanders-in-chief for the Ptolemaic armies; that produced a governor of Egypt (Tiberius Julius Alexander, who, to be sure, was no longer an observant Jew); that produced an Agrippa I, who was such a crucial factor in determining that Claudius should succeed Caligula as Roman Emperor; that at one point was able to control the kingship of half a dozen states, petty though they might be; that was able to get Roman emperors time after time to side with them against their enemies, as we can see alike from the pages of Josephus, the Talmud, and the Acts of the Pagan Martyrs; that was able to get rights and privileges affirmed and reaffirmed in every part of the Graeco-Roman world, and that, with its success in converting so many, came to embrace as much as ten per cent of the Roman Empire, was hardly powerless. Jews were feared and sometimes hated, but this is not the classic anti-Semitism such as we find in the Middle Ages and modern times.

On the contrary, Jews were even admired by some of the greatest thinkers of antiquity. Surely, among the pre-Socratic philosophers, no one had a greater reputation than Pythagoras, since, as Josephus (*Against Apion* 1.162) remarks, for wisdom and piety he was ranked above all other philosophers, presumably including even Socrates and Plato. Indeed, according to Josephus (ibid.), he not only knew of the institutions of the Jews but was an ardent admirer and even imitator of them. Furthermore, Josephus (*Against Apion* 1.163–64) cites a certain Hermippus (who lived ca 200 B.C.E.), known, he says, as a careful historian, who asserts that Pythagoras adopted from the Jews and Thracians three precepts—not to pass a certain spot on which an ass had collapsed, to abstain from thirst-producing water, and to avoid all slander; and he adds that Pythagoras introduced many points of Jewish law into his philosophy. The third-century Christian Church Father Origen (*Against Celsus* 1.15) omits the reference to the Thracians and states that, according to Hermippus, Pythagoras actually brought his own philosophy from the Jews to the Greeks. Moreover, the first-century Antonius Diogenes (ap. Porphyry, *Vita Pythagorae* 11) declares that Pythagoras visited the Egyptians, Arabs, Chaldaeans, and Hebrews, and that he learned from them the exact knowledge of dreams—a skill particularly admired in antiquity. Finally, Pythagoras' condemnation of the use of images (ap. Diogenes Laertius, *Lives of the Philosophers* 1.6–9) is ascribed to Jewish influence.

The most influential philosopher during the Hellenistic period was undoubtedly Plato. The second-century Neo-Pythagorean Numenius of Apamea sums up Plato by saying (ap. Clement of Alexandria, *Stromata* 1.22.150.4), "What is Plato but Moses speaking in Attic Greek?"

The ultimate compliment that an intellectual in antiquity could bestow upon a people was to declare that they were a race of philosophers. It is precisely this compliment that is bestowed upon the Jews by none other than the great Aristotle (ap. Clearchus of Soli ap. Josephus, *Against Apion* 1.179), who was so impressed with the wisdom of a Jew whom he met in Asia Minor that he declared that the Jewish people are actually descended from the renowned Indian philosophers. The compliment is all the greater in view of Aristotle's parochialism (*Politics* 1.2.1252B7–8) in stating that non-Greeks, whom he termed barbarians, are slaves by nature. His student and successor as the head of the Lyceum, Theophrastus (ap. Porphyry, *De Abstinentia* 2.26), reiterates that Jews are philosophers by birth, and he paints a highly complimentary picture of the Jews conversing about the divine while they are conducting their sacrifices. The fact that he adds that the Jews make observations of the stars is a further compliment, since astronomy was the most popular of the four branches of mathematics in Hellenistic times and one of the key subjects in the higher education of the philosopherkings in Plato's ideal state (*Republic* 7.528B–530B).

Among the Romans, none had a greater reputation for learning than Varro (so Quintilian 10.1.95). The ancient Romans, he says, worshipped the gods without an image. If this custom, he adds (ap. Augustine, *City of God* 4.31.2), had continued, "the gods would not be worshipped with greater purity."

In conclusion, it is time to revise the lachrymose view of Jewish history, at least for certain portions of the ancient period. Despite occasional setbacks, Jews were doing well, even counter-attacking, so to speak, through gaining proselytes in large numbers. And even among intellectuals, Jews were sometimes admired.

CONVERSATION FIVE

A Response to Louis H. Feldman

KEVIN MADIGAN

In much of his writing over the course of the past few decades, Louis Feldman has challenged the widely-accepted "lachrymose" view of Jewish history. He does so both here in this essay and in his magisterial study, *Jew and Gentile in the Ancient World: Attitudes and Interactions from Alexander to Justinian.*[1] According to holders of the "lachrymose" view (which has been shaped, understandably, by the traumatic experience of the Holocaust), virtually all of Jewish history can be described in terms of the categories of vicissitude, vulnerability, suffering, and catastrophe. Those who hold this view believe that the history of relations between Jews and non-Jews has been one of virtually unremitting hostility and of bitter hatred. Feldman knows his history too well not to recognize that this lachrymose conception does describe the experience of Jews in *some* times and places. At the same time, he has insisted emphatically that the notion that *all* of Jewish history can be described in these melancholy categories is an unproven assumption and a stereotype which squares poorly with the evidence, particularly the demographic evidence.

In fact, Feldman has found the demographic evidence for the ancient period quite telling. Of particular interest to him have been the results of Salo Baron's analysis of Jewish population patterns in the ancient world.[2] In that study, Baron estimated that there were roughly 150,000 Jews in pre-exilic Judea, the major center of Jewish population at the time the First Temple was destroyed. A little over six centuries later, there were, according to Baron's estimates, something on the order of eight million Jews throughout the Roman empire, an astonishing growth. If these figures are roughly accurate,

Jews would have constituted roughly one in every eight persons in the
Empire. Even if Harnack's much lower estimate of four million is correct, the
population growth is really quite dramatic.[3] Now, the apparent improvement
in agricultural conditions during these six centuries, good Jewish hygiene,
and Jewish refusal to practice birth control, abortion or infanticide all
undoubtedly played a role in the population increase. But are those factors
enough to account for so impressive an increase? Feldman thinks not, and I
am inclined to agree with him.[4]

"How," Feldman has asked, "can we explain why the Jews in antiquity—
so bitterly hated, as so many scholars have insisted—succeeded in winning so
many adherents, whether as "sympathizers" who observed one or more Jewish practices or as fullfledged proselytes?"[5] Of course, the question here contains its own answer: only vigorous missionary activity could have accounted
for so dramatic an increase in population. In order to lay the groundwork for
that argument, Feldman develops two prior arguments connected to the
degree that Jews in the ancient world were Hellenized and to how widespread
and effective prejudice against Jews actually was.

Feldman's thesis with respect to the first issue is that Palestinian Jews
were far less obviously influenced by Hellenistic culture than has usually
been assumed.[6] In fact, Feldman argues, Jews most characteristically regarded Greek culture with contempt, not admiration. Even in the Diaspora, the
extent of assimilation was not very great, and there, too, is evidence for a high
degree of ethnic identification and loyalty to the Temple. In short, Jews were
able "to live in a sea of foreign culture without being enveloped by it." [7] Far
more striking, to Feldman, than the depth of Hellenization was the power of
Judaism to resist it. In fact, in this context, Judaism was able to "counterat-
tack" and to make countless converts.

One of the major reasons, according to Feldman, that Judaism was able
to be so vigorous, self-confident, and vibrant is that, contrary to the widely
accepted view, prejudice against Judaism was neither particularly widespread,
nor ordinarily vicious, nor effective in the long term. This is a motif that,
with P. Schäfer's recent study as backdrop, [8] Feldman pursues with considerable vigor in the essay under consideration here. First of all, neither the

inscriptional nor the papyrological evidence refers (according to Feldman) to anti-Semitic attitudes or activities. "Not a single scrap" of literary papyrus, he argues, has survived to indicate anti-Semitic bias. Feldman is also impressed with the "degree to which," in Greek and Roman writing that has survived, "the Jews were simply ignored."[9] His conclusion is that if anti-Semitism were more profound and more widespread, it would have had to be addressed more fully than it is in the surviving literature. Even where Feldman does find evidence of bias on the part of intellectuals, he argues that it had little influence on Roman policy towards the Jews: "the vertical alliance of Jews and rulers was unaffected by the writings or speeches of philosophers or rhetoricians."[10]

In addition, where anti-Semitic bias is expressed, consideration of its context should discourage us from making sweeping conclusions about widespread or virulent anti-Semitism. Both Feldman and Schäfer have put a lot of weight on Cicero's *Pro Flacco*, though with very different conclusions. In that piece of literature, Cicero describes the Jews as numerous and as influential in formal assemblies and, in fact, describes their cohesiveness in terms redolent of modern anti-Semitism. Feldman makes a number of remarks about the context of this speech which, to his mind, should discourage us from reading the text as Schäfer does. First of all, Cicero was defending a client here who was accused by the Jews of stealing money that was to be sent to the Temple. Second, we know from other evidence that Cicero distinguished his actual opinions from statements he made as a lawyer on behalf of a client. In addition, Cicero, like so many other ancient intellectuals, does not restrict his disparaging comments to the Jews but targets many other groups for similar derogation. (For example, Cicero classes the Syrians with the Jews as a people born to slavery.) Finally, even when the Jews were expelled (as from Rome in 139 B.C.E. and 19 C.E.), it was not because of anti-Semitic attitudes but for attempting, apparently successfully, to win converts. We are told, for example, that the expulsion in 139 occurred because *Romanis tradere sacra sua conati sunt*: because the Jews attempted to transmit their sacred rites to the Romans. Nonetheless, when not proselytizing, the Jews were not merely tolerated but protected and privileged by their Roman political overlords. Even when expelled, they soon returned, their privileges restored. "In no case," Feldman concludes in his essay, "are the Jews expelled simply because they are Jews."[11]

Feldman also spends some time here, and much in his book, on the theme of admiration for the Jews in the ancient period. The Jews, he argues, were admired for their antiquity, for being a "race of philosophers," practitioners of the virtues of temperance, justice, courage, and piety, and for being a "race" that had produced so noble a hero as Moses. For these reasons, as well as the lack of widespread antisemitism, Judaism was attractive to non-Jews throughout antiquity. Even into the Christian period, Judaism remained immensely attractive, as Feldman proves by appeal to Roman imperial legislation, Church canons, the Church Fathers (especially Chrysostom), rabbinic literature, and inscriptional and papyrological evidence. Given the depth of this admiration, it was not, Feldman argues, difficult to win converts. "Despite occasional setbacks," he concludes, "Jews were doing well, even counterattacking, so to speak, through gaining proselytes in large numbers."[12]

What is not clear from the evidence is the precise nature of this missionary activity or its targets. Is it accurate to speak of Jewish proselytism at all? (Some scholars have concluded it is not.) [13] If so, was it coherent, organized, and aggressive enough to be described as a "movement"? And what can we say about those converted, or made interested, in Judaism, particularly about how thoroughly they adopted Jewish practice and identity? Feldman, of course, is well aware that not a single Jewish missionary tract from the era survives and that the only names of Jewish missionaries we know are those who preached the gospel.[14] Consequently, he has laid a lot of weight on "the dramatic new" Aphrodisias inscriptions and their implications.[15] These Feldman views as "the missing link" that seem "to establish for once and for all the existence of a large class of 'Godfearers' or 'sympathizers,' people who adopted certain practices of Judaism without actually converting."[16] But, again, who were these people whom the inscriptions describe as *theosebeis*? And to what extent did they undertake Jewish practice and assume Jewish identity? Feldman's most important response to this question is as follows:

> The term God fearers or sympathizers apparently refers to
> an 'umbrella group,' embracing many different levels of
> interest in and commitment to Judaism, ranging from peo-
> ple who supported synagogues financially (perhaps to get
> the political support of the Jews) to people who accepted
> the Jewish view of G-d in pure or modified form to peo-
> ple who observed certain distinctively Jewish practices,
> notably the Sabbath.[17]

What seems clear is that the *theosebeis* must have been quite a hetero-geneous group. In fact, the religious commitment of some must have been quite minimal, and some, really, could not be described as Jewish, or as con-verts, or as proselytes at all. If this is true, then it surely has implications not only for Jewish demographics in the ancient period but also for the notion of Judaism as a dynamic missionary religion. Judaism may have been such, but it is important to recognize that there is little evidence for this. In the end, Feldman must rely on an *argumentum e silentio*. It is, however, a pretty con-vincing argument from silence.

In fact, there is an awful lot that is convincing about Feldman's picture of Judaism in antiquity, a picture that relies on his unparalleled familiarity with the ancient sources. Even if some scholars remain unconvinced about the degree of Jewish immunity to Hellenization or the significance of Jewish-Gentile conflict (in first century Judea, especially), very few will disagree with Feldman's basic conclusion that "it is time to revise the lachrymose view of Jewish history."[18] Another way of putting this is that the Jewish experience in the Middle Ages and in the twentieth century has caused historians to look back to the ancient world and to expect the same gloomy picture they have found in those periods. What Feldman has demonstrated is that Judaism in the ancient world was, on the contrary, often vibrant, dynamic, self-confident, and even aggressive.

ENDNOTES

1. Princeton: Princeton University Press, 1993. Since many of the remarks Feldman makes in his essay are developed at greater length and in more detail in this book, my response will take into account the analysis he offers there.

2. Salo W. Baron, "Population," in *Encyclopedia Judaica* 13 (1971): 866-903. See Feldman, *Jew and Gentile*, pp. 555–56, note 20.

3. Adolf von Harnack, *The Mission and Expansion of Christianity in the First Three Centuries*, 2d edition, 2 vols. Trans. J. Moffatt. (London: Williams and Norgate, 1904–05), vol. 1: pp. 1–8.

4. Though see the useful cautionary notes sounded by Scot McKnight, "Jewish Missionary Activity: the Evidence of Demographics and Synagogues," in *Jewish Proselytism*, ed. Amy Jill Levine and Richard I. Pervo (Lanham, MD: University Press of America), pp. 1–33; and by Thomas H. Hollingsworth, *Historical Demography* (Ithaca: Cornell University Press, 1969), pp. 259–319.

5. *Jew and Gentile*, p. xi.

6. Especially by Martin Hengel, *Judentum und Hellenismus: Studien zu ihrer Begegnung unter besonderer Berücksichtigung Palästinas bis zur Mitte des 2. Jh.s v. Chr.* (Tübingen: Mohr, 1969; 2d ed, 1973)

7. *Jew and Gentile*, p. 43.

8. Peter Schäfer, *Judeophobia: Attitudes toward the Jews in the Ancient World* (Cambridge, Mass.: Harvard University Press, 1997).

9. "Hatred for and Attraction to the Jews," p. 187.

10. *Jews and Gentiles*, p. 176.

11. "Hatred for and Attraction to the Jews," p. 195.

12. "Hatred for and Attraction to the Jews," p. 204.

13. See especially Edouard Will and Claude Orrieux, *'Proselytisme Juif'? Histoire d'une erreur* (Paris: Les Belle Lettres, 1992).

14. Feldman makes these points on the very first page of *Jew and Gentile*, p. xi.

15. See especially *Jew and Gentile*, pp. 362–82.
16. *Jew and Gentile*, p. xi.
17. *Jew and Gentile*, p. 344.
18. "Hatred for and Attraction to the Jews," p. 204.

CONVERSATION SIX

PETER J. TOMSON

BARBARA E. BOWE

CONVERSATION SIX

Halakic Correspondence in Antiquity: Qumran, Paul, and the Babylonian Talmud

PETER J. TOMSON

Sources and Hermeneutics

Letters require readers, and this is no tautology. They are a written extension of human life, with all its perplexities of understanding and being
understood.

On the one hand letters have something sober and factual. Especially
when dated and exchanged between named persons, they are first-rate historical evidence, comparable in 'hardness' to coins and inscriptions, contracts
and similar datable juridical texts. I focus on halakic letters, i.e. letters with
halakah for their content, with the following considerations: (1) halakah was
(and in certain ways still is) a central determinant of Jewish communal and
individual life and identity; (2) therefore, attitudes on halakah have a high
social significance, especially for the relation to the Jewish community and
tradition; (3) halakah also has a formal, legal aspect, and halakic texts tend to
have a marked documentary value and historical significance.

Yet it is an illusion, typical of late nineteenth century positivism, that
even such "hard" sources offer direct access to historical reality. Reading the
sources, including coins, always implies interpretation or conceptualization in
the reader's mind. And to the extent that no one invents the meaning of letters
all by his own, it also presupposes teaching and learning to read, hence schools
and traditions of interpretation.

Earlier in the nineteenth century, philologists called such ruminations
hermeneutics: philosophical clarification of the process of interpretation.[1] Nor
was this kind of self-critical consciousness entirely new. Rabbinic tradition
ascribes something similar to the sagacious Pharisaic teacher, Hillel (beginning of C.E.).[2] When a candidate for proselytism objected to the Pharisaic

conception of an "oral Torah," i.e., a flexible, ever-innovating tradition of interpretation alongside the written Torah of old, Hillel told him to sit down and read. When the man was able to read out the letters of the alphabet he wrote down before him, Hillel asked whence he knew them. The candid answer, "thus I accepted faithfully," summarizes the philologist's jeopardy. Humans humanly read human letters.[3]

For this reason some rate the humanities lower than the natural sciences. My intuition is that modern developments in theoretical and quantum physics no longer allow such objectivist illusionism. Philology is an aspect of that highest task of "science" or *Wissenschaft*: "Know thyself."

This is why I find some of the ongoing discussion on the historical value of rabbinic literature superficial. It is easy to denounce scholars who are impressed by the wealth of information stored in rabbinic literature and learning as "rabbinocentric." The self-critical question whether such hypercriticism comes closer to philological truth is rarely heard. Here, polemical interests are likely to cause poor observation and biased judgment, and author indexes to be more important than source study.

At a more basic level, the same discussion is going on between what one could call a "philhellenic" and a "philosemitic" approach. When studying the concurrent beginnings of Christian historical criticism and of the "Wissenschaft des Judentums," one is struck by the total dichotomy between two scholarly movements based on the very same philological principles. Leaving the study of rabbinic Judaism to Jews, Christians in the Tübingen tradition preferred to explain Christian origins from what they termed "Hellenism."

A scholar bred in a different culture, such as a Hindu or Buddhist, could perceive at once what we are only beginning to see: the ways in which early Judaism and Christianity are being approached in Western academic circles do not have a separate existence but are interdependent at a deeper level. Paradoxically, this is precisely because they are viewed as two mutually exclusive systems.

On this view, Paul's theology of the law, perceived as being central to Christianity, must of necessity contradict the essence of Judaism. But this is an intellectual myth, and when trying to reformulate it into a historical explanation, scholars like to take recourse to the panacea of Hellenism. Thus they are blind to the fact that Hellenism was no massive monolith but rather an elegant varnish, and that early Rabbinism was about as "Hellenistic" as nascent Christianity, including Paul. It took the formidable independence of mind of an A. Schweitzer to recognize Paul's background in the then recently rediscovered Jewish apocalypses. This was extended to include the world of rabbinic ideas by W. D. Davies and the dualistic apocalyptics of Qumran by D. Flusser. In no way does this exclude Hellenistic phenomena, such as epistolary conventions or popular ideas. If one takes into account the centrality of *halakah* in ancient Judaism, Philo is a most clear example of the coexistence of Hellenistic thought patterns and a Jewish social identity.

This is not to uphold the incredible elasticity of Paul's mind. It is stating the varieties of Jewish experience in antiquity and the inadequacy of any approach which excludes bodies of sources or operates with dichotomies between them. I suspect that Paul mentally had remained much more of a Pharisee than many of his readers (Christian or Jewish) want to accept, precisely in his apocalyptic mysticism. As I found, this quality in no way excluded a halakhic training—just as one could say of the masters of halakic literature. R. Yohanan ben Zakkai, R. Yoshua, and R. Akiva are all said to have been initiate mystics.

As far as the Qumran scrolls are concerned, there is no way of reading them adequately except using the range of other sources at our disposition. For the sect's historical identity, this includes Philo and Josephus; for its apocalypticism, the Pseudepigrapha; and for its halakah, rabbinic literature. Although not very well known, this last element is important. It is becoming very clear that claims of "rabbino-centrism" are futile in face of the relations between Qumran and Pharisaic-rabbinic tradition in the field of halakah.

In sum, I advocate a theologically astute historical science. Following the aspirations of historical criticism as this developed from classical philology, this would involve studying ancient Judaism including its Christian outgrowth in all its expressions, utilizing all possible sources, and integrating continuous self-criticism as to the reader's own position visavis the religions whose early sources he or she is studying and the traditions of interpretation these religions offer.

A Halakic Letter from Qumran (4QMMT)

In 1984 E. Qimron and J. Strugnell announced the publication of a halakhic letter from Qumran.[4] While we are still waiting for this announcement to materialize, Y. Sussman and L. H. Schiffman each recently published a study on the nature of halakic polemics which represent the main body of the letter.[5] The letter, whose beginning is lost, appears to address the ruling priests in Jerusalem. Remnants of six copies were found; apparently it was an important document. Also, it was no longer a letter proper with a onetime address and purpose, but had passed into the category of "published" or "public letters."[6]

The extant parts first present an elaborate calendar of shabbats and festivals, a matter of utmost importance in Judaism and indicative of the sect's separate position. Then some 20 halakic questions are discussed, all having to do with temple ritual and the condition of priests. In the concluding part, the author calls these *miktsat ma'asse haTora*, "some works of the Law." This expression, which the editors chose for the letter's name, had been known in various forms from other Qumran writings and means actual Jewish commandments.[7] It also reminds of the *erga nomou* about the fulfillment of which Paul has his famous polemics. "Some works of the Law" must be an understatement, for the author appears to consider these commandments to be crucial.

Both Schiffman and Sussman come to remarkable conclusions about the letter's halakic positions. They appear to be very similar to the rigid opinions which rabbinic sources ascribe to the Sadducees, in opposition to the much more flexible Pharisees. As is known, rabbinic tradition claims that Sadducee high priests were forced to follow the halakah of the Pharisees, who in this respect were supported by the populace. This claim, which is criticized by some as doubtful,[8] hitherto found confirmation mainly in the bleak assertions of Josephus;[9] now we must add the evidence of this Qumran letter. But the letter offers more. It also forces us to conclude that Qumranites or Essenes held halakic opinions very similar to those of the Sadducee elite! How are we to accommodate this with all we know of the very different world view, theology, and social position of both movements?[10]

The important fact for us is that the letter uses the clear and distinct terminology of halakic polemic, including concepts hitherto unknown and others similar to Pharisaic-rabbinic tradition. I cite some of the latter:[11]

- The term *haarivut shemesh* or "sundown" required for completion of the purification procedure, in rabbinic parlance *heerev shemesh*; the rabbinic correlate *tevul yom* designates one who has immersed but until sunset is in an intermediate state of purity; it is a more subtle conception reportedly rejected by the Sadducees and, explicitly, by our letter;
- the term *mutsakot*, closely related to rabbinic *nitsok*, meaning the stream of liquid being poured from one vessel into another, which according to Pharisaic reasoning preserved in the Mishna *does not* convey impurity (mYad 4.7), but both in the eyes of the Sadducees also cited there *and according to our letter* does transport impurity;
- the words designating halakic practice *al gav* or "in communion" with other persons or movements; also used in rabbinic literature, for example of the "peaceful coexistence" of Shammaites and Hillelites despite their halakhic differences (mYev 1:4).

The expression last mentioned is used in a most remarkable sentence, stating that "we" of the sect "separated" (*parashnu*) from the majority of the people and refrain from observance "in communion with those (others)."[12] This is stating the sect's separatism, and it stands in clear opposition to the Pharisaic pluralism as summarized in Hillel's dictum, "Do not separate (*tifrosh*) from the community" (mAv 2:4).

This draws our attention to the polemical character of the letter, which is born out in the dialectical terminology. Typical expressions are: "But on (. . .) we say (*we-al . . . anahnu omrim*)"; "but on (. . .) we think (*we-al . . . anahnu hoshwim*)"; "but they . . . (*we-hema*)"; "and you know . . . (*we-atem yodim*)." These phrases, and especially the verb *amar*, relate to rabbinic dialectics. A parallel is found in Jesus' polemical statements, "You have heard that it was said to the Elders . . . *but I say* to you . . ." (Mt 5:21–48).[13]

To sum up, the Qumran letter both confirms and challenges our image of the diverse halakic positions of Pharisees, Sadducees, and Essenes; it testifies to the very early existence of developed halakic terminology and dialectics, and it is the hardest possible evidence of halakic correspondence somewhere in the second century B.C.E.

A Halakic Letter to NonJews (1 Corinthians)

The alternative approach on Paul inaugurated by A. Schweitzer includes the view that for Paul the law was not per se a negative entity.[14] From here it is one further step to go on and ask whether his letters do not contain positive affirmations of Jewish law or, in other words, halakah, particularly in the parenetic or practically instructive sections. On this basis, I found 1 Corinthians to be an especially resourceful document. This concurs with previous observations on 1 Corinthians as being a letter of outspokenly practical, not to say "legalistic" or even "Jewish" character.[15]

While 1 Cor 1–4 and 15–16 treat of personal and pastoral themes, chapters 5–14 extensively expound a series of practical questions. In part this is in response to written questions: "Now as to the things you wrote about . . ." (7:1). Further captions announcing new issues appear: "Now as to the unmarried . . ." (7:25); "Now as to the idol sacrifices . . ." (8:1); "Now as to the gifts of grace . . ." (12:1); "Now as to the collection for the saints . . ." (16:1). In addition to written questions, Paul responds to oral reports, possibly originating from "those of Chloe" (1:11) who might also have brought the letter from Ephesus. This concerns the issues of sexual morality (chs. 5–6), traditions relating to worship (ch. 11), and other themes.

It appears that the written questions were preceded by other correspondence.[16] In connection with the unchastity case (chs. 5–6) Paul refers to a previous letter of his: "I wrote *to* you in my letter . . ." (5:9). Furthermore he calls the Corinthian Christians his "children" (4:14) and "the seal of my apostleship" (9:3). This allows us to see Paul as the apostolic founder of the Corinthian church (cf Acts 18:118). Thus this previous letter, the questions written from

Corinth, and 1 Corinthians itself, show us this "apostle of Jesus Christ" (1:1) in his authoritative relationship with the church of his foundation. The absoluteness of his authority is expressed in his staunch verdict on the perpetrator of unchastity (1 Cor 5:3–5).

I stated that Paul's directives are based on halakic traditions. This needs qualification, since halakah denotes the law tradition which in its various branches exclusively applies to the Jewish people. Pharisaic-rabbinic tradition also knew the concept of universal commandments which, while varying in number, from the late second century onwards were termed the "commandments of the children of Noah."[17] The hard core of these coincide with the three central commandments a Jew may never transgress even at the cost of his death: the prohibitions of idolatry, unchastity, and bloodshed. In various forms this tradition is at least as ancient as the book of Jubilees, and of course it has a biblical foothold in the prohibition of bloodshed and blood consumption given to Noah and his progeny in Genesis 9. Apart from rabbinic literature it is also reflected in a range of Greek-Jewish and Jewish-Christian writings touching on relations between Jews and non-Jews. The account in Acts 15 undoubtedly belongs in this category.

Here, however, we run into a minefield of exegetical complications. But while proceeding with care, especially when defusing some of these rather outdated explosive devices, we need not lose our basic direction. True, Acts is not Paul and it portrays Paul in a light different from his own letters. For one thing, we must note the absence in Paul of any reference to the apostolic decree. This does not, however, of necessity imply that Paul was antinomian and anti-Jewish; we have noted the theological biases at work behind such views. Having in mind the idea of a minimum of commandments for all found in a variety of Hebrew, Greek-Jewish, and Jewish-Christian writings, and adding Acts to the lot, we are perfectly justified in asking once again whether Paul's letters to do not contain positive reflections of Jewish law. If so, they would be reproducing some version of the universal code, without mentioning an apostolic decree. The reasons for this silence may vary, from the fantasy of the author of Acts to restrictions imposed on Paul by his conflict with some Jewish brethren over the actual commandments applicable to gentile Christians.

An important element which I cannot elaborate on here is the conclusion that all of Paul's letters, including Romans, read as if addressing gentile Christians only. This conclusion lines up with Paul's self-description as 'the apostle of the gentiles' (Rom 11:13) and his report of the full support given to his "gospel to the uncircumcised" by the Jerusalem apostles (Gal 2:1–10).

I think we made our way through the minefield alive and are free now to address the main question: where is halakah found in 1 Corinthians? Again I skip detailed analysis and jump to the conclusions listing the halakhot I found in the successive sections of 1 Corinthians:

- A halakah prohibiting cohabitation with one's stepmother (1 Cor 5); Several halakot concerning marital sex, divorce, and remarriage (1 Cor 7, incl. v. 10f, v. 39: Apostolic tradition, "the Lord");
- A halakah on sustenance of Apostles (1 Cor 9, "the Lord");
- A halakah defining when gentile Christians should abstain from pagan food because of idolatry (1 Cor 10);
- Two halakot about women during worship, prescribing their head covering and declaring their incompetence for public offices (1 Cor 11 and 14, apostolic tradition);
- Some halakot concerning table order implied in the Eucharist tradition (1 Cor 11, "the Lord");
- Halakot concerning benedictions, their translation and acclamation, and the "representative of the community" (1 Cor 14).

Extremely interesting conclusions for the history of the halakah, of Judaism in general, and of earliest Christianity should not detain us here— such as the evidence of halakah formulated in Greek; the strict halakah on divorce similar to that found in Qumran; and the halakic tradition from the apostles and especially Jesus ("the Lord") as being Paul's supreme authority. I restrict myself to concluding that 1 Corinthians, a letter addressing gentile believers in Jesus as Messiah, answers questions of practical conduct and in so doing relies on halakic traditions; that it proves Paul's persistently positive relationship to Jewish tradition; and that it is a halakic letter to non-Jews of around 55 C.E.

Halakic Letters in Rabbinic Literature

The main part of this paper confronts material of a quite different disposition. 4QMMT and 1 Corinthians each in their way represent entire, real letters. But the numerous reflections of letters contained in rabbinic literature not only are all very brief but also are part and parcel of the discourse of the rabbinic works at hand. In order to evaluate them correctly, we must adjust our perception to the peculiarities of this literature.

First and foremost, a concentration on the correct formulation and teaching of halakah characterizes rabbinic literature—as distinct from early halakic collections (Mishna, Tosefta, Palestinian and Babylonian Talmud). This evokes sophisticated educational and administrative frameworks: academies for teaching and formulating halakah and actual jurisdiction, both in Palestine and Babylonia; the existence of recognized legal authorities and procedures of ordination, and standardized administrative, juridical, and academic procedures.

Then, there is the characteristic brevity of formulation. Concentrating on the essential and the easily memorizeable, the talmudic redactor would tend to omit epistolary embellishment. Also, the original questions and answers may have been re-worded and adapted to the talmudic discussion in which they are quoted. Talmudic dialectics have a certain conventionalism which opts for familiar and effective formulae. This includes epistolary formulae, the authenticity of which may then be hard to decide on. Yet one sometimes comes across unusual formulations which have the smell of the authentic. Furthermore, there is the tendency towards the legendary, especially in the Babylonian Talmud. It must be soberly distinguished from the possibility that indeed historical events are reflected, especially in the unexplainable or seemingly redundant. Finally, there is the difficult question whether a certain message was "sent" by word of mouth, which was entirely imaginable in a culture of oral study, or in writing.

When deliberating on a legal case or studying the text of the Mishna, the Amoraim or later rabbinic teachers would take their cue from the ceremonious oral recitation by so-called *tannaim*, official memorizers who functioned as oral study-books. But in addition we hear of notes and letters being consulted, and since these apparently embodied diverse traditions, they caused another complexity for textual critics. These phenomena are discussed by J. N. Epstein in his *Mavo lenosah ha-Mishna*, an exhaustive introduction (*Einleitung*) to the textual criticism of the Mishna on the basis of penetrating redaction, tradition, and reception criticism.[18] More central to our theme is the importance of halakic letters in the rabbinic discussion, especially in the Babylonian academies, and their influence which sometimes is visible in the literary structure of the end result, i.e., the *sugya* or talmudic pericope of the Babylonian Talmud.

Let us now turn to the texts. The following is based on a partial survey which did not include all of the important but the more inaccessible material from the Palestinian Talmud. This is vital since we seem to be dealing with a divergence between Babylonia and Palestine. Therefore my conclusions are provisional. I develop my theory step by step while citing examples.

1.

Judging from the extant sources, numerous letters were written from Palestine instructing Babylonian teachers about the correct formulation, interpretation, or decision of specific halakot from the Mishna or some parallel compilation. Outstanding are the letters written by Rabin (early fourth century) and other so-called *nehute* or envoys who traveled from Babylonia to Palestine in order to study the Palestinian law tradition and check it against the Babylonian. The way these letters are quoted unmistakably reflects the superior authority assigned to Palestinian teaching. Thus we find four traditions (one being cited twice) brought into the discussion in the Babylonian Talmud as follows: "But this is how Rabin sent by way of his letter. . ."[19] To these, seven traditions can be added in which it is merely said that Rabin "sent," but with the name of his authority being added, one of these figuring in three separate contexts: "Now Rabin sent in the name of Rabbi so and so . . ."[20] A prominent name in these traditions, as also in many similar traditions "sent" by others than Rabin, is that of R. Yohanan, the late third-century leader of Palestinian Amoriam.[21] At best one example deserves to be quoted; remarkably, it transmits prayer formulations which are still in use at the present day:[22]

> Rav Hiya son of Rav Huna sent in the name of Rabbi Yohanan: Concerning the arm phylacteries one says, "Blessed be He who sanctified us by his commandments and commanded us to put on phylacteries"; concerning the head phylacteries one says, "Blessed be He who sanctified us by his commandments and commanded us concerning the commandment of phylacteries."

The inference I am making is that, as in the first five cases where "letters" are mentioned explicitly, so also in the other instances in the Babylonian Talmud, the Aramaic verb *shelah* denotes "to send by letter." I return to this later.

2.

As we see, this phenomenon is evidenced most frequently in Babylonian contexts. In addition to the authority of Palestinian teaching, the geographical distance between Babylonia and Palestine must have been decisive. A couple of times we find partners in lively legal discussions appealing to "a letter from the West"—i.e., Palestine—confirming their position, without an actual quotation being given.[23] However, the phenomenon existed also in Palestinian circles. In one passage of rather enigmatic contents, the Palestinian Talmud cites Rabbi Hizkia as saying in the midst of a halakic discussion: "But I read a letter in which it was written . . ."[24]

3.

A similar situation leads the Babylonian teachers to ask the fundamental question whether it is allowed to write down halakah at all. In fact, this is the major talmudic passage discussing the principle of Oral as distinct from

Written Torah, and it revolves on the permissibility of *letters*. It involves
Rabin's best-known colleague-ambassador to Palestine, Rav Dimi, and has to
do with rules for offerings (mTem 2:1).[25]

> . . . But thus said Rav Yosef: exclude libation offerings
> from this mishna. When Rav Dimi went (to Palestine) he
> found Rav Yirmeya sitting and teaching in the name of R.
> Yoshua ben Levi (. . .) Said he: if I found now (someone
> who is going there),[26] I would write a letter and send to
> Rav Yosef that libation offerings should not be excluded
> from this mishna. (. . .)

> But if he had a letter, would he be allowed to send it? Did
> not R. Ammi son of R. Hiya bar Abba say in the name of
> R. Yohanan: Those who write halakot are like those who
> burn the Tora (. . .) Thus taught R. Yehuda bar Nahmani,
> the interpreter of Resh Lakish: (. . .) Things oral you may
> not recite from writing, and things written down you may
> not recite orally.

> (. . .) They said: But was this a new matter? It is differ-
> ent. For behold, R. Yohanan and Resh Lakish were once
> looking into a book of aggada on Shabbat, and they
> explained this as follows: "A time to act for the Lord, for
> they undid thy Tora" (Ps 119:126)—said they: It is better
> that the Tora be uprooted (i.e. changed) than that the Tora
> be forgotten from Israel.

This discussion has a theoretical character, for it seems certain that the
Mishna itself had been committed to writing in R. Yohanan's days.[27] What he
and his partner in discussion, Resh Lakish, must have meant is the prohibition, apparently still held in their day, to write *targumim* and *berakot*, vernac-
ular Tora translations and prayers. But halakhot were written on notes stored

in the academy's archives and in letters sent to colleagues.[28] What remained, in parallel to the prayers and *targumim* in the synagogue, was the oral recitation during academy sessions—a ceremonious custom which endured into the Gaonic era.

4.

Another story mentions letters apparently also of halakic content which R. Yohanan in Palestine wrote over the years to Rav and Shmuel, founding heads of the two great academies in Babylonia. To the extent that this story, which adds irony to legend, reflects actual history, it shows us a question-answer exchange oriented towards Babylonia, around the middle of the third century:[29]

> All the years of Rav's life, Rabbi Yohanan was writing to him: "To the honor of our Master in Babylonia." When he deceased, he wrote to Shmuel: "To the honor of our Col league in Babylonia." Said the latter: "Doesn't he know I am his teacher?" He wrote and sent him the calculation of intercalation for sixty years (. . .) He also wrote and sent him twelve camel-loads of *kashrut* questions (. . .)

5.

A case in the Yerushalmi refers us to the Palestinian scene, yet another generation back. Rabbi Hiya the Elder passed a question, addressed to him while in Southern Palestine, on to Rabbi, i.e., Rabbi Yehuda the Prince who resided in Galilee in the early third century. The latter answered: "Go and write to them . . ." An identical case involving Rabbi follows in the continuation.[30]

Another interesting story, also from the Palestinian Talmud and involving the same protagonists, allows a glance into the material circumstances of halakic correspondence. It has to do with debts residing on inherited real estate which the heirs subsequently sold or mortgaged:[31]

> Rav wrote to Rabbi: they transgress (read "they act", or:
> "a letter") in respect of the opinion of R. Hiya the Elder.
> For R. Hiya wrote between the lines: If the orphans arose
> and sold it, one collects (the debt) from their livelihood
> but not from their nourishment. If they arose and gave it
> in pledge—as to this pledge I do not know what about it.

This report, however brief, has the touch of the authentic, exactly in its obscurity. The words, "I do not know what about it," are everything but standard. The same case seems reflected in the Babylonian Talmud, but with a different disposition of opinions, a phenomenon met with more often and usually involving imprecision caused by the distance in place and time. The formulation is no less enigmatic:[32]

> Rav appended to Rabbi between the threads (or, lines) (a
> question): If the brothers gave it in pledge, what about it?
> R. Hiya was sitting before him and asked: Did they sell or
> mortgage it? (He answered:)[33] What does this alter?
> Whether they mortgaged or sold it, one may levy from the
> livelihood but not from the nourishment.

Medieval explanations vary from the halakic question having been "appended" to a letter of payment, "stitched between" a row of other written questions, to having been inserted between a batch of deeds.[34] However that may be, and whether it was Rav or R. Hiya who "appended" or "wrote between the lines," it seems the halakic questions came along with other written information. This informality, not to say "marginality," seems significant.

6.

Up till now, we have been reviewing written halakic questions and answers exchanged between Rabbi-colleagues, even if this was not stated explicitly. There are also traces of questions written by communities of simple Jews to what they considered to be halakic authorities.

The men of Kashkar sent to Levi: A curtain, what about it? Kashuta cucumbers in the vineyard, what about it? A corpse on a festival day, what about it?[35]

Levi was of the generation of Rabbi and known for his knowledge of Tannaic traditions. The brevity of expression may be the narrator's or redactor's work. From the context, the following appears to be meant: Is drawing a curtain allowed on shabbat? Do kashuta cucumbers make a prohibited mix with vines? Is it allowed to care for the dead on festival days? This is how the report continues:

> When Levi died and his spirit went to rest, Shmuel said to
> Rav Menasia: If you know (what to say), send to them. He
> sent to them: A curtain—we checked on all aspects of the
> curtain, but found no aspect of permission (. . .) The
> kashuta cucumber in the vineyard: a (forbidden) mix (. . .)
> A corpse— he sent to them: the dead, let no one care for
> them (. . .)

I left out the later comments inserted after each answer, to the effect that more differentiated answers would have been appropriate, and which each time are concluded with the words: ". . . but they were no sons of Torah," i.e., not learned.

7.

We have been reviewing rabbinic texts from the generation of Rabbi Yehuda the Prince onwards, i.e., from around 200 C.E. There is earlier rabbinic evidence of halakic correspondence, but it is few and far between. This paucity must be correctly assessed. First of all, the further one goes back, the less detailed the information about the contributors to Pharisaic-rabbinic tradition becomes. This makes it necessary for us to retroject later situations under the cautious guidance of external evidence. Letters on varying subjects were written in circles close to Pharisaic and early rabbinic Judaism, as is archeologically testified by the Bar Kokhba letters. Written deeds—a genre closely related to halakic letters—are also well in evidence, both in the literary and the archeological sources. The letters of the former Pharisee, Paul, are certainly a significant piece of evidence in this context. Finally, the Qumran letter shows the existence of a fully developed halakic epistolary genre another two centuries earlier.

This places the early rabbinic evidence in perspective.[36] First there is mention of letters from the Great Court in Jerusalem in the tradition cited by R. Yehuda in the Mishna and the Tosefta regarding the capital trial and punishment of false prophets and the like: "They used to execute him at once, and to write and send to all places . . ."[37]

Next there are the rather extensive Hebrew and/or Aramaic letters reportedly sent by Shimon ben Gamliel and/or his son Gamliel the Second, together with Yohanan ben Zakkai, during the last days of the Second Temple, on the subjects of fourth-year tithes and intercalation.[38] The authority assumed by the writers is remarkable and reflects their official function. The Hebrew version is most specific here:

> From Shimon ben Gamliel and from Yohanan ben Zakkai,
> to our brethren in the South, the Upper and Lower, and to
> Shahlil and the seven districts of the South: Peace! Let it
> be known to you . . . (follows the halakic message). And
> we did not begin to write you but our fathers had been
> writing to your fathers.

A story of one or two generations earlier still, well attested in the sources,[39] involves a halakic question which could have been sent in writing:

> Once, Yohanan ben Bag-Bag sent to (*etsel*) R. Yehuda ben
> Batera in Nisibis and said: I heard about you that you say,
> "An Israelite woman who is betrothed to a priest may eat
> of the heave offering." He sent to him: I used to be sure
> about you that you are acquainted with the inner chambers
> of the Torah—but to develop a *Kal wahomer* midrash is

> beyond you? Now as in the case of a Canaanite woman slave . . .

The personal names used here appear in various generations, and the title "Rabbi" given to Yehuda in all versions may or may not be original. But in view of our external evidence this report is not historically improbable by any means. The distance between Palestine and Nisibis seems sufficiently long to have necessitated a written note to be given to the messenger. In fact, a report on another letter written to this teacher from Jerusalem figures in the Babylonian Talmud: "They sent to R. Yehuda ben Batera: Peace to you, R Yehuda ben Bateira, for you are in Nisibis but your net is spread in Jerusalem."[40]

8.

My impression is that the Pharisaic and early Tannaic teachers wrote on halakic matters just as their later Amoraic colleagues, though less systematically and in any case with fewer records in the rabbinic sources.

We do have the references to legal documents sent through messengers; the few mentions refer to a legal practice which must have been standard and frequent. Second, the Rabban (Shimon ben) Gamliel letters are a clear example of another specific kind, transmitting authoritative instruction addressed to extensive regions; these can be called encyclical letters.[41] Nor is their subject accidental: calendar affairs were decided on by the Palestinian Patriarchate till its abrogation by the Byzantine emperor, and we may assume that similar letters were sent all along, certainly to the diaspora.[42] Third, we have the case of a practical question sent by a simple community to a distant authority. Fourth, there is the type of letters prominent in the later layers of the Babylonian Talmud: consultation of colleagues or former teachers on the clarification of the (Tannaic) halakah. This type is attested to for the generation of Rabbi Yehuda the Prince and ascribed already to Ben Bag-Bag. Its specifically Babylonian use must therefore be considered to be a development from a more general phenomenon.

This yields the following division:

(a) *legal documents* sent through a messenger by the court or private persons;

(b) *encyclical letters*, most specifically involving calendar decisions by the Patriarch or Great Court;

(c) *practical questions* addressed by isolated communities to reputed authorities;

(d) *consultation of colleagues or former teachers* on the clarification of the (Tannaic) halakah, recorded especially in the Babylonian Talmud.

9.

A striking example of the function letters could have in later Babylonian talmudic discussion is found in *bBB 127b–129a*. De Mishna passage commented on concerns the accordance of the right of primogeniture (mBB 8:5). After a first survey, two precedents are cited and a collaterally related case is discussed. Then follows this exchange:

> Rava taught: "If two women (of one and the same husband) each bore a son in a (dark) hiding place, they write a declaration to each other (which is the firstborn).
>
> Then Rav Pappa said to him: But Ravin sent us [in his letter]:[43] "I asked all my teachers about this problem but they had nothing to say to me; but thus they teach in the name of R. Yannai: If it was known, but they were interchanged afterwards, they write a declaration, but if it was not known, they may not write a declaration."
>
> Thereupon Rava made his interpreter (*amora*) rise, and he taught: "What I had been teaching you was based on a mistake; but thus they taught in the name of R. Yannai . . ."
>
> The men of Akra de-Agma sent to Shmuel: "May our Master teach us . . ."

Rava and his younger colleague Rav Pappa were leading Babylonian Sages in the first half of the fourth century. This report, which appears to come straight from the academy, shows how the authority of the older Rava yields before a letter of Rabin containing a tradition of R. Yannai, a Palestinian Sage two generations earlier. Without any indication, there now follows the correspondence of the men from Akra de-Agma and Shmuel as a next element of discussion.

After a discussion of further implications, a series of seven "sent" halakot is then cited which touch on various subjects and are commented on one by one. Each of these items begins as follows: "R. Abba sent to Rav Yosef bar Hama: [A halakah] . . ." The combination of an identical address with varying contents gives the impression of a collection of halakot which was kept by Rav Yosef bar Hama and his successors, possibly in the archives of the academy. R. Abba flourished during the late third century in Palestine, Rav Yosef in Babylonia. The series is rounded off by a formal conclusion: "Mar Zutra taught in the name of Shimi bar Ashi: The halakah is as sent by R. Abba to Rav Yosef in each of these traditions."

We see how all of this Babylonian *sugya* is structured by a written halakic correspondence, among which the question of the community in Akra de-Agma stands out. Mar Zutra was the Babylonian exilarch at the beginning of the fifth century, when the basic text of the Babylonian Talmud approached its completion. Moreover his intervention indicates that R. Abba's written halakot were kept in an official archive at that time. These conclusions lead to the suspicion that written notes played a role more often when deciding on the correct halakah, and possibly also in the process of arresting the text of the Talmud and other rabbinic texts.[44]

10.

I must now go into the hypothesis voiced earlier: in the Babylonian Talmud the Aramaic verb *šelah* often conveys the meaning of "sending by letter." First of all, this fully parallels Greek *epistellein* and the noun which informed the theme of this epistolographic conference: *epistolé*.

Tannaic Hebrew *šalah* does not, as far as I see, by itself convey the meaning send by letter (see, however, notes 47 and 48). But it has another prime meaning which is closely related on the practical level: commission, send with a mandate, or send by a messenger. The corresponding substantives are *shelihut* for the mission or mandate, and *shaliah* or *shaluah* for the messenger or legal agent. Greek parallels here are *apostellein, apostolé* and *apostolos*; there is also *pempein*. A messenger would be entrusted with letters or credentials, especially if the commission has a legal aspect and the geographical and social distance is long. Thus Paul says he is going to "send" representatives "with letters" (1 Cor 16:3, *di' epistolon pempso*), just as he himself is reported to have received commissioning letters from the high priest earlier in his career (Acts 9:2). This concurs with the Tannaic expression *korvin wesholhin*, "they write and send by messenger."

"Sending" a message of halakic content orally would be possible only if the messenger was something of a *tanna*, a specialist to whom rabbinic traditions were entrusted orally. The so-called *nehutei* or travelers who brought traditions from the Palestinian academies to Babylonia may have had this quality. But, as we saw, it was precisely they and their most famous representative, Rabin, who are said to have "sent" written messages, in between their oral reportings.

A written document must be involved in the case of missives from the court and similar messages of legal or official halakic content; we saw some examples. This also appears from the fact that *iggeret* means not just letter but "deed" or "document" in general, as expressed in such compounds as *iggeret shevukin* or "deed of divorce" issued by the husband (mGit 9:3) or *iggeret bikoret* or public announcement of the sale of goods circulated by the court.[45]

Whether *shalah* means to send in writing or orally can often be inferred only from the character of the message and the circumstances. My impression is that certainly the many Babylonian Amoraic references to traditions "sent" from the West must concern written messages. That this was a standard procedure appears, in addition to the references I mentioned already, from some 30 occurrences of the expression that "they sent from there," *shalhu mi-tam* or *mihatam*, i.e., from Palestine to Babylonia, sometimes with the specification:

"the halakah is according to . . ." or "not according to . . ."[46] These were decisory letters referred to in passing without quoting them, and tacitly accepted as authoritative by the disputants. Among the circumstances which help deciding in favor of the meaning "send in writing" is certainly the distance, as I observed several times already.

So far the meaning "send by letter" for *shelah* seems specific of Babylonian, not Palestinian, usage.[47] Instead, the Palestinian Talmud uses *shelah ketav* (*mishleh ketev*) or simply *ketav*.[48]

There remain certain margins of uncertainty. Both in the Babylonian and the Palestinian Talmud I found messages involving *ketav* where the parallel has *emar*.[49] Moreover, the ceremonious response which R. Ammi sent to them, *shelah lehu*, is introduced with the frequent expression *ba'u mineh*, "they asked of him." How many times do *ba'u mineh* and the corresponding *emar lehu* conceal the exchange of letters? But these are positive margins: they open the theoretical possibility that many more halakic letters were actually exchanged than those we hear of.

11.

Finally, I sort out the epistolary formulae I found in the rabbinic material.

a) I came across an ordinary greeting in a rather dramatic episode involving a letter which is not halakic in content:[50] *Shelah leh Rav Anan leRav Huna*: "Huna havrin shelam!" "Rav Anan sent to Rav Huna: 'Huna our friend, peace!'" This concurs with the greetings listed by P.S. Alexander.[51] It clearly shows *shelah* as meaning "send by letter."

b) I cited already the honorific address formulae R. Yohanan is reported to have used when addressing Rav: *Li-kedam rabbenu sheba-Bavel*, "To the honor of our master in Babylonia"; and the variant he used to write to Rav's colleague, Shmuel: *Li-kedam haverenu sheba-Bavel*, "To the honor of our colleague in Babylonia."[52] The deferential preposition *kedam* is used in relation to God in the Targumim.

c) Several times we find a question being introduced with the formula: *Yelammedenu rabbenu . . .*, "Let our master teach us."[53] This deferential address was standard to the extent that it caused a definite type of aggadic midrash to be called *Yelammedenu*. It typically opens with a simple halakic question introduced by this formula, which is then used as a peg for ramified aggadic expositions.

d) Questions are typically ended with the question marker *mahu?*[54] or *mani?*[55] "What about it?" And, *ma tiva*, "What is its nature?"[56] Or, after an exposition of the case, the introduction of the actual question: *mahu she* . . . ? "What if . . . ?"[57] This is also attested of questions addressed orally and reflects general usage.

e) R. Ammi's reported response to a question addressed to him[58] starts with the festive opening: *Minni Ammi bar Natan Tora tetse le-kol Yisrael*, "From me, Ammi bar Natan, Torà goes forth to all of Israel."[59] This certainly reflects the honors claimed by the leader of the Tiberian academy.[60]

f) The Rabban Gamliel letters contain two versions of the authoritative instructional introduction involving the verb *yada: yadua yehe lakem*, "Let it be known to you", or *mehodana lekhon*, "We make it known to you." In the Babylonian Talmud we often find: *hawwu yodin*, "Be ye knowing."[61]

Concluding Remarks

I start with a general observation: in all cases, written correspondence must be seen as a natural extension of communication in person. This is illuminated by the *nehute*, the more or less official representatives who in their person were to form the link with Palestinian teaching, and whom we found to be among the better known letter-writers. Letters were an instrument of legal proof or an *aide-mémoire* in the hands of a personal messenger. This holds for all ancient letters, including Paul's (see 1 Cor 5).[62]

The increased evidence of inter-collegial consultative letters in the Babylonian Talmud is intriguing and asks for an explanation. It seems that it must be sought in the vicissitudes of the formulation process of halakah and, paradoxically, of the authority of Palestinian teaching. During the Tannaic period, Pharisaic-rabbinic halakah was taking on definite form, but it was far from uniform. Divergent traditions existed side by side, such as that of Shammaites and Hillelites, without the need to decide (the story of the one-time decision according to the School of Hillel is mere legend).[63] At this time, interpretation of previous halakah was a matter of discussion and dissent. But in the later Amoraic period, the Mishna had become the central halakic document and its correct interpretation a first preoccupation. Meanwhile the distant Babylonian academies had risen to importance, which involved communication problems and certainly necessitated extensive use of letters. The enduring authority of Palestinian teaching accounted for a predominantly oneway direction of the questions and answers.

Incidentally, this explanation throws light on the relationship between Palestine and the Greek diaspora in earlier days, which involved frequent communication also in the field of halakah; the use of letters and other written documents must have been equally indispensable. The difference is that no Alexandrian Talmud has been preserved, nor indeed do we have indications that something similar was developing when Alexandrian Jewry was extinguished during the insurgence of 115–117 C.E. Therefore the remarkable preservation of so many traces of halakic letters within later Amoraic Babylonian tradition seems to be the result of the rise to dominion of Babylonian Jewry and its Talmud during the subsequent Gaonic period.

It was during this post-talmudic period that the type of correspondence arose which nineteenth century scholars termed Responsa literature. Circumstances had changed: the dominance of the Palestinian Patriarchate had been replaced by the Babylonian Gaonate, and the clarification process of the Mishna had been summarized into a Babylonian Talmud. From all over the world, questions in all areas of life including halakah were sent to the Geonim in their splendid authority. Their numerous responses came to constitute a new stage in the history of Jewish literature. Two examples which mark the advent of a new era deserve mention: the description of synagogue prayers contained in Rav Amram's *responsum*, and the history of talmudic tradition given in Rav Sherira's letter.

In one aspect there is a closer comparison with the legal *responsa* of early imperial Rome, which lent their name to the Gaonic *responsa*. One of Emperor Augustus's innovations was the investment of a class of authorized lawyers with the *jus respondendi*: they were awarded an official, strategic function in deciding and formulating imperial law.[64] While the aspect of central authority more resembles the Gaonic situation, the creation and accumulation of these socalled *quaestiones, responsa, epistulae,* or *digesta* and their importance for the codification process is reminiscent of the type of letters so often found in the Babylonian Talmud: intercollegiate consultation on the clarification of halakah. Decisive differences need not be ignored: in the Jewish context there never was anything comparable to the Emperor's power, and during the Tannaic and Amoraic periods the formulation of halakah could emerge only from the interaction of divergent, inherited traditions alive within the community.

Overviewing all the material, my final impression is that early letters of halakic content such as 4QMMT, Yohanan ben Bag-Bag's correspondence, 1 Corinthians, Acts 15, and (Shimon ben) Gamliel's encyclical letters are diverse and incidental in character and do not yield one category. Starting from the classification I proposed for the halakic letters preserved in rabbinic literature, the following overall division could be made, here integrating the material from all sources:

a) *Legal missives*: document sent via a messenger by the court or private persons (cf. mSan 10:4; tSan 11:7; 1 Cor 16:3; Acts 9:2);

b) *Encyclical letters*: the (Shimon ben) Gamliel letters; the Apostolic letter (Acts 15);

c) *Practical questions and responses*: to the Jews of Kashkar (bShab 139a); to the Jews of Akra de-Agma (bBB 127b); to the non-Jewish Christians of Corinth (1 Cor);

d) *Consultation of colleague-halakists*: especially most of the letters reflected in later Babylonian Amoraic text layers, but in evidence since the beginning of the era;

e) *Adhortations on halakic topics with polemical aim*: 4QMMT (on calendar, temple procedures, priests—against Pharisees); Galatians (on circumcision for gentile Christians, against "judaizing" Christians, i.e., those proselytizing for life according to Jewish law).

ENDNOTES

Scripture references are the author's own translation.

1. Cf A. W. Boeckh, whose program of classical philology influenced both Jewish and Christian historical scholarship: *Encyclopädie und Methodologie der philologischen Wissenschaften* (Berlin 1886) p. 5S: 'Das absolute Verstehen behandelt die *Hermeneutik*, das relative die *Kritik*.' "Kritik" implied textual and literary criticism, "Hermeneutik" linguistic, stylistic, and historical interpretation. Without being preposterous we can now add that this needs adjustment in view of the interpreter's "historical" position.

2. ARN a 15 (ed. Schechter fol. 31a); ARN b 29 (ib); bShab 31a.

3. Similarly, Boeckh (see note 1) defined philology as "das Erkennen des vom menschlichen Geist *Produzierten*, d. h. des *Erkannten*" (p. 10, italics in original).

4. E. Qimron, J. Strugnell, "An Unpublished Halakic Letter from Qumran," in J. Amitai, e.a., *Biblical Archeology Today. Proceedings, International. Congress on Biblical Archeology* (Jerusalem, 1984), pp. 400–407. Publication followed ten years later: E. Qimron and J. Strugnell, *Qumran Cave 4*, V: MIQSAT MA'ASE HA-TORAH, (DJD 10). Oxford 1994.

5. Y. Sussman, "The History of the Halakha in the Dead Sea Scrolls: A Preliminary to the Publication of 4QMMT," *Tarbiz* 59 (1990): pp. 11–76 (Hebr); L. H. Schiffman, '*Miqsat ma'aseh haTora* and the Temple Scroll,' *RdQ* 14 (1990): pp. 435–457; id, 'The Temple Scroll and the Systems of Jewish Law of the Second Temple Period,' in G. J. Brooke, ed., *Temple Scroll Studies: Papers Presented at the International Symposium on the Temple Scroll.* (JSP Sup 7), (Sheffield, 1989), pp. 239–255. Sussman's paper appeared in somewhat shorter form in English in Strugnell-Qimron, *Qumran Cave 4*, pp. 179–200. See also E. Qimron, "The Halakha," ib., pp. 123–177 (124–130, bibliography).

6. For a recent study on publication of letters in antiquity, see David Trobisch, *Die Entstehung der Paulusbriefsammlung: Studien zu den*

Anfängen christlicher Publizistik. Novum Testamentum et Orbis Antiquus 10. Freiburg (CH)/Göttingen, 1989.

7. See Qimron-Strugnell, "An Unpublished Halakhic Letter from Qumran," n. 5; Sussman, n. 62.

8. E.g., E. P. Sanders, *Jewish Law between Jesus and the Mishnah: Five Studies*, London-Philadelphia, 1990, *passim*; see my review in *JSJ* 12 (1991), 274–283.

9. *War* 2: pp. 162–166; Ant 13: pp. 288, 297f; 18: pp. 12–17.

10. Schiffman, 'Temple Scroll' (n. 5 above), stresses the slightly separate position of 4QMMT and 11QTemp over against other sectarian documents. Sussman (n.5 above) considers the identity of *Baitusin*, "Boethusians" (hitherto seen as a Sadducee sub-group) with "Essenes," an explanation proposed in 1953 by Y. M. Grintz and ultimately descending from Azaria de Rossi in 1575—see Sussman, n.141 and J. M. Baumgarten, "Halakhic Polemics in New Fragments from Qumran Cave 4," in *Biblical Archeology Today* (above n. 4), (pp. 390–399) p. 399, n. 32. For the broader evidence on the identity of the Sadducees, see M. Stern, 'Aspects of Jewish Society; the Priesthood and Other Classes,' in CRINT 1/2, (561–630) 600–612.

11. Qimron-Strugnell, "Unpublished Letter," pp. 403–406; Sussman p. 27.

12. Qimron-Strugnell, ib. p. 402f; Sussman p. 38f.

13. Cf also the tradition where R. Shimon ben Yohai cites four (nonhalakic) teachings in which he disagrees with his master, R. Akiva, saying: "R. Akiva interpreted . . . , *but I say* . . . , and I prefer my words over his" (tSot 6:6–10).

14. On this section see my *Paul and the Jewish Law: Halakha in the Letters of the Apostle to the Gentiles* (CRINT III/1) Assen-Philadelphia, 1990; introduction ibidem for history of research.

15. ib. 69.

16. J. C. Hurd, *The Origin of 1 Corinthians*, London 1965, remains indispensable.

17. See D. Flusser – S. Safrai, 'Das Aposteldekret und die Noahitischen Gebote', in E. Brocke and H. – J. Barkenings (eds), *Wer Tora vermehrt*,

mehrt Leben: Festgabe für Heinz Kremers zum 60. Geburtstag, Neukirchen-Vluyn 1960, pp. 173 192; and my *Paul and the Jewish Law*, pp. 50, 99, 178 181.

18. Mavo le-nosah ha-Mishna, Jerusalem 1948, rev. ed. 1964; pp. 673–726; specifically on letters p. 699f.

19. bKet 49a = bBB 139a (here interestingly involving Rava's opposition to the letter, ib. 139b, on the basis of yet another tradition); bBM 114a; bBB 127a (see below); bNid 63a.

20. bMen 57b and bHul 49b in the name of R. Yohanan; bSan 51a and bHul 101b in the name of R. Yose be-R. Hanina; bYev 48b and bBB 144b in the name of R. Ilai; bBB 135b = bBB 152 = bGit 9b in the name of R. Abbahu who quotes R. Elazar in the name of Rav.

21. See previous note: R. Yose be-R. Hanina was a student-colleague of R. Yohanan, and R. Ilai his most famous student. See also Rav Yitshak bar Yaakov bar Giori in the name of R. Yohanan (bEr 62a; bTaan 29b; bMK 18a; bKet 46a; bHul 101b); Rav Hanina in the name of R. Yohanan (bYev 58a; bMen 79b; bKer 27a); Rav Kahana in the name of R. Yohanan (bYev 46b); and see next note.

22. bMen 36a; ib 42b.

23. bShab 115a citing R. Yohanan; the others anonymous: bBB 41b; bSan 29a; bShevu 48b.

24. yNed 6, 39b.

25. bTem 14ab; of bGit 60ab. See Epstein ib. pp. 696, 701.

26. Thus Rabbenu Gershom's version; cf Rashi.

27. For these and the following remarks see Epstein ib.

28. See especially bHor 14b bottom.

29. bHul 95b, see version in *Iggeret de-Rav Sherira Gaon*, ed. Levin p. 81; Epstein p. 699.

30. yNed 3, 50c.

31. yGit S. 46d; for *avrun* ('brwn) Epstein ib p699 proposes to read *'avdun [te'avdun]* (t'bdwn); Kosovski, *Concordance* s.v. *'iggeret, 'igrin*.

32. bKet 69a. For the issue see mGit S:2; mKet 6:6.

33. Not in the Munich ms.

34. Rashi and the Tosafot clearly knew the Yerushalmi parallel; R. Yeshaya de- Trani (RY"D) seems to read *benei hoze* for *benei hitte*.
35. bShab 139a.
36. On the Tannaic evidence cf D. Pardee et al., *A Handbook of Ancient Hebrew Letters*; A Study Edition, Chico, 1982, pp. 183–211.
37. mSan 10:4; tSan 11:7. The formula, *kotvin wesholhin bekol hamekomot*, seems borrowed in bSan 88b.
38. Cf Pardee *ib.* pp. 184–96. These are either two sets of letters, one in Hebrew and another in Aramaic, or one set transmitted in both languages. MidrGad Deut 26:13 (ed. Margulies, p. 597f.)—two Hebrew letters to Galilee and the South about tithes from Shimon ben Gamliel and Yohanan ben Zakkai. The addresses of these letters are very detailed; also, the narrative introduction which involves R. Yoshua is remarkably specific (see also the word *hala*, Margulies *ib.* note to line 2). tSan 2:6; yMaasSh 5, 56c; ySan 1, 18d; bSan llb—three Aramaic letters from Gamliel and Yohanan, two on the same tithing issues and the third one written to the diaspora about intercalation.
39. SifN 117 (pl37); tKet S:1; yKet 5. 29d; bKid ib.
40. bPes 3b. See Pardee ib. pp. 203f.
41. Thus also P. S. Alexander, 'Epistolary Literature,' in M. E. Stone (ed), *Jewish Writings of the Second Temple Period.* (CRINT II/2), Assen/Maastricht/Philadelphia, 1984, pp. 579–596.
42. yEr 3, 21c mentions a letter sent by the Amora R. Yose to Alexandria "on the cycle of the festivals" (*katavnu lakem sidre moadot*).
43. Thus mss Munich and Hamburg, and R. Asher.
44. Written halakhot were used in Palestine before the Mishna was committed to writing, see bHor 14b in the archives of R. Meir and others, second half of the second century. See also bTem 14a–b; bGit 60 a–b, on which Epstein, ibid. 696, 701.
45. yMeg 4,75b: R. Yehuda bar Pazzi explains this Tannaic term as *akraza*, announcement.
46. E.g., bHul 59b; ib. 76b; bBB 135b.

47. bPes 3b ("they sent" to R. Yehuda ben Batera in Nisibis) is Babylonian adaptation of a Palestinian tradition.

48. yEr 3, 21c (both forms, cf. Ginzberg, *Yerushalmi Fragments*, 101); yMeg 3, 74 (quotes from 8 or 9 nonhalakic letters, both forms); yNed 3, 50c (*ketav*); yGit 5, 46d (*ketav*). yHag 1, 76c could involve *shelah* as "send by letter": after two messages exchanged via *šelah* the third goes by *shelah ketav* (but see next note!). Significantly bHul 95b about R. Yohanan preserves Palestinian usage.

49. Compare yHag 1, 76c on yPes 3, 30b; bNid 47b, two variants on the same page!; bBB 127a printed editions vs. ms. Hamburg. And cf. bBB 139a and bShevu 46a, *'emar* in answer to *shelah/shalhu*.

50. bKet 69a. The contents quoted are standard, the same sentence appearing four lines up in another reported letter. This makes the greeting contained here stand out.

51. See above, Endnote 42.

52. bHul 95b. Does the difference reflect Shmuel's nonordained status?

53. bShevu 46a; bBB 127b; bBB 139a.

54. bShevu 46a; bBB 127b; bBB 139a.

55. bYev 104b, referring to a *yevama*.

56. bShevu 48a.

57. bGit 44a; bBM 114a; bBB 165b.

58. The formula *ba'u minei* here appears to imply a written question!

59. bGit 44a, ms. Munich; cf. versions quoted by Rashi, Rabbenu Asher, and R. Yeshaya deTrani.

60. Of course it echoes Isa 2:3, but through the mediation of tHag 2:9 (and parallels, see Lieberman a.l.), *misham halakha (Tora) yotset urowahat beYisrael.* And cf bNed 81a *hizharu bivene eniyim shemehen teitsei Tora.*

61. bRH 20a, R. Yehuda Nesia interestingly instructing R. Ammi about R. Yohanan's usual teaching; bB8 135b, 152a, introducing a decisive teaching of R. Elazar.

62. Similarly Pardee (*Handbook*, p. 2) defines a letter as "a written docu-
     ment effecting communication between two or more persons who can-
     not communicate orally."

63. S. Safrai, 'The Decision according to the School of Hillel in Yavneh,'
     Proceedings, World Congress of Jewish Studies 7/3 (1981), pp. 21–44
     (in Hebrew).

64. See W. Kunkel, *Römische Rechtsgeschichte: Eine Einführung*, 5th ed.
     Cologne-Graz, 1967, pp. 103–108, 113f.

CONVERSATION SIX

A Response to Peter J. Tomson
BARBARA E. BOWE

Readers are indebted to Peter Tomson for this paper in which he examines common halakic elements found in the letter from Qumran known as 4QMMT, in Paul's first letter to Corinth, and in the selected examples from the Rabbinic literature of the post-200 C.E. era as illustrated in both the Palestinian and the Babylonian Talmud. That these sources all reflect some form of what Tomson calls "inter-collegial consultative letters" is surely true, although their variety in form and content argues against any fixed formal stereotypes at this early date. Common patterns do emerge in what Tomson identifies at the end of his paper as five different types of material: "a) legal missives, b) encyclical letters, c) practical questions and responses, d) consultation of colleague-halakists, and e) adhortations on halakic topics with polemical aim."

In responding to Tomson's paper, I'd like to raise a number of issues that, for me, still remain in need of clarification before we are permitted to draw conclusions about common halakic traditions or common epistolary methods. The first concerns the comments on the nature of letters at the opening of his paper. That letters are historical sources open to widely divergent interpretations and not "hard" sources with transparent meanings is, as Tomson notes, the essential starting point for any discussion of these texts. Tomson's five "types," noted above, in themselves point to very different forms of communication between sender and addressee, and each type yields very different degrees of halakic teaching. Reviewing this material, several questions pose themselves and beg for an answer. How precisely are we to draw the distinctions among these five different types of material? When, for example, Paul responds to various practical questions (Tomson, "type c") in 1 Corinthians

5–14, is he not at the same time adopting a polemical stance (Tomson, "type e")
towards other opinions held in the community? And how can we be sure that
halakhic topics are presented *in response to* specific questions generated
among the addressees (Tomson, "type d"), rather than judge them as authoritative initiatives sent from an individual to a group for the purposes of establishing control over the conduct of the group? Even the so-called formal
indicator *peri de* (1 Cor 7:1, 25; 8:1, 4; 12:1) of Paul's first Corinthian letter
cannot be used to establish with certainty that each of the topics so introduced
responds specifically to a question posed by the Corinthians.[1] The matter is
more complex. As Antoinette Wire has suggested in the case of Paul, it could
just as easily be argued that "Paul is not so much answering questions put to
him as he is '*questioning answers*' that found currency in the community and
challenged his leadership and authority."[2]

A second issue that calls for further clarification is the one implied
above: namely, the nature and the effect of the polemical and/or rhetorical
character of the examples surveyed. 4QMMT offers Tomson an excellent
illustration of a polemical letter. Its repeated phrases and dialectical terminology ("But on (. . .) we say (*we-al . . . anahnu omrim*)"; "but on (. . .) we
think (*we-al . . . anahnu hoshwim*)"; "and you know . . . (*we-atem yodim*)"
signal, he maintains, the kind of exchanges common in Rabbinic dialectics.
But as is the case with all such one-sided polemical evidence, one cannot
assume that the position or opinion implied or *attributed* to the addressees
reflects their actual position. Nor can one say with certainty that the matters
debated were of equal significance to both parties implied in the exchange. As
historical sources, therefore, these types of letters must be approached with a
healthy dose of caution in trying to reconstruct the actual historical debates
they seem to reflect.

Recent studies on epistolary rhetoric also remind us of the danger of
equating the "rhetorical situation" of a letter with the actual, historical situation that may have engendered its contents. Recently in this regard, Dennis L.
Stamps has made a case for rethinking the whole notion of rhetorical situation
and urges that we see it as "the way in which the text presents a selected,
limited and crafted entextualization of the situation."[3] Whether reading

MMT, 1 Corinthians, or Rabbinic material, Tomson sometimes gives the impression that he believes the letters in question give reliable access to actual historical debates about halakic traditions when their rhetoric may signal something much less reliable than that.[4]

Another factor, not developed in Tomson's work, is the nature of the rhetorical and/or epistolary topoi in the letters and how these rhetorical clichés function within the different examples Tomson cites. For example, the final section of MMT (4Q397–398) contains several formulaic expressions that elsewhere John White has identified as typical of letter closings in the Greek letter corpus.[5] According to White's analysis, five elements often appear at the close of letters: "(1) the disclosure-motivation for writing formula, (2) responsibility statements, (3) polite requests for a letter, (4) formulate references to a coming visit, and (5) conditional clauses employed formulaically as a threat."[6] The author of MMT concludes his letter with just such a reminder about why the letter was written:

> And we have (written) to you so that you may study (care-
> fully) the book of Moses and the books of the Prophets and
> (the writings of) David (and the) (events of) ages past.[7]

In a similar vein, the author employs repeated statements to the addressees to remember their duty to hold fast to the path of Torah. He punctuates these with threats of evils to come if they fail to do so. He mentions blessings and curses and uses an "expression of confidence" in their "wisdom and knowledge of Torah." These phrases all display common epistolary conventions identified by White. It remains a matter of further study to determine just how these conventions may have been modified or emended in the halakhic literature, and how they functioned to punctuate patterns of communication about legal matters in these letters.

Tomson's listing of seven halakot identified in 1 Corinthians raises another question for me. By what precise criteria is ethical advice, and even specific exhortation about moral conduct, judged to be, in a formal sense, halakhot? Reviewing Tomson's list, the case seems to me to be strongest in the examples of the halakot prohibiting cohabitation with a stepmother (1 Cor 5), those concerning marital sex, divorce, and remarriage (1 Cor 7), that dealing with abstaining from pagan food because of idolatry (1 Cor 10), and table order in the Eucharistic tradition (1 Cor 11). In each of these examples, Paul draws on authoritative tradition specific to Judaism. Whereas, in the cases of sustenance due to apostles (1 Cor 9), the conduct of women at worship (1 Cor 11 and 14), and benedictions in the community (1 Cor 14), Paul draws on a method of argument that combines both Torah citation (e.g., the quotation of Deut 25:4 about not muzzling the ox cited by Paul in 1 Cor 9:9) and general moral precepts common to Jews and non-Jews alike. For example, in the case of 1 Corinthians 9, Paul is equally influenced by the Hellenistic philosophical debates concerning the proper means of support for the philosopher.[8] Should not a clearer formal distinction be drawn in these examples, therefore, in order to establish the specific distinguishing characteristics of a developing *halakic* tradition?

In his treatment of the Rabbinic material, Tomson begins his discussion by noting the importance of "the so-called *nehutei* or those who traveled from Babylonia to Palestine in order to study the Palestinian law tradition and check it against the Babylonian." He goes on to raise the important question of how to assess the difference between the Oral and the Written Torah at this stage. He even documents the questioned permissibility of such things as *halakic letters* themselves. Once the practice of consultative letters had been established, however, the *envoys* and *couriers* of such letters became crucial factors in the developing tradition.

The role and function of these envoys and how they contributed to the development of halakot is a subject requiring further study and clarification. In the development of early Christianity, for example, we assume that the couriers and envoys who functioned as part of the Pauline mission surely exercised some latitude in the way they delivered Paul's letters to their destined recipients and in the manner in which they freely *interpreted* the letters' contents. In a similar vein, Peter Borgen's study comparing the role of Jesus in the gospel of John and the role of the delegate or envoy in the formation of Rabbinic halaka identifies six halakic principles of agency shared with the fourth gospel, including the central role of the delegate or agent in the exchange.[9]

Another resource for understanding the dynamic relationship and function between the one sent and the authoritative sender are the important social and diplomatic conventions in the ancient world that shed light on how these delegates and letter couriers might have contributed to the development of authoritative teaching communicated by letter.[10] Contrary to Robert Funk's judgment about the "apostolic parousia," the presence of the authoritative figure is not always the most effective means of presence or communication.[11] Sometimes the letter is a *more* effective means of communication (especially in a delicate matter) than even personal presence precisely because the delegate or envoy can mediate the letter's contents to the intended audience.[12] In the case of Paul, it was not always the best strategy to appear in person! The accusation against Paul that "His letters are weighty and strong, but his bodily presence is weak and his speech of no account" (2 Cor 10:10) is, of course, the strongest case in point. But if this pattern is true elsewhere, then letters sent by envoys such as Tomson's *nehutei* must have been even more significant in the development of halakhot than we have hitherto acknowledged, as Tomson's own example from mTem 2:1 illustrates. Further study of the development of this oral halakhot would seem to be in order

These few questions raised by Peter Tomson's paper, I hope, point to its value and importance in our ongoing study of what he has called the "intercollegial consultative letters" of early Christianity and first and second century Judaism.

Endnotes

Scripture references are from the Revised Standard Version. Nashville: Thomas Nelson, 1952.

1. 'So Ernst Bansland, "Die 7 *peri*-Former und die Argumentation (situation) des Paulus," *ST* 42 (1988) 69–87, and Margaret M. Mitchell, "Concerning *peri de* in 1 Corinthians," *NovT* 31 (1989) 229–256.
2. Antoinette Wire, quoted from an unpublished address.
3. Dennis L. Stamps, "Rethinking the Rhetorical Situation: The Entextualization of the Situation in New Testament Epistles," in Stanley E. Porter and Thomas H. Olbricht, eds., Rhetoric and the New Testament: Essays from the 1992 Heidelberg Conference JSNTSup 90; Sheffield: JSOT Press, 1993) 193–210.
4. A recent article by James D. G. Dunn ("4QMMT and Galatians," NTS 43, 1997, 147–153), on the other hand, also points to 4QMMT as a reliable example of the kind of "theological attitude and halakhic practice which in the event determined the attitude and action of Peter and the other Christian Jews in Antioch (Gal 2: 11–14)." This position would support Tomson's conclusions.
5. John L. White, *The Form and Function of the Body of the Greek Letter: A Study of the Letter-Body in the Non-Literary Papyri and in Paul the Apostle* (SBLDS 2, Missoula, MT: Scholars Press, 1972) 11, 42.
6. Ibid., 66.
7. Translation from Elisha Qimron and John Strugnell, Qumran Cave 4 V, *Miqsat Ma'ase HaTorah, Discoveries in the Judean Desert*, vol. X (Oxford: Oxford University Press, 1994).
8. See especially the study of Ronald F. Hock, *The Social Context of Paul's Ministry: Tentmaking and Apostleship* (Philadelphia: Fortress, 1980) 52–59. Hock demonstrates the debate especially by reference to the tractate of Musonius Rufus, "What Means of Support is Appropriate for a Philosopher?"

9. See Peter Borgen, "God's Agent in the Fourth Gospel," in *Religions in Antiquity: Essays in Memory of E. R. Goodenough* (ed. J. Neusner; Studies in the History of Religions 14; Leiden: Brill, 1968) 137–148, esp. 143–144.

10. Margaret M. Mitchell, "New Testament Envoys in the Context of Greco-Roman Diplomatic and Epistolary Conventions: The Example of Timothy and Titus," JBL 111:4 (1992) 641–662.

11. See the now classic study by Robert W. Funk, "The Apostolic Parousia: Form and Significance," in *Christian History and Interpretation: Studies Presented to John Knox* (W. R. Farmer, C. F. D. Moule, and R. R. Niebuhr; Cambridge: Cambridge University Press, 1967) 249–269.

12. Mitchell, "New Testament Envoys," 641.

CONTRIBUTORS

BARBARA BOWE, R.S.C.J., is Associate Professor of New Testament at Catholic Theological Union.

CELIA DEUTSCH is Professor in the Department of Religion at Barnard College/Columbia University.

LOUIS FELDMAN is Professor of History at Brandeis University.

LESLIE HOPPE, O.F.M., is Professor of Old Testament at Catholic Theological Union.

KEVIN MADIGAN is Assistant Professor of Church History at Catholic Theological Union.

JOHN T. PAWLIKOWSKI, O.S.M., is Professor of Ethics at Catholic Theological Union.

HAYIM GOREN PERELMUTER is Chautauqua Professor of Jewish Studies at Catholic Theological Union.

ALAN SEGAL is Professor in the Department of Religion at Barnard College/Columbia, Columbia University.

MICHAEL SIGNER is Professor of Jewish Thought and Culture at the University of Notre Dame.

CLEMENS THOMA is Professor of Jewish Studies at the Universitäre Hochschule in Lucerne.

PETER J. TOMSON is Professor of New Testament at the Free Protestant Faculty of Theology in Brussels.

ELIOT WOLFSON is the Abraham Lieberman Professor of Hebrew and Judaic Studies at New York University.

INDEX

A

Abraham, 56–57
Adler, William, 83
Against Apion (Josephus), 175, 178
Agrippa I, 172, 184, 188
Akiva, Rabbi, 203
Alexander, 169–170
Alexander Polyhistor, 174, 176
Amidah, 59
Analogical Imagination, The
        (Tracy), 4
anti-Semitism, 60, 113, 167, 171, 175,
        187, 193
Apion, 168
apocalypse, 77–80, 91, 106
Apostolic Decree, ix, 125–128, 132,
        141–142, 144, 153
Aristeas, 123
Aristotle, 176, 189
Armstrong, A. Hilary, 90
Augustine, 10, 20
Avodah Zara(h), 10, 11, 120

B

Baeck, Leo, 16
Bar Cochba, 66, 187
Barnabas, 10, 142
Baruch, 80–81, 85–86
Be Fertile and Increase (Cohen), 19
been Hyrcanus, Eliezer, 67–68
Ben, Augustin, 27
ben, Johanan, 65, 68, 203, 216, 221
Benjamin, Walter, 5
berit (= covenant), 6
Bockmuehl, Markus, 87, 90
Body of Faith, The (Wyschogrod), 15
Borgen, Peter, 234
Bornkamm, 83
Boron, Salo, 191

Bowe, Barbara, x
Boys, Mary, 40, 43
Brown, Raymond, 31, 41
Buber, Martin, 16, 43
Burden of Freedom, The,
        (van Buren), 29

C

Cassiodorus, 175
Cataline, 168, 185
Charlesworth, James, 35
*Christian Theology of the People of
        Israel, The* (van Buren), 29
Cicero, 168, 173, 186, 193
circumcision, 116
Claudius, 181
Claudius Ptolemy, 183
Clement of Alexandria, 174
Cleomenes, 179
Cohen, Jeremy, 19
Cohn, Norman, 78
collegium, 147
Collins, John, 78–79, 89, 93
conversion, 117
Corinthians (1), 206–208, 233–234
covenant, viii, 4–5, 144; double
        model, 34–43; single, model,
        28–34
Cyrus of Persia, 8

D

Daniel, viii, 9, 79, 84, 89, 107–108
Daniélou, Jean 27
darshan, 54–55
David, 36
Davies, W. D., 93–94, 203
*Death and Resurrection of the
        Beloved Son, The* (Levenson), 33

De Divinatione (Cicero), 168
Derrida, Jacques, 88
Deutsch, Celia, ix, 141–142
Diaspora, 170
Didache, 129
Discerning the Way (van Buren), 29
Domitian, 183

E
Eckardt, A. Roy, 42
Edom, 11–12, 53
eidolothuta, 126, 129, 151
Eliezer, Rabbi, 118
Ennius, 168
Enoch, 80, 121
Epicurus, 179
Epstein, J.N., 210
Eusebios, 129
Ezekiel, 7
Ezra, 81–82, 173

F
Feldman, Louis, ix 191–194
Flaccus, 171–172, 193
Flusser, David, 52, 203
Fraenkel, Jonah, 52
fundamentalists, 108
Funk, Robert W., 235

G
Gaius Caligula, 171, 187
Gamaliel, Rabbi, 119, 217, 222
Garber, Zev, 43
Geiger, Abraham, 16
ger, 131, 143
ger Toshav (semi-converts), 12–13
Greenberg, Irving, 14
Gregory the Great, 10
Guest in the House of Israel, A
        (Williamson), 40

H
haima, 126–127, 129, 151
halakah, 208

Hanson, Paul, 91
Hartman, David, 19
Hebrews, 9–10
Hecataeus, 180
Heliodorus, 174
Hellwig, Monica, 28–29, 43
Herodotus, 173, 180
Heschel, Abraham Joshua, 18
Hillel, 201, 205, 223
Hippolytus, 175
Hizkia, Rabbi, 211
Holocaust, 42
Hope, 86
Hoppe, Leslie, viii
Hurd, John, 129

I
idolatry, 7–8, 11
incarnation, 39
Isaiah, 134
Ishmael, 11–12

J
James, 68, 143
Jeremiah, 7, 81
Jesus Christ, 9, 30, 37, 69, 206
*Jew and Gentile in the Ancient
        World* (Feldman), 191–192, 194
Joel, 117
John, 84
John Paul II, Pope, 5, 13, 28
Josephus, 169, 172, 174–175, 178, 182,
        184, 187, 189, 204
Joshua b. Hananiah, 118–119
Journet, Charles, 27
Jubilees, 121–122
Judeophobia (Schäfer), 167
Justin, 129
Juvenal, 180–181

K
Keller, Catherine, 85
Ketuvim (= covenant), 8
Klappert, Bertold, 5

Klausner, Joseph, 16
Knitter, Paul, 40
Kritik, 225 n 1

L
Langmuir, Gavin, 185, 188
Lauer, Simon, 63
Leib, Moshe, 70
Letter of Aristeas, 169
Levenson, Jon, 33
Levinas, Emmanuel, 43
Lieberman, Saul, 179
Lohfink, Norbert, 5, 33–34, 40, 43
Lucerne Institute for Jewish-Christian Studies, 52
Luke, 116, 127, 130, 142–143, 146
Luke and the Law (Wilson), 127

M
Maccabees, 9
Madigan, Kevin, ix
magic 149–150, 161 n 43
Maimonides, Moses, 12
Major Trends in Jewish Mysticism (Scholem), 70
Mani, 83
Marquardt, F. W., 5
Martini, Carlo, 35
mashal, 53
Mekhilta, 11–12, 22 n 8
Melito of Sardis, 10
Metz, Johannes, 41–42
midrash, 69
Midrash Pesilta de Ray Kahana, 52
Millar, Fergus, 170
Minucius Felix, 129
Mishnah, 13
Moore, James, 43
Moses, 8, 12, 70, 116–117, 180, 194
Mussner, Franz, 37–40, 42
mysterion, 86
mystery, 97 n 23

N
Nachmanides, 70
nehutei, 234–235
Nero, 186
Neusner, Jacob, 41
nimshal, 53, 58, 61
Noah, 121, 207
Noahide Commandments, 120, 124, 130
Nostra Aetate, 3, 25–27, 55
Novak, David, 12, 121

O
Origen, 151, 189

P
parable, viii, 51
Parkes, James, 35–37, 42
Paul, ix-x, 9, 16, 25, 59–60, 115, 117, 129, 132, 133–137, 142, 150, 202, 204, 207, 220, 231–232, 235
Paul the Convert (Segal), 132
Pawlikowski, John, viii
Perelmuter, Hayim, viii, 37-38, 40–41, 43
Perrin, N. 87
Peter, 57
Phan, Peter, C., 14
Philo, 117, 169, 174, 176, 203
philology, 225 n 3
Plato, 173, 180, 189
Pliny, 147
pniktos, 126–127, 129, 139 n 14, 151
polytheism, 168, 180
porneia, 126, 151–152
Porphyry, 173, 175
Price, Jonathan, 170
Protocols of the Elders of Zion, 177
Psalms, 18
Pseudo-Longinus, 174
Pseudo-Phocylides, 123
Ptolemy IV Philopator, 184
Pythagoras, 189

Q
Qimron, Elisha, 204

Qumran, 9, 82, 86, 122, 204–205, 216

R

Rabin, 210
rainbow, 120
Ratzinger, Joseph, 5
Rav Dimi, 212
Rav Yirmeya, 212
Revelation, viii, 84
Rinat Yisrael, 14
Rivkin, Ellis, 42
Rosenzweig, Franz, 16, 114
Ruether, Rosemary, 40
Rule of the Community, 82
Russell, D. S., 92
Rylaarsdam, J. Coert, 36–37, 42

S

Sabbatai Sevi, 93
Saldarini, Anthony, 35
salvation, 117, 142
Schäfer, Peter, 167, 169, 177–178,
    185–186, 188, 192
Schiffman, L. H. 204
Schillebeeckx, Edward, 42
Scholem, Gershom, 64, 66, 91, 94
Schweitzer, Albert, 203, 206
Scroggs, Robin, 35, 41
secrecy, 78, 84
Segal, Alan, ix
selah, 219–220
Seneca, 177
Shmueli, Efrain, 41
Shoah (= holocaust), vii, 14
Sibylline Oracles, 123, 129
Signer, Michael, viii, 25–26
Smith, Morton, 77–78
Stamps, Denis L., 232
Star of Redemption, The
    (Rosenzweig), 17, 114
stasis, 147
Stern, David, 52, 173
Stone, Michael, 82
Strugnell, John, 204

Suetonius, 184, 106
Sussman, Y., 204

T

Tacitus, 177, 183–184, 186
Tcherikover, 171
Tertullian, 129, 147, 152
Teshuvah (= turning), 7
Teucer of Cyzicus, 176
theology, 4
*Theology of the Jewish-Christian
    Reality* (van Buren), 19, 29
Theophilus of Antioch, 175
Tiberius, 171
Tomson, Peter, ix, 231, 233–235
Tosefta, 119
Toward a Definition of Anti-Semitism
    (Langmuir), 185
Tracy, David, 4
trefah, 126–127

V

van Buren, Paul, 19, 29–35, 40
Varro, 190
Von Balthasar, Hans Urs, 27
von Harnack, Adolf, 16, 192

W

Way, 153, 156 n 8
White, John, 233
Wiesel, Elie, 114
Wilken, Robert, 35
Williamson, Clark M., 40–41, 43
Wilson, Steve, 127–128
Wire, Antoinette, 232
Wolfson, Elliot R., viii, 105–106
worship, 26
Wyschogrod, Michael, 15–16

X

xenophobia, 180, 185

Y

Yalqut Shim'oni, 19

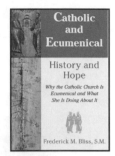

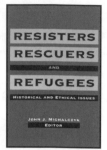